Subjectivity and Religious Belief

Subjectivity and Religious Belief

AN HISTORICAL, CRITICAL STUDY

by
C. Stephen Evans

CHRISTIAN UNIVERSITY PRESS

A Subsidiary of Christian College Consortium
and William B. Eerdmans Publishing Company
Grand Rapids, Michigan

Copyright © 1978 by *Christian College Consortium*
11 *Dupont Circle, N.W., Washington, D.C.* 20036
All rights reserved
Printed in the United States of America

Available from Wm. B. Eerdmans Publishing Co.
255 Jefferson Ave. S.E., Grand Rapids, Mich. 49503

Library of Congress Cataloging in Publication Data

Evans, C. Stephen
    Subjectivity and religious belief.

    Bibliography: p. 215.
    1. God—Proof, Moral—History of doctrines. 2. Subjectivity.
3. Faith. 4. Kant, Immanuel, 1724-1804. 5. Kierkegaard, Søren Aabye,
1813-1855. 6. James, William, 1842-1910. I. Title.
BT98.E85   200′.1   77-13851
ISBN 0-8028-1712-2

Selections from Immanuel Kant, *Critique of Pure Reason,* transl. by
Norman K. Smith (copyright © 1965 by St. Martin's Press, Inc.). Reprinted
by permission of St. Martin's Press.

Selections from Søren Kierkegaard, *Concluding Unscientific Postscript,*
transl. by David Swenson and Walter Lowrie (copyright 1941 © 1969 by
Princeton University Press; Princeton Paperback, 1968), pp. 38-510.
Reprinted by permission of Princeton University Press and the American
Scandinavian Foundation.

To Jan

Acknowledgments

I should like to express my appreciation to the many people who helped make this work possible, whether by giving me original insights and suggestions, reading and criticizing the manuscript in various forms, risking their own well-being to get it typed, or just contributing to my general philosophical development. Chief among these are John Smith, Arthur Holmes, Merold Westphal, Paul Holmer, George Mavrodes, David Schlafer, and most of all, three delightful sisters: Linda Schlafer, Debbie Elliot, and Marcia Wegner.

Contents

vii

Abbreviations

References to primary sources refer to the following works. Page numbers refer to the editions and translations listed in the bibliography, except where otherwise noted.

KANT

Gw   *Groundwork of the Metaphysic of Morals*
(First number refers to the pagination of the original second edition; second number refers to the pagination of the Royal Prussian Academy Edition as cited in Paton's translation.)

KPV   *Critique of Practical Reason*
(First number refers to the pagination of the Royal Prussian Academy Edition; second number refers to the pagination of Beck's English translation.)

KRV   *Critique of Pure Reason*
(Numbers refer to the pagination of the first and second German editions as cited in Kemp Smith's translation.)

KU   *Critique of Judgment*
(First number refers to the pagination of the Royal Prussian Academy edition; second number refers to the pagination of Meredith's English translation of the *Critique of Teleological Judgment*.)

Rel   *Religion Within the Limits of Reason Alone*

WOT   *What is Orientation in Thinking?*
(First number refers to the pagination of the Royal Prussian Academy edition; second number

refers to Beck's English translation as found in his *Critique of Practical Reason and other Writings in Moral Philosophy*.)

KIERKEGAARD

AR	*On Authority and Revelation*
CD	*The Concept of Dread*
ChD	*Christian Discourses*
FSE	*For Self-Examination*
FT	*Fear and Trembling*
Jour	*The Journals of Kierkegaard* (Selections edited by Dru)
JY	*Judge for Yourselves!* (Published with *For Self-Examination*)
PF	*Philosophical Fragments*
PH	*Purity of Heart Is to Will One Thing* (Harper Torchbook edition)
Post	*Concluding Unscientific Postscript*
PV	*The Point of View for My Work as an Author*
Rep	*Repetition*
SD	*The Sickness Unto Death* (Published with *Fear and Trembling*)
TC	*Training in Christianity*
WL	*Works of Love* (Harper Torchbook edition)

JAMES

Quotations from all the articles except "Reason and Faith" and "Philosophical Conceptions and Practical Results" are taken from *The Will to Believe and other Essays in Popular Philosophy*, and page numbers refer to that volume. "Philosophical Conceptions and Practical Results" is taken from *The Writings of William James*, edited by John J. McDermott. "Reason and Faith" is cited as it appeared in *The Journal of Philosophy*, XXIV (April 14, 1927).

HI	*Human Immortality*

ILWL   "Is Life Worth Living?"
MPML   "The Moral Philosopher and the Moral Life"
MT   *The Meaning of Truth*
PCPR   "Philosophical Conceptions and Practical
           Results"
Prin   *Principles of Psychology* (Vol. II)
Prag   *Pragmatism*
PU   *A Pluralistic Universe*
RAT   "Reflex Action and Theism"
RF   "Reason and Faith"
SR   "The Sentiment of Rationality"
Var   *The Varieties of Religious Experience*
WPR   "What Psychical Research Has Accomplished"
WB   "The Will to Believe"

1

Introduction: Subjective Justifications of Belief in God

THAT RELIGIOUS BELIEF IS CLOSELY BOUND UP WITH THE satisfaction of subjective needs and obligations is undeniable. This is especially evident at the level of popular consciousness, where the connection of religious belief with subjective satisfaction is usually frankly acknowledged. It is scarcely less evident among more sophisticated thinkers, where it usually serves to undercut religious belief. Freudians and Marxists are not the only thinkers who have charged religious conviction with being a form of wish-fulfillment but they are perhaps the most influential. The intimate connection between religious belief and subjective satisfaction makes those who have a developed logical conscience uneasy. After all, beliefs should be determined by rational evidence, not by subjective wants.

It is obvious that many religious beliefs are cases of irrational wish-fulfillments, although it would be rash to claim that this is always the case. One would not wish to use guilt by association to tar all religious beliefs because some are offenders. The question which I wish to raise, however, is whether the connection of religion with subjective need is necessarily incriminating. Are there situations where it is reasonable to take some of one's subjective needs into account in forming beliefs? I shall try to argue that indeed there are. I shall not claim that it is legitimate to abandon reason in favor of subjective need; rather I shall argue that in certain situations, the reasonable thing to do is to take certain of one's subjective needs into account in forming one's beliefs. As is the case with so many contemporary philosophical issues, we

1

can best begin our discussion of this claim by looking at Immanuel Kant.

The significance of Kant as a watershed for philosophy of religion can hardly be overestimated. One can hardly find a discussion of any of the theistic proofs after Kant which does not refer to him either implicitly or explicitly. It is equally significant that Kant's negative critique of the theoretical proofs for God's existence has had an influence which has far outstripped his later defense of divine existence as a postulate of practical reason. To put the matter bluntly, the positive support Kant offered religion as a replacement for the traditional proofs has seemed to many to be terribly weak, so much so that Heine's outrageous suggestion that Kant's defense of religion was a sop thrown to his old servant has even been taken seriously by some.[1]

Regardless of the generally harsh judgment which has been made about Kant's defense of religion, I believe that its significance and worth have been underestimated. One reason that this is so is that many thinkers have not realized the extent to which Kant's critique of the traditional theistic proofs and the denial of the claims of theoretical reason to be able to surpass the phenomenal world and attain knowledge of the noumenal world are an integral part of his defense of religious belief. Kant did not just abolish knowledge to make room for faith; he believed it was *necessary* to do so, and he also felt that in doing so he was building an equally strong case against those who claim to have knowledge which is contrary to the religious position. The destructive work of critical reason, the fixing of the boundaries of theoretical reason, was an important part of the Kantian strategy of defending theistic belief.

And the overall strategy employed by Kant has its attractions. Whether or not Kant's arguments in the *Critique of Practical Reason* seem weak, the approach embodied in those arguments has struck many as suggestive and promising. The

1. Though Kant's mòral argument has been ably defended as of late, particularly by Allen Wood, *Kant's Moral Religion* (Ithaca: Cornell University Press, 1970).

strategy underlying Kant's moves seems to be more cogent than the moves themselves.

Of course Kant was not the first to abandon theoretical proofs of divine existence and advance on behalf of theism considerations derived from man's practical reason and experience. There are echoes of at least the first part of this strategy in the "learned unknowing" of Cusanus, and very forthright statements of similar views in some of the Renaissance and Enlightenment skeptics. Montaigne, Charron, and Gassendi all voiced the view that an enlightened skepticism with regard to theoretical knowledge of God's existence was a friend of true religious faith, as did Bayle and Hume.[2] However, none of these thinkers developed such a non-theoretical *justification* of religious belief in the rigorous and systematic form in which Kant did. The Kantian approach to theism is further distinguished by its utter lack of fideism. Even though Kant wished to ground religion in belief rather than in knowledge, he thought that these beliefs were rational in an important sense and could be defended.

What is a non-theoretical justification of belief in God? We can perhaps characterize it in a preliminary and crude way by pointing out just two features. We have already noted the first of these, which is the claim that with regard to the divine existence, no theoretical knowledge[3] is possible, either of a positive or negative character. The most that is claimed for religion is that some form of faith or belief can be given a rational defense.

The second feature concerns the sort of considerations

---

2. See Richard H. Popkin, "Kierkegaard and Scepticism," *Kierkegaard*, ed. Josiah Thompson (Garden City, N.Y.: Doubleday and Co., 1972), pp. 342-372, for an historical account of fideists who have been philosophical skeptics.

3. I shall consistently use the qualifying adjective "theoretical," despite the fact that such defenses of religion generally presuppose a conception of knowledge in which the qualifier is redundant. Generally speaking, such defenses do not claim religious propositions constitute a special, non-theoretical kind of *knowledge*, but are content to rest on a belief/knowledge disjunction. The qualifier is used, however, to indicate that this conception of knowledge is not beyond question; i.e., other defenders of religious beliefs might argue that the considerations advanced in such non-theoretical arguments provide a kind of religious knowledge.

which are advanced in that defense. These are considerations which are derived from or closely related to practical human existence. Rather than arguing from the sheer fact that the world exists, or arguing from certain features of nature, one begins with certain pervasive features of human existence, particularly those features which concern man as a responsible agent. These arguments appeal to the desires, needs, and felt obligations of the existing human being. We shall henceforth refer to non-theoretical justifications of religious belief which derive from these aspects of the human subject as *subjective* justifications of religious belief.

The term "subjective" is of course a problem-laden one. Many critics of this type of argument would no doubt claim that the term is quite apt. Such critics would charge that these arguments are indeed subjective, meaning that they lack any objective validity and represent an irrational abandonment of genuine evidence. An argument which appeals to the desires, needs, and sensed obligations of the human self seems to play right into the hands of a Freudian critic of religion, who charges that religion is merely wish-fulfillment, a projection of human desires. Such charges are no doubt frequently justified when directed against the reasons many religious believers give for their faith. However, I shall argue that such criticisms are not always justified, and that some subjective arguments are in no way irrational.

The term "subjective" has at least two distinct, though sometimes confused, meanings. There is first a pejorative sense which connotes arbitrariness and bias on the part of an individual. When a teacher is accused of being a subjective grader, the charge is that he is irresponsible and biased; he lacks objectivity. But there is a second sense of the word which lacks these pejorative connotations. We sometimes say that a person who is not very understanding of his fellows is too objective. He seems cold and heartless because he treats the people around him as if they were simply objects to be manipulated. Such a person, we might be inclined to say, needs to gain an understanding of those around him from a *subjective* point of view. He needs to understand that other individuals are persons in their own right, with feelings, desires, and needs of their own. He needs to see things from the other person's point of view. This point of view is that of a subject. In this sense of the word, "subjective" implies "that which pertains to a subject." It does not necessarily connote bias, arbitrariness, or lack of rationality.

Obviously, it is this second sense I have in mind when I term the justification of belief I want to consider "subjective." Nevertheless, some will charge that these arguments are subjective in the first sense as well. Whether that is so cannot be decided by assertion, but only by reasoned reflection and argument. That is the purpose of this essay.

In any case it is not hard to see why the sort of approach we are going to consider should seem attractive since Kant's time and even today. At least three reasons can be given. The first stems from the failure of the traditional natural theology. As the criticisms of the cosmological, teleological, and ontological arguments given by Hume and Kant found widespread credence, those wishing to give a philosophical defense of religion naturally began to look elsewhere. What I have called the subjective approach not only suggested a new area to make that defense; it also contented itself with the seemingly modest and (and hence more secure) claim that one could rightfully believe in God, even though certain knowledge was lacking.

A second factor in the attractiveness of such an approach is its effectiveness in safeguarding a distinctively religious concern. Even in medieval philosophy there had been a strong undercurrent which viewed with suspicion the Aristotelian synthesis by which God was made an object of scientific knowledge. To be sure, this knowledge was not just knowledge of another object in the world; it was the culmination and crowning glory of scientific endeavor. But it was open to suspicion from two quarters. First, the tradition of negative theology, with its roots in neo-Platonism, preserved an appreciation of the radical discontinuity between an infinite God and all finite, created objects. This discontinuity made problematic any positive knowledge of God derived from knowledge of that creation. Secondly, scientific knowledge of God seemed to supplant or make superfluous the Biblical conception of faith. The question of whether knowledge of the Thomistic sort and faith are compatible with regard to the same object or proposition depends of course on the particular conception of faith involved. (Obviously faith could supplement knowledge with regard to more specific doctrines such as the Trinity; the problem centered on the question of God's existence.) But the possibility of tension is surely evident. There was a tendency to downgrade faith, to regard it as the means whereby the unlearned and unsophisticated came to learn that there is a God.

As modern science and mathematics developed in the Renaissance and afterwards, this tension continued. Knowledge was increasingly identified with mathematical knowledge and knowledge of the laws of the physical world. But philosophical rationalists, particularly Descartes, continued to incorporate knowledge of God within the emerging scientific world view, regarding such knowledge as essential to a proper explanation of the physical world.[4]

For many modern religious thinkers this sort of knowledge of God just will not do. They feel that such metaphysical schemes, in addition to being poor science, simply do not do justice to the uniqueness of religious knowledge. There is a tendency to use God to fill up gaps in scientific knowledge; and as the gaps recede so does God. According to these critics, a God who could be known via scientific methods would not be the God who is the object of religious faith. For example, given a Kantian epistemology, to be known, God would have to be an object within the empirical world. Such a God would simply not be God as he has traditionally been understood in the West. A Humean epistemology leads to equally unpromising results. If factual knowing and empirical knowing are equated, and all empirical knowledge is merely probable, then knowledge of God would seem to be merely the result of calculating empirical probabilities. Many religious thinkers found such a result unappealing. For example, Kierkegaard thought that such an approximation process was a

---

4. For an illuminating discussion of the "functional" role God played in rationalist systems see James Collins, *God in Modern Philosophy* (Chicago: Henry Regnery Co., 1967), chap. 3, pp. 55-89.

world away from the appropriation process which constitutes true faith; the two are mutually exclusive. A similar concern is present in Marcel, who argues that God's existence is not a problem to be solved, but a mystery which by its very nature resists solution. When Tillich argues that the man who affirms God's existence is really denying God, because God is not another being in the world, he is motivated by a similar concern.[5] All of these thinkers feel that to make God an object of scientific knowledge is to degrade or deny God's nature. For someone who holds this view it is easy to see the attractiveness of an approach which "denies knowledge in order to make room for faith."

A third reason for the attractiveness of a subjective approach is a constantly growing concern for the distinctive character of human existence, which involves an emphasis on man as a knowing-willing-feeling agent. Even as science progresses in its task of placing man within the scope of its world-picture, or perhaps because of that progress, there has been an increasing concern since Kant's time with those aspects of man which will not fit into that picture without distortion. Though the two are not identical, there is a relationship of continuity between those aspects of human experience and thought which Kant termed "practical" and those aspects which are today identified as "existential." Both are concerned not with man as an object to be known but as a reflective agent who must make choices and act on these choices. An approach to religion which begins from and appeals to these aspects of man quite naturally partakes of this concern. It seems more likely to lead to a conception of a God who is intimately related to personal and human needs. There is the added bonus that a religious apologetic grounded in these concerns seems, at least to some, less likely to conflict with a scientific world-view than one which appeals to teleology in nature or to a causal principle which is to be applied to the universe as a whole to demonstrate God's existence.

Of course such an approach will also have its critics.

---

5. Paul Tillich, *Systematic Theology* (Chicago: University of Chicago Press, 1951), I, 205.

There will be those who perhaps have nothing against the approach in general, but simply believe that no particular attempt to justify belief in divine existence in this way is very good. But aside from criticisms of particular forms of this approach, there are also those who would characterize the whole approach as wrong-headed in principle. In general we might classify these "wholesale" critics into two camps. If we remove from the terms the pejorative connotations they usually possess, we might call these two types of critics dogmatists and fideists.

Dogmatists reject any subjective justification of belief in God because they claim to have some theoretical knowledge over the issue. They come in two varieties, those who claim to know that God exists and those who claim to know that God does not exist. Someone who claims to have such knowledge will naturally be opposed to an approach which as an integral part of its argument denies that such knowledge is possible.

Fideists, on the other hand, as I shall use the term, reject the subjective approach because it is overly rationalistic. They feel that a "rationally justified belief" sounds suspiciously like knowledge, and is equally far removed from genuine religious faith. As we shall see, there is a strong fideistic element in Kierkegaard, side by side with elements which are characteristic of a subjective justification of religious belief as we have described it.

It is clear that in order to show that a subjective justification of belief in God is sound, these positions must be discredited or at least disarmed. But it is not really fruitful to attack or defend such an approach in general. Indeed, it is quite obvious that up until now the description we have given of subjective justifications of belief in God has been both general and vague, and could be taken as applying to many different defenses of religion both before and after Kant. To determine the viability of such an approach, it is desirable to put it into some particular historical form. In this essay I shall attempt to look at three historical examples of thinkers who offered a justification of belief in God, while denying any objective, theoretical knowledge of God. They are Immanuel Kant, Søren Kierkegaard, and William James. From one point of view it is a mistake to regard these three thinkers as proponents of the "same" approach to religious belief. I have chosen them partly because of the great contrasts between them. They represent not only different historical eras, but also very different approaches to philosophy. The content of their arguments is very different. Indeed, in the case of Kierkegaard it is difficult to assert that there is an argument or defense of religious belief present at all. We shall note these differences by designating Kant's way "the practical approach," that of Kierkegaard "the existential approach," and that of James "the pragmatic approach." Nevertheless, despite these differences I hope to show that it is illuminating to regard these different approaches as possessing a common *structure*.

What is this structure? The basis of it is surely the thesis that the practical and existential elements of human existence are real and important, and that they are not inherently irrational but intimately related to man as a cognitive being. It must be shown that there are at least two very basic and different kinds of thinking. In thinking one adopts a certain standpoint, either the standpoint of theoretical thought, or the standpoint of the agent, the doer, the existential man who must choose.

The thesis that there are such standpoints and perspectives certainly seems initially plausible. We do apply terms like "thinking," "inquiry," and "reflection" to very different sorts of activities. A scientist may be thinking about an experiment, perhaps trying to discern why a certain gas behaves as it does when heated. His thoughts are interrupted by the sound of the lab assistant closing the door. This sets his thought going in a completely different direction. The lab assistant has been pilfering supplies from the laboratory. Ought the scientist to report him? Perhaps when he himself leaves the laboratory, the scientist will be assailed by doubts as to the worth of his vocation. Ought he to continue his endeavors, when he knows that his discoveries may well be misused, just as the lab assistant misuses the supplies? It is clear that the sort of thinking which these last two questions ("Ought he to report the lab assistant?" and "Is his work worthwhile?") necessitate is of a different order from the thinking he was engaged in while doing the experiment.

In doing the experiment he asked such questions as "Why did the temperature increase by so much when I added gas B?" This may ultimately raise questions about the general properties of gas B, or the general way in which gas B behaves, or even questions about gases in general. These sorts of questions differ significantly from such questions as "Does being a scientist give me true fulfillment as a person?" This latter question may lead to such general questions as "What is fulfillment?" "What does it mean to be a person?" "What is the meaning and value of science?" Both types of questions may be specific or they may be quite general, but the second type of question seems to be related more fundamentally to the scientist as human being, an agent who must act and make decisions and take responsibility for those decisions.

The first sort of thinking we might characterize as the standpoint of the observer. The scientist wishes to know something about an object or set of objects, or about what is the case. He may be intensely interested and involved in his work, but it is plausible to regard the object of his experiments as not *essential* to the man's being. Even if he is personally crushed by his failure, the failure is essentially grounded in his lack of success as a scientist; it is his failure to discover something significant which depresses him; it is his success in showing something new which elates him. The gas itself is external to his being as a human; it becomes related indirectly to him through his choice of science as a vocation.

The second sort of thinking definitely represents something other than the standpoint of the observer. It is generated by questions about what the man *ought* to do. It is precisely the mark of this sort of question that it seems to involve a man's being or identity immediately and essentially. *He* must make the decision. *He* must take the responsibility for his decision and his action. So we will characterize this sort of thinking as done from the standpoint of the agent. This seems to be the sort of concern which has generated such identity questions as "Who am I really?" and "What is the point of my life?"

We could easily imagine the scientist adopting the first standpoint, that of the observer, with regard to his lab assistant. In this case, rather than asking, "What ought I to do?", he might ask "What makes the lab assistant behave as he does?" With a little relevant knowledge of the man and his situation and with a little psychological or sociological sophistication, the scientist might be able to give a good account of why the man behaves as he does. And this knowledge will be an invaluable aid to him when he is reflecting on the different question: "Ought I to report him?" But it is also clear that the scientist may have to make a decision even if he does not have all the relevant knowledge he would like to have. To postpone his decision is equivalent to temporarily deciding not to turn the man in. And even if he has all the relevant knowledge, his decision still has to be made; it is not made for him. *He* must weigh the relative values of loyalty to a co-worker and loyalty to an employer; he must decide whether the harm done to the man by reporting him will be greater than the harm done to him by allowing him to continue in his dishonesty. This requires him to weigh the relative values of physical suffering and the deterioration of moral character. Regardless of all the countless ways in which these two types of thinking are related, and even though they both clearly are forms of thinking, it is plain that in moving from one to the other, a significant shift of perspective occurs. This difference seems even more pronounced when the scientist is thinking not just about whether he ought to do a particular action, but about how he ought to live his life as a whole. It is some such distinction as this which underlies the subjective justification of belief in God. God must be shown to be necessitated or justified by *practical* or *existential* thinking.

With this distinction between the perspective of the agent and the perspective of the observer in mind, we can usefully distinguish several elements of the structure which we shall attempt to use in examining and evaluating Kant, Kierkegaard, and James. These elements do not necessarily occur in any particular order and are not emphasized to the same degree in each of these three philosophers.

The first element that can be distinguished I shall term "theoretical skepticism" with regard to divine existence. This element involves an argument, or at least an assumption that could be defended on the basis of the philosopher's other views, that from the observational standpoint, which is the standpoint of theoretical or scientific knowledge, no knowledge of God's existence, either positive or negative, can be attained. Obviously no belief in God could be said to be a rationally justified belief if one had knowledge that God's existence was not actual or possible. One might also plausibly argue that such an approach would be superfluous or unnecessary if knowledge that God does exist is possible.

Theoretical reason, to do even this much, must show the *meaningfulness* of the problem via an explication of the concepts which purport to refer to the object of religious faith. So it is also important to show that despite our lack of knowledge, the existence of God is *thinkable*, at least as a problem. Even though a serious thinker might not be able to resolve the problem, the question of God's existence is a question which inevitably confronts a person. These two tasks — showing the meaningfulness of the problem and the impossibility of knowledge which would resolve the problem — are not incompatible with a third — that of showing the *plausibility* of religious belief on theoretical grounds. A belief which could not amount to knowledge could nonetheless be judged plausible or implausible. As a matter of fact, to be judged merely plausible or implausible, it is essential that a belief be meaningful and yet fail to amount to knowledge. It will be helpful in our study to regard the negative denial of knowledge and the positive demonstration of meaningfulness as part of the work of theoretical reason in establishing the plausibility of belief.

A second major element of the approach is an attempt to undermine the agnostic position. I shall call this element the "repudiation of the neutral attitude." It requires an argument to show that despite the lack of theoretical knowledge, suspension of judgment is either impossible or undesirable. What must be shown here is that some compelling human interest is at stake; it is not a question which one can or ought to ignore. Or perhaps it can be shown that the decision to ignore the question of God's existence is equivalent to deciding not to believe.

Closely related to this repudiation of neutrality, and perhaps in most cases even identical with it, is a shift of perspective on the question. The question of God's existence must be shown to be a question which is not purely theoretical; it is a question which concerns what I ought to do and be. In one sense this is undeniable of course, in that what is being asked is "Shall I adopt the attitude of belief or disbelief?" What must be shown is that deciding whether or not to believe in God is very closely related to the sorts of questions one is led to when considering one's existence in the world from the viewpoint of the agent. The relationship between God's existence and such questions as "What is the point of my life?" and "What sort of life ought I to live?" must be shown. If God does exist, what difference would it make to the individual, considered as an agent, a person who makes decisions, acts, and takes responsibility for his actions? To use a legal metaphor, there is a change of venue. The case of religion is shifted from the court of theoretical reason which decides certain kinds of cases according to strict criteria, to the court of practical reason, which in order to arrive at its decisions may and must rely on other types of evidence and pay attention to different sorts of concerns.

What finally must be shown of course is that, considered from this practical standpoint, either belief in God is rational or disbelief is irrational. It is not just that neutrality is impossible, and that something important is at stake. Rather what is at stake is something that is required in a fully rational being who is also a practical agent. The refusal to believe in God is in some way inconsistent with some essential feature of my existence as a practical agent and thinker.

As a corollary to this structure, it seems necessary to give some account of the relationship of these two thought-perspectives, which I shall term the theoretical and practical standpoints. It will not be enough to distinguish them. The boundaries and functions of each must be drawn, and they must be shown to mesh harmoniously.

Such a procedure as I have outlined is, of course, fraught with difficulties. I have no intention of minimizing the extreme differences both in style and position which one finds in a close examination of Kant, Kierkegaard, and James. However, I believe that such an endeavor will be as rewarding as it is difficult. In seeking to discover a viable defense of religious belief in the face of a confessed ignorance with regard to theoretical knowledge of God's existence, it seems advisable, as Hume says in another context, to beat the bushes in a wide area and look at the most diverse and original versions. I hope to understand and evaluate each thinker's work on its own merits, but I hope to show that despite the differences, some common problems and assumptions are present which make such a comparison fruitful, and even that their approaches show deep, underlying similarities, particularly of a formal or structural sort.

The underlying issues concern the nature of knowledge, belief, and rational thinking. On what view of knowledge does it become impossible to know anything about God or his existence? What is the nature of belief? In what manner are beliefs held and what is the relationship of belief to evidence? What is rationality, and how is being rational related to man as a willing-feeling-acting being? These are the fundamental issues which are raised by each of these three philosophers' defenses of religious belief, and these are the issues one must ultimately tackle to evaluate properly a subjective defense of theism.

2

Kant: Belief as a
Postulate of Practical Reason

To show that Immanuel Kant provides an example of a subjective justification of religious belief should not be difficult inasmuch as Kant served us as something of a model in developing the concept. Kant is the pre-eminent example of a thinker who carefully denies any knowledge whatsoever of God's existence or nature, but who equally firmly holds that belief in God is completely and thoroughly rational. "For although we have to surrender the language of *knowledge*, we still have sufficient ground to employ, in the presence of the most exacting reason, the quite legitimate language of a firm *faith*" (*KRV* A745, B773).[1]

PRACTICAL AND THEORETICAL REASON

In our introductory chapter we introduced the notion of two types of thinking, and we tried to make this notion more concrete by characterizing these two types of thinking in terms of standpoints or perspectives. In particular we looked at thinking from the standpoint of the observer and thinking from the standpoint of the agent, and pointed out the basic role some such distinction must play in a practical justification of divine belief.

Kant himself does not speak of two types of thinking but of reason in its practical and theoretical employment. Even within the theoretical sphere, Kant uses the term "reason" in two ways. At times he uses "reason" as a general term for the

---

1. Such abbreviations in the text refer to primary sources. For the system of abbreviations used in this book see the list of Abbreviations.

faculty of knowledge. He uses it in this sense in the title *Critique of Pure Reason*.[2] At such times he speaks of the limits of theoretical reason in a way which is almost equivalent to what we might mean if we spoke of the limits of theoretical knowledge. When used in this sense, theoretical reason includes what Kant terms the understanding, and presupposes what he terms intuition.

In the more strict sense, theoretical reason is for Kant the faculty which endeavors to unify experience under principles — to systematize our various bits and kinds of knowledge by subsuming particular facts under conditions and seeking more general conditions for those conditions in turn (*KRV* A305, B361). Reason is concerned with principles, and it strives always for principles which are universal. It is in this sense that reason gives rise to what Kant calls speculative ideas, the most important of which for our purposes are the ideas of God and freedom. What is important to note is that whether he is speaking of reason in the broad sense or in the more restricted sense, by *theoretical* reason Kant means knowing, or at least attempting to gain knowledge. To know for Kant is to adopt what we have termed the standpoint of the observer, the one who is attempting to *explain*. However, when actions are being considered, Kant says reason may not only look at them from the standpoint of the observer, of the one who wishes to explain their law-abiding character, but from the standpoint of the agent, who is concerned with producing an action (*KRV* A550, B578). This is reason in its practical employment.

Strictly speaking there is a form of knowing involved here as well. Kant says that reason is always involved in knowing something a priori; the marks of reason are universality and necessity. But Kant says, "this knowledge may be related to its object in one or other of two ways, either as merely determining it and its concept (which must be supplied from elsewhere) or as also *making it actual*" (*KRV* Bix,x).

---

2. Although this book also deals with reason in its practical employment.

Kant uses the term practical reason interchangeably with will, at least in the *Groundwork*[3] (*Gw* 36, 412). This may seem strange at first, but only until we realize that Kant does not mean by will everything that we might mean when we use the term. He is singling out the cognitive factor in what we regard as willing, and he regards this factor as decisively important. Kant defines the will as "a faculty either of bringing forth objects corresponding to conceptions or of determining itself, i.e., its causality to effect such objects (whether the physical power is sufficient to this or not)" (*KPV* 15, 15). Kant is calling attention to the fact that human beings are able not only to understand, but also to will an action as being of a certain kind. "Only a rational being has the power to act *in accordance with his idea* of laws — that is, in accordance with principles — and only so has he a will" (*Gw* 36, 412). Persons not only will and perform acts which can be understood or viewed as falling under principles or laws; they will them because or in virtue of the fact that the act is the kind of act it is. Or at least this is how we view action and willing when we look at them from the perspective of the agent and willer, someone who is faced with a choice or who has made a choice. We must agree with Beck that "the phenomenon of responding to meanings according to conceptions of rules and laws and of mobilizing our resources to withstand the importunities of momentary impulse is the essential, though often agonizing, kernel in consciousness of the kind of action which makes us men."[4]

Kant calls this rational element in willing practical *reason* to emphasize the role that principles or practical rules play in willing, reason being the faculty of principles.[5] Even so simple an action as sharpening a pencil may be expressive,

---

3. The distinction between *Wille* and *Willkür* is not really made clear before *Religion Within the Limits of Reason Alone*. See John Silber, "The Ethical Significance of Kant's *Religion*," in the introduction to *Religion Within the Limits of Reason Alone*, Harper Torchbook (New York: Harper and Row, 1960), pp. lxxix-cxxxiv.

4. Lewis White Beck, *A Commentary on the Critique of Practical Reason* (Chicago: University of Chicago Press, 1960), p. 36.

5. Whether Kant is using "reason" in strict accordance with his own technical sense in his conception of "practical reason" is a matter of dispute.

not merely of some momentary impulse, but of a settled policy, which might be expressed, for example, in the rule, "Always start off the work-day by sharpening all one's pencils." Such a principle as this Kant terms a maxim, a maxim being defined as "a subjective principle of volition" (*Gw* 15, 401). Maxims are contrasted with laws, which are objective principles which would serve as a maxim for a rational being if he were fully rational.

In addition to being a maxim, this pencil-sharpening principle is a principle which holds for the agent in virtue of the fact that he has adopted a certain end. We might express this by putting the principle in hypothetical form: "If one wishes to have plenty of sharpened pencils always at hand, then one ought to start off every day by sharpening all one's pencils." And even when dealing with this sort of principle, involving the category of means and ends, it is no accident that the principle takes the form of an imperative. For beings like man who are not fully rational, the prescribing of actions as means to an end takes the form of an "ought"; if one wills the end, he ought to will the means (*KPV* 20, 18). It is just this necessitation which is the mark of reason.

Of course this necessity is, as we have seen, a conditional necessity. Even the imperative that one ought to seek one's own happiness, which Kant says one can presuppose with certainty as present in every man (*Gw* 42-43, 415-416), is still a hypothetical imperative which commands an action as a means to some further purpose. As every introductory stu-

---

Paton claims that by "practical reason" in general Kant means something which is more like the work of the understanding than of reason in the more restricted sense. Paton himself adopts the term "practical intelligence" and reserves "practical reason" for what Kant terms "pure practical reason." See H. J. Paton, "Can Reason Be Practical?" *In Defense of Reason* (London: Hutchinson, 1951), footnote 1, p. 131. Beck, however, defends the appropriateness of regarding reason as the prime practical faculty, and argues that Kant does recognize a distinct practical function of the understanding (Beck, *A Commentary*, p. 38). Though this issue is not merely one of terminology, since it bears on the nature of reason itself and how it differs from the understanding, it falls beyond the scope of this essay. What we must examine is Kant's thesis that there is a rational element in willing, and that in some cases this element may be "pure," i.e., that the will may be determined in virtue of this rational element alone.

dent knows, however, Kant holds that reason is practical not only in this sense, but in the sense that it enjoins imperatives absolutely or categorically. Such an imperative is a moral law. It is practical reason in this sense which is crucial in Kant's defense of religious belief, and we will examine it more closely as we proceed with our examination.

As a matter of fact, both theoretical and practical reason must be examined much more carefully as we examine the structure of Kant's justification of what he termed moral or practical faith. Now that they have been distinguished in a preliminary way, we must see what Kant actually says about the way practical and theoretical reason properly function. We must discern not only the boundaries and scope of each; we must see the intimate way in which Kant believes they interrelate.

THE TASK OF THEORETICAL REASON

The general strategy of Kant's defense of belief in God is spelled out in the preface to the second edition of the *Critique of Pure Reason.* Speculative or theoretical reason forces us to transcend the limits of experience and think the unconditioned. In so doing it gives rise to what Kant calls ideas. But if it can be definitively shown that "the unconditioned is not to be met with in things, so far as we know them . . . that is, so far as they are given to us, but only so far as we do not know them, that is, so far as they are things in themselves," then speculative reason will have presented us with an extension of our ideas, a place in the structure of knowledge, which it is compelled to leave empty (*KRV* Bxx). This makes possible the hope that in the field of practical reason, data may be found which are sufficient to justify our occupation of this place or room (*KRV* Bxxi-xxii).

It is plain that this program delegates to theoretical reason the first major element which we described in the first chapter as common to the three approaches we are examining. Theoretical reason must show that (1) the concept of God is thinkable, and (2) no knowledge of God is possible. We suggested that these two elements may be subsumed under a more general project: (3) to show that God is a *possible* object of rational belief, or that belief in God is plausible.[6] We shall argue that this conception of theoretical plausibility or believability illuminates Kant's complicated estimate of the relations between religious belief and theoretical reason. One might think that with regard to (2), all that would be necessary would be to show that no *negative* knowledge is possible, that one could not know that God does not exist. However, we shall see that for Kant, because of the special way in which he construes knowledge, positive knowledge of God would be equally destructive. If a philosopher views faith in God and knowledge of God as mutually exclusive, then to justify religious faith, he must reject all knowledge of God.

The Role of Theoretical Reason in Giving Rise to the Idea of God

First, we shall examine Kant's defense of the thesis that reason[7] can and must think the concept of God. That Kant should have given so much careful attention to this problem is remarkable. In our own day, when there has been no shortage of philosophers willing to claim that propositions about God are neither true nor false but strictly meaningless, it is easy to see the importance of showing that the concept of God is meaningful. However, even without the spur of logical positivism Kant gave a close analysis of this problem. This is partly because Kant felt that it is important not only to know that statements about God are meaningful, but to understand just how they are meaningful. He expresses this by seeking to determine how these concepts arose.

Near the beginning of the transcendental dialectic of the *Critique of Pure Reason* Kant asks an important question:

> Can we isolate reason, and is it, so regarded, an independent source of concepts and judgments which spring from it alone, and by means of which it relates to objects; or is it a merely subordinate faculty, for imposing on given modes of knowledge a certain form, called logical? (*KRV* A305, B362)

---

6. See above, p. 12.

7. In this context Kant uses "reason" in his restricted, technical sense and usually in the sense of theoretical or speculative reason as well. Unless otherwise noted, I shall also use "reason" in this sense in this section.

Unfortunately, Kant himself does not give an altogether clear answer to this question. That is, in his treatment of reason and the ideas to which reason gives rise there is, at the very least, a decided difference of emphasis at times, which has led some commentators to the conclusion that Kant was of two minds on the subject. One of these tendencies we might term the "low" view of reason; it corresponds to what Professor Kemp Smith terms the "skeptical interpretation." The other tendency we shall term the "high" view of reason, and it corresponds somewhat to Kemp Smith's "idealist interpretation."[8] On the high view reason is said to be an independent source of important concepts and principles, while on the low view reason is entirely subordinate to the understanding. The low view of reason interprets the ideas as concepts of the understanding which have been illegitimately extended. This is certainly an important area of Kantian thought. As Kemp Smith's nomenclature implies, the dispute over the status of reason and its ideas is in large part responsible for the wide divergence between the idealist interpretation of Kant and the more anti-metaphysical interpretations.

Very early in the dialectic Kant forthrightly announces the high view of reason:

> Reason, like understanding, can be employed in a merely formal, that is, logical manner, wherein it abstracts from all content of knowledge. But it also is capable of a real use, since it contains within itself the source of certain concepts and principles, which it does not borrow either from the senses or from the understanding. (*KRV* A299, B355)

However, that these concepts are not "borrowed" is obviously forgotten later:

> Reason does not really generate any concept. The most it can do is to *free* a concept of *understanding* from the unavoidable limitations of possible experience, and so to endeavour to extend it

---

8. Kemp Smith gives A645 = B673, A650 = B678-679, A653 = B681, A656 = B684, and A660-661 = B688-689 as passages which support an idealist interpretation; and A646-649 = B674-678, A663-668 = B691-696 as passages which lean towards a skeptical interpretation. See Norman Kemp Smith, *A Commentary on the Critique of Pure Reason* (2nd ed.; New York: Humanities Press, 1962), pp. 425-431, 543-561.

beyond the limits of the empirical, though still, indeed, in terms of its relation to the empirical. (*KRV* A409, B435)

The low view is given support by Kant's contention that reason never applies itself directly to experience or objects, but is concerned merely with the unification of the knowledge gained by the understanding (*KRV* A302, B359). The high view is given added weight by Kant's firm belief, important for his ethics and defense of religion, that reason is *necessarily* a source of concepts and questions which are totally distinct from the sorts of questions dealt with by the understanding (*KRV* A763, B791).

Perhaps a solution to this ambiguity can be found by looking at what Kant says in the light of his philosophical intentions as a whole. He makes it very plain in the preface to the second edition of the first *Critique* that it is absolutely essential for the *Critique* to show that we can and must think the idea of God, but equally essential to show that no speculative knowledge of God is possible (*KRV* Bxxvii-xxix). Only thus could the integrity of both science and religion be preserved. Kant clearly anticipated the two directions in which his thought would be pulled, and he sought vigorously to discourage both. He knew that some would regard him as the destroyer of morality and religion, and he knew that the temptation to build a metaphysical system on the ideas which reason necessarily thinks was strong. Both of these alternatives were abhorrent to him. In such a book as the *Critique* it is natural, even to be expected, that Kant should at times, in his concern to deny the pretensions of speculative reason, emphasize the limitations of the ideas, and that at other times, thinking of the vital use which these ideas of reason must play in the practical sphere (and of their regulative use in the theoretical sphere), he should emphasize their unique, necessary, and unavoidable character.[9]

Thus, at times, in his concern to check the pretensions of speculation, Kant even says that the ideas of reason, divorced as they are from any possible experience, are ideas of which we have "no concept" (*KRV* A338-339, B396-397). At other

---

9. Necessary in the sense that they necessarily arise.

times he seems almost to imply that the ideas are objectively meaningless. He tells us that "concepts are altogether impossible, and can have no meaning, if no object is given for them, or at least for the elements of which they are composed" (*KRV* A139, B178). But Kant here means by a concept "a concept that allows of being exhibited and intuited in a possible experience." That is, he is using the term "concept" in a special, technical sense. So, he continues, to avoid being misunderstood, we should say, instead of claiming we have no concept, that we have a problematic concept, a concept that can never result in knowledge (*KRV* A339, B397).

Now Kant certainly held that the field of the thinkable is broader than the knowable, and even broader than the conceivable in that narrow sense in which the conceivable means the possibly knowable (*KRV* B146). To assert that the ideas are thinkable is not necessarily to say that they are empirically conceivable or knowable. And, as a matter of fact, it is important for Kant to show that the idea of God is thinkable in just this way. It is necessary that the ideas be ideas of which we have only a problematic concept. For if the concept of God is an empirical concept, then its object will be an empirical object, a finite object in space and time. But nothing could be more disastrous than this for religion; to free itself of idolatry, theology must not identify its ultimate concept with some object or characteristic in the world experienced by sense.

> Necessity, infinity, unity, existence outside the world (and not as world-soul), eternity as free from conditions of time, omnipresence as free from conditions of space, omnipotence, etc., are purely transcendental predicates, and for this reason the purified concepts of them, which every theology finds so indispensable, are only to be obtained from transcendental theology. (*KRV* A641-642, B669-670)

There is indeed, says Kant, "something absurd and far from edifying" even in the attempt to realize an ideal (an idea conceived as an archetype or particular being) in the field of appearance. For example, someone who tried to depict the perfectly wise man in a romance might through his failure cast suspicion on the good itself "by giving it the air of a mere fiction" (*KRV* A570, B598).

How then does reason give rise to the idea of God? We have seen that reason is for Kant that aspect of thought which involves the unification of knowledge under principles or universal conditions (*KRV* A305, B361). Thus, says Kant, reason is always involved in seeking for the conditioned knowledge obtained by understanding some further universal condition. Expressed in terms of the traditional logic, "a power which infers conclusions must equally seek grounds for its premises."[10] Kant contends that such a power can never be content with an indefinite series of grounds stretching on *ad infinitum*. There is something unsatisfactory about such a chain of conditions. To achieve the unity and completeness which reason demands, at least the possibility of an ultimate ground must be considered. Reason necessarily gives rise to the notion of a condition for which there is no further condition, the concept of the unconditioned (*KRV* A307, B364). However, Kant is careful to point out that nothing is thereby secured with regard to knowledge of the unconditioned; it is only an idea which must be entertained as a possibility.

This notion of the unconditioned, when applied to different types of inferential reasoning or seeking of conditions, gives rise to the ideas. The idea of God is said by Kant to be not merely an idea but an *ideal*, which is an idea not merely viewed as real but as a particular being (*KRV* A568, B596).

Considering reality as completely determined either positively or negatively with regard to every possible predicate, Kant argues that this presupposes the concept of "the sum total of all possibilities" (*KRV* A572, B600). Kant means that the logical determination of the universe presupposes a disjunctive proposition giving all the positive alternative attributes which any object might possibly have. This concept contains only positive attributes, since Kant says that negations presuppose the corresponding positive attribute. (Unless the concept "good" has some meaning, it is meaningless to say that an object is not good.) This concept is the concept

---

10. Paton, *In Defense of Reason*, p. 134.

of a single thing, that which possesses all reality, "the supreme and complete material condition of the possibility of all that exists" (*KRV* A575-577, B603-605).

Some have charged that Kant's derivation of the idea of God is artificial, and we may indeed ask whether the concept which is generated when the disjunctive syllogism — one of the standard forms of inference — is expanded to the unconditioned is identical with the *religious* conception of God. While Kant's notion is far from capturing the richness and moral content involved in most religious conceptions, it would be a mistake to assume that his conception is fundamentally non-religious. Many theologians have viewed the concept of God as the concept of the Ground of all possible beings. Such a conception of God has its origins not merely in Greek philosophy; it could be argued that it is one way of expressing the Biblical doctrine of creation. St. Paul, in affirming Christ's divinity, taught that "he is before all things, and by him all things consist" and gave a recognizable formulation of the "highest reality" concept by affirming that this is possible because in Christ "all fullness dwells."[11] We can reasonably regard Kant's account of the origin of the ideal as an abstruse and abstract formulation of one fundamental aspect of the traditional conception of God.

Men often ask the question, "Why is this thing like this rather than being like that?" And they usually answer in terms of some finite condition or set of conditions. But as the process of questioning proceeds, whether legitimate or not, there is a natural tendency to ask this question of the whole of the universe. Why this set of conditions, this universe, with its set of objects and characteristics and relationships, rather than another one? This question seems to demand some ground or sufficient reason why this universe is actualized out of the whole range of possible universes, and Kant conceives this ground as that which possesses in itself the possible reality of all beings, the highest reality. Put in personal terms, this is none other than the concept of a God who wills this universe to exist, who chooses this universe from the

---

11. Colossians 1:16-19.

range of universes which are possibly real in virtue of his creative power.

With this account of the origin of the concept of God, we can now understand Kant's ambivalence toward reason and the ideal. From one perspective, it does seem that reason has taken the concept of the condition of a finite object's being the particular object it is, and radically extended it, or "freed it from every empirical condition." We do give explanations of why Johnny is fat rather than thin, and why a bird has two wings rather than one. To ask this sort of question about reality as a whole is indeed merely a problematic extension of a concept of the understanding, problematic because we have no way of answering the question or even of determining whether there is indeed an answer to it.

But for equally good reasons one could argue that this concept, extended in this way, is radically transformed, is qualitatively different in such a way that reason could be said to engender a new concept and question. The question, "Why this universe and not another?" has seemed to many to be a real question,[12] and such a question seems of a completely different order than any asked by the understanding. The question "Why this rather than that?" is one asked by the understanding, but when one extends this question to the universe as a whole it really does seem to be a new question, one which engenders a new concept as a purported or possible answer. And it is certainly, as Kant says, a problematic concept, a concept which can never itself be made completely determinate by exhibiting its object in experience. We can therefore understand Kant's contention that though we can certainly think the idea, there is a sense in which we have no concept of it. It is too big for our understanding. The question even engenders a certain feeling of giddiness or dizziness, as if our intellect had reached the very boundaries of theoretical thought. And Kant believed that the ideas of reason did mark precisely that boundary.

Even though this concept is problematic, it is important

---

12. See for example William James, who considers this question "the parent of philosophic craving" (SR, p. 72).

that theoretical reason can think it. Kant argues that theoretical reason, though it may not be adequate to obtain knowledge of God, can and must produce this ideal. Though it is a problematic concept, a "mere" ideal, it is "an ideal without a flaw" (*KRV* A641, B669).

> For if, in some other relation, perhaps on practical grounds, the *presupposition* of a supreme and all-sufficient being, as highest intelligence, established its validity beyond all question, it would be of the greatest importance accurately to determine this concept on its transcendental side, as the concept of a necessary and supremely real being, to free it from whatever, as belonging to mere appearance (anthropomorphism in its wider sense) . . . is out of keeping with the supreme reality. (*KRV* A640, B668)

Not only does theoretical reason provide an ideal which at least shows the possibility of a harmonious dove-tailing with practical reason (*KRV* A329, B386), but it also determines the ideal in a way which prevents any idolatrous identification of God with finite objects, or harmful ascription to him of finite characteristics which belong to the world of appearance, but in a way which leaves open the possibility of the ascription to God of ideal moral attributes.

And in producing this ideal, theoretical reason is not being unfaithful to her calling and surreptitiously introducing moral and practical conceptions into the theoretical endeavor. The ideas are not arbitrarily conceived. Reason, in the continuous advance of empirical synthesis, is necessarily led up to them "whenever it endeavours to free from all conditions and apprehend in its unconditioned totality that which according to the rules of experience can never be determined save as conditioned" (*KRV* A462, B490). There is thus a theoretical need to think the idea of God, to unify our explanations of the world by referring them all to a single principle. This theoretical need is justified in part by what Kant calls the regulative function of the ideas, their role as ideal guides for thought, always calling us to seek greater and greater unity in our explanations of the world, preventing us from identifying any particular stage of explanation as that final unity. These ideas provide, Kant says, a signpost or compass by which the thinker can orient himself (*WOT* 142, p. 301). This metaphor of orientation is very apt, and it helps to underscore Kant's view of the theoretical concept of God as the highest reality and the conceptual notion of logical space which underlies his derivation of the idea.

Reason takes a concept of the understanding and by extending it to its limit transforms it into a concept which transcends any possible experience. No intuition of the object of such a concept is possible; its relationship to the world of appearances cannot be thought via the schematized categories which the understanding employs; the relationship can only be thought in terms of pure or formal concepts (*WOT* 136, p. 296). We remove from the idea the conditions which limit the concept, but which also enable us clearly and definitely to conceive the object. We then think the idea as "standing to the sum of appearances in a relation analogous to that in which appearances stand to one another" (*KRV* A647, B702). This denial of any empirical concept of God is precisely what is to be desired from the practical standpoint. For if "reason is denied the right of being the first to speak of things which concern supersensuous objects, such as the existence of God and the future world, a wide gate is opened to fanaticism, superstition, and even atheistic opinions" (*WOT* 143, p. 302).

To summarize Kant's view, rational reflection on the process of empirically conceptualizing the world naturally leads one to the concept of an ultimate ground or unconditioned condition which completely determines the real universe with regard to all possible positive attributes. This concept is none other than the concept of an *ens realissimum*.

The correspondence of Kant's account of how we think the idea of God to what has traditionally been viewed as a theistic proof can easily be seen. However, Kant does distinguish between the origin of the idea, which is necessary for the conceptual determination of the universe, and the proof, which argues from the actual existence of the universe to the existence of a necessary being.[13] That is, an argument that

---

13. Chapter 3, Section 2 of the first *Critique* is an account of how reason

reason must form a concept of the highest reality to adequately conceive the finite universe is different from an argument that the existence of the contingent universe requires such a highest reality as its ground. However, that the derivation of the idea and the proofs should be closely related or even confused by Kant is not surprising in view of Kant's analysis of the cosmological proof, or at least of the basis of the proof, which really amounts to the claim that the proof is an account of the subjective necessity of reason to think an idea, which has been confused with an objective necessity.[14] Of course such a subjective necessity on Kant's view establishes nothing with regard to the objective reality of the object of the idea, but the necessity for reason remains. Thus "human reason has this peculiar fate that in one species of its knowledge it is burdened by questions which, as prescribed by the very nature of reason itself, it is not able to ignore, but which, as transcending all its powers, it is also not able to answer" (KRV Avii).

Of course in claiming that the question of God's existence is a question which man cannot answer, we have already turned from the first part of the task of constructing a non-theoretical justification of belief in God, which is showing that the concept is meaningful or thinkable, to the second, which is showing that no theoretical knowledge of God is possible. And it is this element which we must now consider.

However, before doing so, in anticipation of some later remarks and the sort of argument given by William James, we might ask if Kant has not shown something more than merely that the concept of God is thinkable. One of the conditions which James attaches to any justification of religious faith is that its object must not merely be thinkable but believable. The introduction of such a psychologically laden term raises many problems. Believability is obviously in part a function

---

produces the ideal (the conception of God), while Section 3 introduces the proofs with which reason supports that ideal.

14. See for instance Kant's treatment of Mendelssohn in What is Orientation in Thinking? Kant says that Mendelssohn accurately showed the need of reason to think the idea of God in his theistic proofs, but criticizes him for confusing this "need of reason" with knowledge.

of many non-rational and subjective factors. But there is also a cognitive or rational element involved in belief, or at least there is in many cases. To say of an account of a crime that it is believable implies that it is rationally convincing, that it does justice to the facts known, that it is at least not implausible. The question which I should like to pose is whether Kant, in showing that the idea of God is thinkable, is really showing that one of the conditions for believability has been met, and whether or not his attempt to show that the idea of God is meaningful is part of a larger effort to show the believability of God's existence.

Granted that Kant would not have posed this question himself, one still is faced with Kant's very puzzling contention that reason's ascent to God is a *necessary* ascent. Granted, it is only subjectively necessary, but this sort of of subjectivity does not refer to the particular thinker's idiosyncratic conditions; the ascent is subjective in the sense that it is grounded in the nature of reason or thought itself. The ideas "are not fictitious and have not arisen fortuitously but have sprung from the very nature of reason" (*KRV* A339, B397). It is this subjective necessity which produces what Kant calls "a natural and inevitable illusion," which "does not cease even after it has been detected and its invalidity clearly revealed by transcendental criticism" (*KRV* A297-298, B353-354). Though we will leave this question for now, this peculiar status which the ideas have will become increasingly important as we look at Kant's critique of any claims to knowledge of God, and particularly at his ambivalent attitude toward the physico-theological proof.

The Role of Theoretical Knowledge in Showing that No Knowledge of God Is Possible

Kant's critique of natural theology has often been viewed as a negative, even shattering analysis. And of course it is negative in the sense that Kant denies that any positive or theoretical knowledge of God is possible. But Kant himself was far from viewing his work as negative in the sense of "harmful to religious belief." As he puts it, "to deny that the service which the *Critique* renders is positive in character, would thus be like saying that the police are of no positive benefit, inasmuch as their main business is merely to prevent the violence of which citizens stand in mutual fear, in order that each may pursue his vocation in peace and security" (*KRV* Bxxv).

Kant thought the criticism of claims to have theoretical knowledge of God rendered a positive service for several reasons. First and most obvious, but amazingly neglected, is the role of this criticism in silencing objections to religious belief. Kant believed that he could demonstrate that no knowledge of God is *possible*, either positively or negatively. He did not merely content himself with criticism of theistic proofs, or merely assert that we have no good reason to suppose that God exists. Kant wished to show that no knowledge of God is possible, that the attempt to gain any such knowledge is in a certain sense misguided, and to reproach religion with its lack is even more misguided. His undertaking was an attempt to show a necessary ignorance derived from principles (*KRV* A761, B789). Thus Kant actually felt that the critique would forever silence all objections to morality and religion, "and this in Socratic fashion, namely, by the clearest proof of the ignorance of the objectors" (*KRV* Bxxxi). The grounds upon which Kant was to show the inability of reason to maintain the existence of God served equally well, he thought, as grounds to show the invalidity of all counter-assertions (*KRV* A640-641, B668-669).

The second kind of positive service rendered by the *Critique* involves protecting against the identification of God with the sensible. We have already seen that it is necessary that the idea of God be an idea of reason and not an empirical concept. It is equally valuable and necessary for reason to show that no empirical knowledge of the object of this idea is possible. And of course reason can do this if it attains to a correct understanding of empirical knowing and also maintains the idea of God in its purity. When pure reason attempts to attain knowledge of the supersensible, it threatens an identification of the real with the sensible which would make impossible any practical knowledge of God. Reason, in attempting to gain theoretical knowledge of God, threatens to transform God into an object of experience and establish an identity between the empirical and the real. By limiting one sort of knowledge, theoretical knowledge, reason actually makes possible the extension of knowledge in another area (*KRV* Bxxiv-xxv, xxx).

The third positive service which the *Critique* renders becomes finally clear only after practical reason has shown how morality does provide a ground for belief in God. It is then evident that this is the route to be preferred for moral and religious reasons, because a theoretically grounded religion could and easily would degenerate into a gnosticism divorced from true moral and religious concerns. Speculative knowledge would render "theology and morals, and through the union of these two, likewise *religion*, and therewith the highest ends of our existence, entirely and exclusively dependent on the faculty of speculative reason" (*KRV* Note to A337, B395). But this would mean that morality would have to conform to the dictates of an "external legislator" (*KU* 460, p. 131). A theoretical proof would lead to a religion of fear and compulsion; objective proofs ask only submission. Morality, on the other hand, leads to a free presentation to us of the final end of our being, a Being to be accepted in a free moral act, through our reverence and veneration for the moral law (*KU* 481-482, p. 159).

Kant is here certainly moving towards what we would today term an existential approach to religion. Though he would be the last to deny the cognitive or rational element in religion and morality, he recognizes clearly that religion and morality do not *merely* consist in the acceptance of factual truths. Though religion and morality do embody objective truth, they embody it in a way which is essentially related to man's ethical and religious existence. Belief in God, though certainly not a mere attitude, nevertheless is not merely a matter of accepting some fact about the world. The relationship of religion to morality must be for Kant an essential one, not a mere accident. The acceptance of the truth of religion is dependent on one's being a moral person, and the acceptance of that truth is itself a free moral act.

And it is precisely in this direction of turning man's

attention away from speculation and towards the business of becoming a moral person that Kant thought the denial of theoretical knowledge of God's existence would lead. In every area in which reason seeks knowledge of the unconditioned, its failure to gain satisfying answers is to be taken as a hint to turn from speculation in the direction of more fruitful practical employment (*KRV* B421). The difficulty into which theoretical reason falls in its dialectic is "the most fortunate perplexity in which human reason could ever have become involved" since it compels us to seek the "key to escape," which is the discovery of "a higher immutable order of things in which we already are" (*KPV* 107, pp. 111-112).

How then does Kant go about attempting to show that such knowledge is impossible and thereby perform these various positive services? It is clear that mere criticism of proofs of God's existence would not accomplish this, even if Kant were correct in asserting that all such proofs are of the types which he criticized, a claim which is unlikely to be granted.[15] Kant must show why such proofs *must* fail, which is seemingly a rather tall order. However, there is certainly a sense in which Kant attempts to do just that. To some extent the criticism of the theistic proofs is merely corroboration of what we knew in advance must be the case. Given the analysis of knowledge and its conditions which Kant has given in the Transcendental Aesthetic and Transcendental Analytic (and the support given to that analysis by the Antimony of Pure Reason), *and* Kant's account of the nature of the ideas of reason and their origin, his conclusions as to the impossibility of any knowledge of these ideas follows immediately.

Kant has concluded already that "the categories as yielding knowledge of *things* have no kind of application, save only in regard to things which may be objects of possible experience" (*KRV* B147-148). And we have already seen that one of the defining characteristics of an idea of reason, such as the idea of God, is that its object can never become the object of

15. For example, a typical Thomist response to Kant is that the Kantian version of the cosmological argument stems from Wolff and Leibniz and differs significantly from Aquinas' argument.

any possible experience (*KRV* B383, A327). On Kant's analysis of knowledge, intuition is one of its essential conditions, and in this case intuition is by the nature of the case impossible. If knowledge depends on the categories, and if the application of the categories can only be justified via the mediation of the concept of a possible experience, then Kant seems to be on solid ground in claiming that in the absence of any possible experience, a concept is a "mere idea" (*KRV* A489, B517).

Of course the conception of knowledge and experience that Kant is advocating can be attacked. One might wonder whether claims to theistic or atheistic knowledge can be disposed of so readily; it seems almost as if Kant has made such knowledge impossible by definition. This type of criticism is important, and it centers precisely on one of the points which we will consider in our evaluation of Kant's practical approach and the general structure of this type of justification of religious belief. The conceptions of experience, or what is to count as evidence, and of knowledge are crucial and require close scrutiny.

But it also must be noted that Kant's conception of knowledge is far from arbitrary. The theses that knowledge is impossible in the absence of experience and that it is impossible to experience God have been adopted by a great many modern thinkers. They certainly cannot be dismissed as mere prejudices. Almost the whole of the *Critique of Pure Reason* is a sustained attempt to justify this view of knowledge. Kant has attempted to show that experience is necessarily spatiotemporal, and that the justification of the application of the categories of the understanding is possible only in relationship to experience of space-time objects. He then has given an account of certain ideas of reason, whose objects, it is plain, are never to be met within such experience.

And what we have called the corroboration of the argument, the detailed arguments of the dialectic, should not be forgotten. Having argued that no knowledge of the ideas is possible, Kant then takes particular varieties of claims to such knowledge and attempts to unmask them individually. Particularly significant as corroboration for Kant's thesis are the antinomies. If the attempt to apply the categories to that unconditioned reality which transcends any possible experience involves reason in contradictions, then one would certainly be justified in restricting the application of those categories. Kant himself even seems to give the antinomies a central role in the discovery of the proper limits of theoretical knowledge.[16]

> But the illusion [of transcendent knowledge] would never be noticed as deceptive if it were not betrayed by a conflict of reason with itself in applying to appearances its principle of presupposing the unconditioned for every conditioned thing. Reason is thus forced to investigate this illusion, to find out how it arises and how it can be removed. (*KPV* 107, p. 111)

One should also keep in mind that as corroboration Kant offers a painstaking critique of three types of theistic proofs. While these criticisms are important, they are also well known and I do not intend to summarize them here.[17] They have generated an enormous amount of literature, and in some respects do not represent much of an advance beyond Hume's *Dialogues Concerning Natural Religion*. As a matter of fact, Kant's treatment of the proofs is, in my opinion, interesting not so much for his criticisms of them, as for his obvious ambivalence towards these proofs. Given the Analytic, it is not surprising that Kant should reject these proofs; his contention that they are nevertheless not mere mistakes, but natural illusions, which retain a certain force even after criticism, is a far more interesting and significant claim.

We thus see how Kant claims to show a necessary ignorance about the question of God's existence. Even if we are prepared to grant that this has been shown, it might be doubted whether Kant has really "forever silenced all objections to morality and religion." Kant has attempted to show that no one can claim to know that there is no God by showing

---

16. Norman Kemp Smith maintains that the sections on the antinomies were the earliest part of the Dialectic to be written and that they played a key role in the revolution in Kant's thought which led to his critical views. See his *Commentary*, pp. 425, 431-440.

17. A. C. Ewing offers a brief and lucid summary in *A Short Commentary on the Critique of Pure Reason* (Chicago: University of Chicago Press, 1938), pp. 241-245.

that no knowledge with regard to God's existence is possible. But it may be asked whether positive and negative existential affirmations function in the same way and bear the same relationship to evidence.

Someone might claim that in deciding whether an entity exists there is some sort of presumption on the side of the negation.[18] Thus, if scientists are looking for evidence that a certain particle exists, if they can find no positive evidence, then it does not follow that the assertions that the particle exists and that it does not exist are equally well supported. Though perhaps their lack of success does not show the particle does not exist, it at least seems to be more supportive of that conclusion than the opposite. If we have *no* knowledge of such a particle, then that is supportive of the truth of the proposition "No such particle exists." Similarly, the fact that I have no knowledge of there being a unicorn in the office next to mine, and no evidence that there is a unicorn there, lends support to the thesis that there is no unicorn there. In the absence of any knowledge, the two assertions "There is a unicorn in the next office" and "There is no unicorn in the next office" are not on the same par.

Whatever one wishes to make of the status of this "negative presumption" within the realm of experience, it is not a valid objection to Kant's contention about knowledge of God. When considering the question as to the existence of a possible object of experience, the lack of any evidence or experience suggesting the existence of such an object may offer *prima facie* support for its non-existence (or it may not). But this is not a realm where we have no knowledge in Kant's sense. The scientists looking for the particle know a great deal. If there is such a particle, they may know the conditions under which it is likely to be discovered. The failure of those conditions to produce such a discovery constitutes negative evidence. (Though of course the scientists are fallible.) Similarly, I have walked into the office next door to mine many times and I have never seen a unicorn. In the lack of any

---

18. Sidney Hook makes such a claim in *The Quest for Being* (New York: St. Martin's Press, 1961), p. 97.

evidence to suggest the existence of a unicorn there, there is a strong presumption against the existence of any such entity.

The situation with regard to God is completely different, at least according to Kant. No one can specify any set of conditions under which God ought to be experiencible. If Kant is right, we know in advance that such empirical verification is impossible. Even to demand it or seek it would be wrong-headed and betray a serious misunderstanding. In *this* case positive and negative existential affirmations are equally risky. One has no more reason to believe there is no God than to believe there is.

Very well, our critic might respond. Let us construct a case which is exactly parallel. Let us suppose some entity, say a fairy, which is defined in such a way that experience of it is impossible. This entity will be a fairy who can be neither seen, heard, smelled, nor experienced in any way. There are therefore no conditions under which one could ever know anything of this fairy. Would we really say that a belief in this fairy and belief in his non-existence are equally risky? Even if it should be granted that the hypothesis of such a fairy is meaningful (and of course many would not grant this), common sense would surely dictate that belief in such an entity would be illogical and absurd.

This is a penetrating criticism and goes right to the heart of the Kantian approach. Kant's answer to it surely lies in his contention, which we have already discussed, that the idea of God is a natural idea of reason, an idea which reason must necessarily consider, not merely a fortuitous and fantastic construction, as in the case of the fairy. The idea of God, though it is an idea of a particular entity, is an idea which bears an integral relationship to reality as a whole. It is a metaphysical idea, the embodiment of a way of viewing the universe. And it is not surprising that the sort of evidence and the arguments which are appropriate in this arena are significantly different from that which is offered for particular, finite entities.

What the fairy criticism makes clear is that if theoretical reason is to make rational belief in God (even on other grounds) *possible*, it must do more than show that the idea of

God is thinkable merely as a logical possibility and that we have no knowledge whatsoever with regard to it. Theoretical reason must show that the object of the idea is a *believable* metaphysical view. This certainly does require that we have no knowledge that there is no such object and it does require that the existence of such an object be logically possible. But it can be argued that these are merely the entrance requirements; it must also be shown that the idea is meaningful, that is, not silly, as in the case of the fairy. It must be shown that it is natural for a reflective person to think of this idea, or even regard it as plausible, or perhaps the most plausible alternative, when considering the nature of reality as a whole. In short, the idea must be shown to be believable. Given Kant's restricted sense of knowledge, this is perfectly compatible with his holding that no knowledge of God's existence is possible.

Conclusion: The Role of Theoretical Reason
in Showing that the Idea of God Is Believable

We have already noted the ambiguity which is present in the term "believable." To say that a proposition is believable is to make a judgment about the psychological make-up of someone. If a proposition is believable, then it is a potential object of belief for some person. Therefore, if any person A does believe a certain proposition P, then it is certain that for A, P is believable. However, A might find P believable even if he doesn't in fact believe in its truth.

The types of factors involved in determining whether a proposition is believable for any person A are of course legion. Psychologically it may be possible for A to believe some proposition P for any number of reasons, including such subjective factors as A's father believed P, A's father did not believe P, A belonged to a club which required belief in P as a membership requirement, and so on. Therefore, one certainly cannot deduce from the fact that P is believable for A, that A has good reasons for believing P (though he may in fact have such reasons), nor does the fact that P is not believable for A entail that P is not true or that A has no good reasons for believing P. (A might have some reasons for believing which he does not recognize as good reasons.)

Nevertheless, I believe that some of the factors which sometimes make a proposition believable to a person are rational in nature. Thus, on some occasions P might be believable to A because it satisfactorily explains certain types of phenomena, or because A is in the possession of certain kinds of evidence which suggests that P is true. If A's finding P believable *is* the result of some such factor as this, which is at least more rational than many such factors, then it is likely (though not certain) that other persons, if they are attempting to form their beliefs on a rational basis, will also find P believable. In general, we can say of those factors which go into making a proposition believable to a person that the less subjective (in a different sense of "subjective" than in the title of this essay) they are (the less they depend on having a particular father or being born in a particular town, etc.), the more effective they will be in making P believable to others. Or in other words, the more rational these factors are (the more they are the result of A's weighing of cognitive evidence), the more potent they will be in making propositions believable to others. Of course since those others form some of their beliefs as the result of non-rational factors, from the fact that P is believable to A in virtue of some rational evidence he knows, it will not follow that everyone who is acquainted with that evidence will believe P or even find P believable.

We have been attempting to discuss the grammar of "believable." If our analysis so far has been correct, we can now introduce the concept of a proposition whose truth is not known with certainty, but which is believable to all fully rational beings. Such a proposition is not logically absurd or impossible. If there were such a proposition, it would by no means entail that it was known by those beings or that it was true. There might even be two such propositions, whose truth is mutually exclusive. It would only entail that the proposition made some kind of claim, or was recognized as plausible by these fully rational beings, for reasons which were independent of any idiosyncratic, non-rational factors. It also does not entail that every fully rational being would actually believe such a proposition to be true, and it certainly does not entail that all human beings, who are not fully rational, would believe it, or even that all human beings would find it believable. How such a proposition could be recognized is of course very problematic, but it would seem that belief in a proposition P for reasons which are non-subjective by a significant number of intelligent thinkers, and the finding of P to be believable by an even larger number of intelligent thinkers for similar reasons, would be at least a *prima facie* distinguishing mark of such a proposition. What I would like to suggest is that Kant's ambivalence towards the theistic proofs is clarified if we interpret Kant's assessment of those proofs, particularly the physico-theological proof, as that they are adequate to show that God's existence is rationally believable, but not known. Of course to show that a proposition is rationally believable in no way entails that it ought to be believed. It merely entails that the proposition is a meaningful alternative, perhaps merely one alternative among others. Nevertheless, if a person should actually believe in the existence of God, if it is such a rationally believable proposition, he could not be reproached with having made an irrational decision or sacrificed his intellect. And of course it is always possible that new evidence will be found, perhaps of a different kind, which will tip the scale in favor of one alternative, making it a proposition which ought to be believed.

Let us look at what Kant actually says about the idea of God, and about the theoretical proofs for God's existence. We have already seen that Kant holds that the idea of God is a necessary but problematic idea. It is necessary in the sense that it inevitably arises as a possible answer to reason's quest for a final unifying explanation of the universe in its totality. The idea of God is the concept of the unconditioned condition of all conditions. However it is a problematic idea because reason has no grounds for holding that there is an answer to this quest, and we have seen that on Kant's view of knowledge, it could never be known that there is an object which would satisfy reason's demand.

However, this is not all Kant has to say on the subject.

Not only is the idea of God natural; it gives rise to an illusion which is also said to be natural. Reason employs certain fundamental rules or maxims in its work of unifying our knowledge, and it is the application of these rules to the whole of reality which gives rise to the ideas. But as these rules or maxims are not arbitrary, but fundamental for reason's work (*subjectively necessary* for our thinking), reason goes further and by a natural illusion takes this subjective necessity to be an objective necessity (*KRV* A297, B354). This illusion results from our regarding the conditions which are *necessary* if the universe is to be fully known or fully intelligible, to be objectively necessary conditions of being. It is very much in the interest of reason to proceed on the assumption that reality is fully intelligible, and there is a strong, almost irresistible tendency for reason to argue that since she must necessarily proceed in this fashion, it is necessary that reality conform to these conditions.

Kant holds that this is not merely a mistake or fallacy, but a temptation which is deeply rooted in the very nature of thought or rational investigation.

> There exists, then, a natural and unavoidable dialectic of pure reason — not one in which a bungler might entangle himself through lack of knowledge, or one which some sophist has artificially invented to confuse thinking people, but one inseparable from human reason, and which, even after its deceptiveness has been exposed, will not cease to play tricks with reason and continually entrap it into momentary aberrations ever and again calling for correction. (*KRV* A298, B354-355)

Kant even says that the illusions spring "from the very nature of reason" and that the "wisest of men cannot free himself from them" (*KRV* A339, B397). From this we may conclude at least that for Kant himself there was something attractive about those pseudo-rational conclusions, even after he himself clearly rejected them as giving knowledge, and even gave clear reasons why one ought to reject them as illusions.[19]

Before attempting to determine whether this remarkable

---

19. Nathan Rotenstreich argues that Kant shows that the illusions are explicable, but not that they are "natural." His argument is that Kant shows only that the formation of the concepts is inevitable and necessary; it is

position is philosophically important or merely gives us some revealing psychological insight into Kant, let us examine Kant's specific treatment of the proofs, where the ambivalence is equally pronounced. This is not surprising since the illusion of reason is fundamentally of the same nature in all its forms: the taking of a subjective necessity for an objective necessity.

Kant's discussion of reason's attempt to demonstrate the existence of God begins with an account of what he terms the natural procedure of human reason. He first gives an account of the subjective need of reason to presuppose a foundation for the complete determination of its concepts which we examined earlier in our discussion of the idea of God. However, Kant says that reason is far too conscious of the merely ideal character of this concept to be persuaded on this ground alone that "a mere creature of its thought is a real being" (*KRV*, A583-584, B611-612). We are led to believe in the existence of God not because of our need to think of the world as completely determined with respect to all possible predicates, and the subsequent need to think of a ground of that determination, but by a train of thought which begins with common experience and seeks support for the existence of those objects which we encounter in that common experience.

> If we admit something as existing, no matter what this something may be, we must also admit that there is something which exists *necessarily*. For the contingent exists only under the condition of some other contingent existence as its cause, until we are brought to a cause which is not contingent, and which is therefore unconditionally necessary. This is the argument upon

---

clearly not necessary to believe in the hypostatized objects, as Kant himself shows. Hence the illusion is not really natural, though it is explicable. However, it seems clear that Kant himself wishes to hold that it is the illusion itself which is natural, not in the sense that reason is necessarily deceived, but in the sense that the deception is a constant temptation. Kant evidently feels that the belief that the conditions of rational intelligibility are conditions of being to be more than a mere mistake. In addition, Rotenstreich ignores the extent to which the illusion may be rooted in our practical reason. See Nathan Rotenstreich, "Kant's Dialectic," *Review of Metaphysics*, 7 (March, 1954), 389-421.

which reason bases its advance to the primordial being. (*KRV* A584, B612)

After reason has persuaded itself of the existence of some necessary being, it "looks around for the concept of that which is independent of any condition, and finds it in that which is the sufficient condition of all else," which is none other than the concept of the highest reality, conceived as absolute unity and as a single being, which is precisely the transcendental concept of God to which theoretical reason gives rise (*KRV* A586-587, B614-615).

All this is preliminary to Kant's discussion of the three types of proofs themselves, but it is clear that the germ of these proofs is already present in this discussion of the procedure of the common understanding. For Kant really does not view the proofs as completely separate. The cosmological argument depends on the ontological argument to establish that the necessary being is that perfect being who is God, and in a similar way, the physico-theological proof presupposes the cosmological argument (and hence also the ontological argument) to establish that the cause of the order in the world is a necessary being.[20] This preliminary discussion is an account of how "in all peoples there shine amidst the most benighted polytheism some gleams of monotheism, to which they have been led, not by reflection and profound speculation, but simply by the natural bent of the common understanding as step by step it has come to apprehend its own requirements" (*KRV* A590, B618).

This natural procedure is developed by reason into formal proofs, which either begin from "determinate experience, or the existence of something in general," or else argue completely a priori for the existence of God on the basis of concepts alone (*KRV* A590-591, B618-619). These three proofs, called by Kant the physico-theological proof, the cosmological proof, and the ontological proof respectively, all share in the illusion of reason, which is to regard as objectively necessary what is subjectively necessary for the employment of reason. For example, the need of reason to

---

20. Whether Kant is right on this point is unimportant for our purposes.

view certain objects as designed persuades her to assert that these objects must in fact have been designed by a designer.

In his discussion Kant does not merely criticize these arguments as not proving what they attempt to prove, though he does do that. He also maintains that despite this failure, at least the cosmological and physico-theological proofs, which begin not merely with the way in which reason must necessarily form concepts but with the way reason must necessarily view existing objects, have a certain plausibility. Thus, he maintains that the cosmological argument "enters upon a course of reasoning which, whether rational or only pseudo-rational, is at any rate natural, and the most convincing not only for common sense, but even for speculative understanding" (*KRV* A604, B632).

In the case of the physico-theological argument this muted praise becomes much more extravagant. Not only should this proof be treated with respect because "it is the oldest, the clearest, and the most accordant with the common reason of mankind," but it is such a help in our examination of nature, and is in turn so confirmed by that examination that it "acquires the force of an irresistible conviction." And in a remarkably poetic passage Kant exclaims:

> It would therefore not only be uncomforting but utterly vain to attempt to diminish in any way the authority of this argument. Reason, constantly upheld by this ever-increasing evidence, which, though empirical, is yet so powerful, cannot be so depressed through doubts suggested by subtle and abstruse speculation, that it is not at once aroused from the indecision of all melancholy reflection, as from a dream, by one glance at the wonders of nature and the majesty of the universe — ascending from height to height up to the all-highest, from the conditioned to its conditions, up to the supreme and unconditioned Author (of all conditioned being). (*KRV* A624, B652)

Kant himself says he has nothing but commendation for this procedure; he only wishes to criticize the claim that this proof logically possesses "apodictic certainty," and also to argue that the assent which reason gives to it is founded in part on "support from other quarters," that is, from practical reason (*KRV* A624, B652). As we shall see later, in the *Critique of Judgment* Kant asserts that there is a close relationship between the physico-theological argument and Kant's own "moral argument."

Despite this praise, however, it is clear that Kant's considered judgment on the physico-theological argument is that, taken alone as a speculative proof of God's existence, it fails because it rests on the cosmological and hence the ontological argument, and thus shares with them the illusion of taking what is subjectively necessary to reason as objectively necessary for things. And Kant explicitly holds that reason must show the existence of God as apodictically certain. To attempt to establish the probable existence of an idea of reason is as absurd as attempting to prove that a proposition of geometry is probably true. Reason has no dealings with opinion; she judges with certainty or she must refuse to judge at all (*KRV* A775, B803). There is thus an obvious tension if not contradiction between Kant's praise of the theistic proofs, particularly the physico-theological argument, and his criticisms of them.

This tension is the result of Kant's holding three theses. (1) The arguments which reason uses to attempt to prove the existence of God have a certain plausibility about them; their claim to acceptance is based on rational grounds, which are open to the inspection of any rational being, and which possess some force even after criticism. (2) Despite this plausibility, these arguments fail to establish God's existence apodictically because a crucial premise is not known to be valid: that the conditions which the world must satisfy to be completely intelligible are in fact satisfied. (3) There is no place for hypotheses or any judgments which are not apodictically certain in the field of speculative reason.

While there is no logical contradiction in holding these three theses, there is a tension. What I should like to argue is that (1) and (2) represent valuable insights by Kant which must be retained, and that the tension must be resolved by giving up or modifying (3). In effect (1) is an attempt to show that "God exists" is a proposition which is believable and not believable merely to certain groups of people in virtue of certain accidental features of their experience or existence, but inherently believable, believable for any fully rational

being. This is fully compatible with (2): it is quite possible
that a proposition might be regarded as plausible but not
sufficiently grounded to be known. For instance, a thinker
might find both (a) "the physical universe is a self-sustaining
system which has no beginning or end," and (b) "the physical
universe requires for its existence some necessary being as its
ground" to be plausible theses to which he feels a certain
attraction, yet might not regard either as established truths.
The introduction of thesis (3), on the other hand, makes the
status of either (1) or (2) problematic.

And of these theses, it is (3) that has the least to recom-
mend itself. Kant's view of reason is a very exalted one, to say
the least. Speaking in the preface to the first edition of the
Critique of Pure Reason, he claims that in the work he has
solved every metaphysical problem, or at least provided the
key to such a solution. This thoroughness was possible because

> Pure reason is, indeed, so perfect a unity that if its principles
> were insufficient for the solution of even a single one of all the
> the questions to which it itself gives birth we should have no
> alternative but to reject the principle, since we should then no
> longer be able to place implicit reliance upon it in dealing with
> any of the other questions. (*KRV* Axiii)

This remarkable need for a certain solution to all its problems
is due to the fact that reason has to deal only with "reason
itself and its pure thinking" and to the fact that there is no
need to go "far afield" to discover answers to its problems
since "I come upon them in my own self" (*KRV* Axiv). Kant
offers logic as an example of another field where all questions
can be answered completely and systematically. Of course
few logicians would admit such a claim today.

I do not find Kant's view of reason's capabilities plausible
at all. First, with regard to the theistic proofs, it is not true
that reason "deals only with itself," as Kant himself clearly
holds that in two cases these arguments begin from experience . Though a crucial premise may depend on the nature of
reason, the proofs themselves concern the nature of the objective world.

In any case, that a science, faculty, or inquiry should

prove unable to solve a particular problem in no way entails that it is inherently unreliable and untrustworthy. It seems to me that Kant, working from the framework of Continental rationalism, with its Cartesian demand for certainty, and accepting Wolff's dogmatic claims at face value, has proceeded to impose those claims on the proponents of theistic proofs as a requirement. As F. E. England notes, Kant "while rejecting the content of Wolffian metaphysics, still conforms to its method."[21] But most modern defenders of the theistic arguments, such as F. R. Tennant, neither make such claims nor regard them as necessary.

Kant was firmly in the tradition of those philosophers who identified knowledge with certain knowledge. He himself did not believe that the theistic proofs did or could produce knowledge in his sense, yet he did think they possessed a certain plausibility. However, on his view, in the field of reason, it is all or nothing. There is no such thing as a proof that God probably exists. Nor is there a place for plausible opinions or hypotheses. Nevertheless, he continued to hold that the physico-theological argument possesses such force that it could never be undermined by abstruse criticism. The lack of any such notion as we have developed with the concept of "believability" forced him to make such strange assertions as that there is a natural illusion or temptation which is inherent in the nature of reason itself.

With a more realistic view of the potentiality and nature of metaphysical arguments, Kant's treatment of the theistic proofs can not only be shown to be consistent, but also plausible. Kant is groping towards what we might term a phenomenology of this type of argument. He is not so much engaged in proving God's existence as stepping back and seeing what such proofs accomplish. And his central insight is that the proofs, though they fail as logical demonstrations, are convincing expressions of a certain insight or way of viewing reality, an insight which strikes us as plausible to a greater or lesser degree, but one which we have no way of conclusively

---

21. F. E. England, *Kant's Conception of God* (London: George Allen and Unwin, 1929), pp. 180-181.

verifying. What these proofs show is that God's existence is a possible object of rational belief.

What are we to make of the phenomenon of theistic proofs? Over literally thousands of years a long and unresolved debate has continued. Some thinkers have regarded the proofs as conclusively establishing God's existence. Others have held that the proofs have no force whatsoever. A third group, in which we may place Kant, has held that though the arguments possess some plausibility, which some may rate very high and others very low, they are not completely conclusive. Into this group we may place such diverse thinkers as David Hume, who rated the plausibility on the low side, and F. R. Tennant, who regards the cumulative force of theistic arguments to be so great as to make theism far more plausible than any other alternative.

Now there are several possibilities which would account for this situation of disagreement. It is possible that no such proofs have any force at all, that either the inferences are invalid or one or more of the premises are absurd. In this case we must account for the fact that these arguments have been regarded as sound by many intelligent proponents over thousands of years, even after they have read and studied the criticisms which point out the errors contained in the proofs. We must also explain the plausibility attributed to the proofs by that group of thinkers who do not accept the proofs as conclusive. This could be accounted for in a number of ways. Perhaps some of those who accept the arguments are not very intelligent. More plausibly, as many of these proponents of the arguments are committed to some particular religion, it might be held that they are unable to be fully neutral on the issues; their religious beliefs interfere with their ability to see the issues dispassionately. Or perhaps they are emotionally unable to face the truth of a world without God for any number of reasons, such as those given by Freud for example. Or it might just be that these logical errors were engrained in these thinkers through education or cultural indoctrination; they were absorbed at an early age as part of a world-picture which has unfortunately been shown to be erroneous.

Another possible alternative is that the arguments do

possess demonstrative logical force, that the inferences are valid and the premises are known to be apodictically certain. In this case it is the failure of critics to appreciate the force of the arguments which must be explained, and again this could conceivably be done by pointing to the various factors which cause people to fail to recognize truth: mistakes, emotional prejudices, and the like. This sort of account inevitably carries a reductionistic flavor. There is a parallel between the theologian who dismisses the objections of critics as stemming from a rebellious, sinful heart, and the charges of skeptics that theistic arguments are rationalizations of wish-fulfillments. Each of these strategies seems to me to be not only inadequate factually, but dehumanizing as well.

I submit that far more attractive than either of these alternatives is the view that these arguments possess some degree of plausibility, no doubt conditioned by subjective and irrational factors, but that there is no way to determine with certainty the truth or falsity of their conclusions. On this interpretation the inferences are regarded as valid, but one or more of the premises is regarded as merely plausible, either in a high or low degree, but not established as certain.

A proof, such as the cosmological proof, is integrally related to a way of viewing the world. It expresses a certain insight into the way things are said to be. The belief that the world is *contingent*, in the sense that it requires a necessary being to sustain it, is a way of viewing the world which some people find completely convincing, and many others find convincing at times or at least to a certain degree. The belief that the universe is a self-sustaining system requiring no ground or explanation outside itself is another possible way of viewing the universe which many accept as correct, and others perhaps are drawn to at certain moments. The important point is that both of these ways of viewing the world represent metaphysical stands; neither may be regarded as certain knowledge. But if this is indeed the case, then one might be on firm ground in asserting that at least the proposition "God exists" is a *possible* object of rational belief. God's existence is believable to rational beings as such, and not merely believable for irrational and subjective reasons.

This is precisely what Kant needs to establish in the *Critique of Pure Reason*. All he needs to show is that rationally speaking, among the various metaphysical positions which are options, theism is a viable alternative. He does not need to establish the truth of theism or even speculate as to the probability of its truth, for as Kant rightly saw, probability in such a case has no clear meaning. This position of "one plausible alternative among others" is sufficient for his purposes because he intends to show that (1) skepticism, neutrality, and suspended judgment on this issue are logically undesirable, and (2) we have evidence of a different type from that considered by speculative reason which tips the balance in favor of theism.

Thus we can characterize the general work of theoretical reason as establishing the existence of God as a possible object of rational belief. To accomplish this Kant attempts to do three things. First he attempts to show that the concept of God is a meaningful concept — that it can be thought. Secondly, he attempts to show that no one could ever have knowledge that the object of such a concept does not exist, nor speculative or theoretical knowledge that God does exist. Finally, he attempts to show that, in rationally understanding the world as a whole, the view that God exists has a certain plausibility, which, though it does not suffice to prove God's existence as an item of knowledge, shows us that if we had other grounds for accepting God's existence, and it became necessary for us to arrive at a decision, we should have no intellectual difficulties in doing so.

THE REPUDIATION OF THE NEUTRAL ATTITUDE: THE INTEREST OF REASON IN THE QUESTION OF GOD'S EXISTENCE

The Interest of Theoretical Reason

One of the most interesting sections of the *Critique of Pure Reason* is the section following the Antinomy entitled "The Interest of Reason in These Conflicts." The conflicts are of course over whether the world is infinite or finite with regard to space and time, whether there exists any simple substance in the world, whether there are any events which can truly be said to be the result of freedom, and whether there must exist an absolutely necessary being either as part of the world or as its ground. It is certainly surprising that reason, that austere, rigorous judge, suddenly gets an interest in this litigation at hand, and alternately puts in appearances for the parties in this dispute. It must be admitted that it is not very clear initially as to how reason gets such an interest or even what it might mean for reason to have such an interest. However, perhaps it will become clear as we seek to determine just what those interests amount to.

The interest with which we are most concerned is reason's stake in the question of God's existence. It might be thought that in speaking of interests or needs we have already left the sphere of theoretical reason and moved to the practical sphere. And it is true that this area provides a crucial link or transition between theoretical and practical reason. Nevertheless, Kant speaks of theoretical needs and interests as well as practical interests (WOT 139, p. 298).

The striking characteristic of theoretical reason's stake in the question of God's existence is that it seems to have an interest in both sides of the controversy. Kant gives us a picture of reason which involves an actual split. On the one hand, the proposition "God exists" provides reason with that unified complete explanation which she must seek and avoids that endless series of conditions which is itself ultimately inexplicable and unintelligible (KRV A467, B495). On the other hand, the proposition "God does not exist and hence there is no unconditioned condition" offers to reason the inestimable advantage that the chain of explanation is completely a matter of sure-footed empirical investigation. The laws which are discovered are empirical laws and the objects known can one and all be exhibited in intuition (KRV A468-469, B496-497).

One can immediately see that it is the claim to know these propositions on both sides which generates reason's self-estrangement. It is only the claim to know God's existence, to have completed the explanation of reality via a non-empirical concept, which is a threat to empirical investiga-

tion; and it is only the claim to *know* that there is no unconditioned condition which could unify and complete our
knowledge that makes speculative reason unhappy. Thus, a
solution which allowed reason to believe in God, while carefully denying that this belief amounted to knowledge of why
things go on as they do in the physical world, would satisfy
the interests of both parties.

Kant believes that it is to reason's advantage to *believe*
that the universe is ultimately rational and orderly, but he
doesn't want the belief that the universe is rational to replace
the search for that rationality. He doesn't want the belief that
the world is ultimately explainable and intelligible to replace
the process of actually explaining it. He is adamantly against
a certain misuse of the concept of God, that mentality which
in its most crude form is willing to take "It was God's will" as
a sufficient explanation for any occurrence.

> For in this field of enquiry, if instead of looking for causes in the
> universal laws of material mechanism, we appeal directly to
> the unsearchable decrees of divine wisdom, all those ends
> which are exhibited in nature, together with the many ends
> which are only ascribed by us to nature, make our investigation
> of the causes a very easy task, and so enable us to regard the
> labour of reason as completed, when, as a matter of fact, we
> have merely dispensed with its employment — an employment
> which is wholly dependent for guidance upon the order of na-
> ture and the series of its altercations, in accordance with the
> universal laws which they are found to exhibit. (*KRV* A691,
> B719)

On the other hand, it is very much in the interest of
reason to regard the world as possessing the sort of order
which it would possess if it originated in the purpose of a
supreme intelligence. Such an assumption cannot but contribute to our knowledge the greatest possible systematic unity. "The assumption of a supreme intelligence, as the one
and only cause of the universe, though in the idea alone, can
therefore always benefit reason and can never injure it"
(*KRV* A687, B715).

This theoretical assumption is not strictly speaking a belief in God, but a belief that the world is as it would be if it
were created by God. Kant certainly does not attempt to jus-

tify religious belief in God merely on this basis. Nevertheless, as we have seen, one of the characteristics of metaphysical beliefs, such as belief in God, is that they embody and express beliefs about the world. If Kant can show that belief in God (not knowledge) is required on other grounds, one can certainly say that theoretical reason is favorably disposed towards such a result. This positive theoretical function which the *concept* of God plays, provides grounds, if practical reason does require belief in God, for a harmonious dovetailing of theoretical and practical reason. And, as we shall argue in our concluding chapter, it is just this sort of overall coherence which is one of the most important criteria in the evaluation of metaphysical positions.

The Interest of Practical Reason

Though he recognized reason's theoretical need with regard to God's existence, Kant clearly felt that these interests were relatively unimportant in comparison with the needs of practical reason, the interest man has in the question of God's existence when the question is considered not merely from the viewpoint of the detached knower, the observer, but from the viewpoint of the engaged knower, the responsible agent who must make decisions and act. The reason for this is that Kant felt that the interest of theoretical reason in God's existence is merely conditional. "If one wishes to achieve systematic knowledge of the world, he ought to regard it as if it were created by a supreme reason."[22] Kant, however, believes that practical reason has needs which are unconditional (WOT 139, p. 298).

Practical reason is the realm in which at least the possibility arises of situations where suspension of judgment or neutrality with regard to a question may be impossible, irrational, or undesirable. For practical reason is concerned with man as an actual being in the world, with needs and ends to fulfill, and decisions and actions to make. It is the introduction of action which is crucial. As Paton notes, "It is not

---

22. However, one might argue that this condition is very important and significant, even inescapable.

always intelligent to refrain from outward action till we have gathered all possible relevant knowledge, if this means that the opportunity for relevant action will have been gone forever."[23] And action, Kant believed, is itself intelligent. Our actions, or at least many of them, must be seen as presupposing, or even as the embodiment of, certain beliefs about the way things are.[24]

As long as we are merely speculating, we can waver back and forth between various positions. But in some cases, of which the problem as to whether man is free is the most notable example, as soon as men are summoned to action "this play of the merely speculative reason would, like a dream, at once cease, and they would choose their principles exclusively in accordance with practical interests" (*KRV* A475, B503). When acting, we do and must believe that we are free, at least implicitly, because it is the presupposition of meaningful choice and action. Thus we have at least one example of a cognitive belief which is justified on practical grounds.

It must not be thought that Kant is here arguing that one should allow one's beliefs to be determined by one's arbitrary emotional needs or preferences. He is merely introducing a realm where in *some* cases action and rational decision as the ground of action may be necessary even though certain knowledge is lacking.

Man is a being with needs and interests; he is a being who acts. To ignore these needs or to ignore this fact about man would be irrational indeed. Even our theoretical knowledge is useless if we do not propose ends to ourselves (*KRV* A816, B844). And it is Kant's view that at least one end is presented to man by reason itself, and that the fact that he finds himself under this obligation constitutes a kind of self-knowledge of the highest order. To ignore this rational end and this self-knowledge when one is acting would be the height of irrationality as well as immorality, and it is not inconceivable that this knowledge, along with the action that

---

23. Paton, *In Defense of Reason,* p. 123.

24. For a clear account and defense of Kant's view of the relation between action and belief see Wood, pp. 17-25.

it entails, could be shown to presuppose or embody other beliefs. This is of course precisely what Kant thinks: God's existence is a necessary postulate of practical reason.

Kant therefore believes that indifference or neutrality towards God's existence is itself fundamentally irrational. The end of being a moral being is the highest end given to man. This is not an end that a man can ignore; he is a conscript in the army of beings who ought to be moral. If it can be shown that this end requires actions which are irrational in a universe without God, or if it can be shown that morality is integrally related to God's existence in any way, either via some sort of entailment or perhaps by way of theism being a "presupposition of the intelligibility of moral obligation" it follows that man ought not to be neutral with regard to the question of God's existence. It is the first of these possibilities that Kant is most interested in showing; if it can be shown that belief in God is a presupposition of intelligent moral *action*, the case for suspension of judgment will have been undercut completely.

Kant was not unaware of a certain intellectual puritanism which holds that in cases where we have no conclusive rational evidence, the rational procedure is to withhold or suspend judgment. Indeed he certainly possessed an abundant measure of the air of intellectual rigor which gives birth to that view. Nevertheless Kant saw clearly that there are certain situations or questions in which the luxury of intellectual detachment is, if not impossible, at least irrational.

> One can be assured against all error by not undertaking to judge where he does not know as much as is required for definitive judgment. ... But where it is not just an arbitrary matter whether one will judge definitively or not, i.e., where a real need associated with reason itself makes judging necessary even if ignorance with respect to the details required for judging limits us, a maxim is necessary by which we can form a judgment, for reason insists on satisfaction. (*WOT* 136, p. 296)

We have seen that Kant rejects this intellectual puritanism because he believed that some needs, and particularly man's obligation to be a moral being, are not irrational and subjective, but real human needs, the very existence of which gave man genuine knowledge about himself and the human situation.

In speaking of human needs and actions, it must not be imagined that an alien intruder or appendage has been introduced into theoretical reason. Rather, it can be seen that reason has been practical, as well as theoretical, all along. Kant recognizes that even forming a theoretical judgment is an *act* which requires a decision. Theoretical knowledge is something which is achieved; one must decide to investigate the world, and such an investigation presupposes truth as a value, an end to be pursued. Ends have been present to reason from the very beginning, even in its theoretical employment. "Every interest is ultimately practical, even that of speculative reason being only conditional and reaching perfection only in practical use" (*KPV* 122, p. 126). And Kant holds that the end with which God's existence is connected is an end which is laid on us by reason itself. It must not be forgotten that theoretical and practical reason are not two different reasons; they are merely Kant's terms for the rational faculty of inference in two different employments.

Thus we now see what Kant means by "the interests of reason." I think it would be more accurate to characterize them as rational human interests. They are fundamental human needs, which it would be irrational to ignore, and at least one of which, Kant argues, is constituted by the mere fact that man is a rational being. Kant must now make the nature of this highest end clear, with its resulting self-knowledge, and show just *how* it is connected with God's existence. He has shown already, at least, that it is possible that skepticism with regard to God's existence is irrational, even in the absence of certain knowledge. Kant himself seems to feel that this sort of neutrality is psychologically impossible as well.

> But it is idle to feign indifference to such enquiries, the object of which can never be indifferent to our human nature. Indeed those pretended-indifferentists, however they may try to disguise themselves . . . inevitably fall back into those very meta-

physical assertions which they profess so greatly to despise. (*KRV* Ax)

Kant is here calling attention to the fact that those who deny the truth of metaphysical positions are themselves doing metaphysics. Those who assert that there is no God are themselves dogmatists.

THE TASK OF PRACTICAL REASON: MORAL OBLIGATION AND BELIEF IN GOD

The most crucial step in Kant's justification of belief in God is obviously establishing the link between morality and theism. Many philosophers, sympathetic to Kant's view of moral obligation and even sympathetic to his religious conclusions, have nonetheless been unable to accept Kant's view of belief in God as a necessary postulate of morality. Indeed most have been of the opinion that no relationship of entailment exists between moral obligation and the existence of God. The crucial question here concerns the nature of the link between God and morality. Is it a relationship of entailment at all? If not, what sort of link is possible?

The situation is complicated by the fact that Kant's moral argument is stated many different times and in a bewildering variety of forms. There does not seem to be any one clear, definitive account of the relationship between morality and God.[25] Rather, in general we can say that Kant offers us a variety of mediating concepts or third terms which provide the link he is seeking, the most important of which is the concept of the highest good, which we shall discuss presently.

The most obvious and simple way of linking morality and God would be to assert that moral laws are divine commands, and that they owe their status as moral laws to the fact that God commands them. To say that an action is right on this account would simply be to say that God commands it to be done. The objections to such a view are well-known and were

---

25. Robert Whittemore distinguishes seven distinct formulations of Kant's moral argument in "The Metaphysics of the Seven Formulations of the Moral Argument," *Tulane Studies in Philosophy*, 3 (1954), 133-161.

stated at least implicitly in Plato's *Euthyphro*. In any case
Kant clearly and emphatically rejects this interpretation of
morality and condemns it as moral heteronomy.

Though Kant never held the view that moral laws arise
from divine fiat, he does, in the *Critique of Pure Reason*, seem
to hold the view that these laws, though not constituted as
moral laws by God's command, are nonetheless in their application to men dependent upon God for their obligatory
power (*KRV* A634, B662). Exactly what he means by this is
not completely clear. He says that though these laws are
completely valid in themselves, unless there were a supreme
being to give "effect and confirmation to them" they would
"in their application to ourselves . . . be lacking in all reality."
This means that they would be "obligations to which there
would be no motives" (*KRV* A589, B617).

These statements are fully in accord with his statement
of the highest good argument in the "Canon of Pure Reason,"
where Kant states that without the postulate of a Moral Ruler
we should be compelled to regard the moral laws as "empty
figments of the brain" (*KRV* A811, B839). It must be admitted that on their face these statements are obviously in conflict with Kant's view of morality, which entails that the only
motive for a moral act is simply respect for the moral law as
such. Or as Ewing tactfully notes, these statements are "not
in accord with Kant's usual view," which was that the moral
law is binding and certain, whatever our metaphysical beliefs.[26]

Even though this does not represent Kant's mature view,
it is instructive to seek to determine why Kant thought at this
time that the obligatory force of the moral law depended on
God's existence and exactly what he meant by asserting this.
For even at this time Kant did not think that the moral law
must be or could be derived from God's existence or nature,
either as commands or in any other way.

> For it is these very laws that have led us, in virtue of their inner
> practical necessity, to the postulate of a self-sufficient cause, or
> of a wise Ruler of the world, in order that through such agency

---

26. Ewing, p. 265.

effect may be given to them. We may not, therefore, in reversal of such procedure, regard them as accidental and as derived from the mere will of the Ruler, especially as we have no conception of such a will, except as formed in accordance with these laws. So far, then, as practical reason has the right to serve as our guide, we shall not look upon actions as obligatory because they are the commands of God, but shall regard them as divine commands because we have an inward obligation to them. (*KRV* A818-819, B846-847)

When Kant says that God is necessary in order to give effect and confirmation to the moral law, and to give motives to our obligations, he does not mean that the moral laws are binding because God commands them. He is rather attempting to describe, in an admittedly confused and seemingly contradictory way, a phenomenon which Allen Wood terms "moral despair," which arises out of a recognition of a discrepancy between moral obligation itself and the possibility of achieving the end which moral obligation lays upon man.[27] Moral despair is the awareness of an incommensurability between the ideal which man recognizes and the world of which man is a part and in which he must act. In the grip of moral despair, a man believes that the moral law is a "mere" ideal, an ideal which has no impact on the actual world.

What Kant seems to be saying in the first *Critique* is this. If there were no God, then the world really would be as it seems to be at certain moments; that is, a world which follows mechanical laws blindly and takes no account of moral ends. In such a world, moral action, which aims at bringing about the maximum amount of virtue and happiness proportional to virtue (the highest good, which we shall discuss shortly) is doomed to systematic frustration, especially with regard to the achievement of material goods, such as happiness. If this is indeed true, then morality must inevitably seem a figment, or a mere ideal. In such a world I would be in the situation of a man who recognizes certain obligations as valid and necessary, but who is simultaneously aware that the actions which those obligations enjoin cannot possibly succeed. Such an awareness, though it would not preclude

---

27. See Wood, pp. 155-160.

my recognition that those duties are valid in themselves, says Kant, would inevitably remove from those duties the force of their obligatoriness.

When put in these terms, the connection established between the existence of God and morality seems to be psychological in nature. As Beck puts it, belief in the possibility of the highest good (and hence in God) may be necessary to a semblance of morality.[28] But it can be only a semblance of morality, since the admixture of any motive other than morality itself inevitably destroys autonomy.

However deficient, this account possesses very real value as a phenomenological description of the situation in which I find myself as a moral being in an amoral world, a world which is not seen as created and ordered by a supreme Moral Person. It shows great insight into the sort of self-doubts and temptations which may plague a man who is aware of an unconditional obligation which he necessarily lays on himself, but who views this unconditional obligation and the self-knowledge it gives rise to as fundamentally divorced or alienated from reality, or the actual nature of things. Unfortunately, Kant expressed his insight here in a confused and misleading way, by implying that this divorce would remove the "obligatory power" of the moral law and that thereby God's existence is necessary as a motive to morality. But of course if the man is truly morally aware, he will know that no other motive than the desire to be a moral person can possibly lead to a moral act. His despair is really a despair over the possibility of rational moral action. There is a kind of absurdity or contradiction inherent in his situation if he acts as a moral being. It is perhaps his awareness of this absurdity which might tempt him to discount the reality of the moral law itself. We must not forget that though Kant thought that the moral law is in itself certain, and can be known with certainty, men can and actually do convince themselves that morality is an illusion, a "figment of their brain," a remnant of childhood fear, or a product of cultural mores. But to say that the belief that God does not exist may tempt a man to

---

28. Beck, *A Commentary,* p. 244.

consider the moral law an illusion is not to say that belief in
God's existence is necessary as a motive for morality, or even
that it is ever in fact a motive for a truly moral action.[29]

To understand the absurdity or contradiction which
arises when a moral being acts morally and at the same time
refuses to regard the world of which he is a part and in which
he acts as grounded in and governed by a Moral Person, we
must explicitly discuss the concept of the highest good, and
its relation to moral obligation. For it is Kant's view that the
highest good, as he conceives it, is the necessary end of moral
action, and it is this thesis which, when combined with the
absence of religious faith, gives moral action its absurd or
contradictory character.

Kant's view of moral obligation, though often subject to
misinterpretation, is well known, and it is outside the scope
of this essay to explore it in depth. We have already discussed
Kant's belief that reason has a practical employment — that
men will actions as actions which conform to a rule or principle. The subjective rule of an action Kant terms a maxim, and
maxims are said to possess both a form, which consists in its
general character as a principle or rule, and matter, which is
an end or object of desire. The distinctive feature of Kantian
morality is of course the thesis that the *motive* for adopting a
maxim lies in the form of the maxim, rather than in its material. If I adopt a maxim merely in virtue of the fact that I
desire certain ends, my actions are heteronomous, immoral.
If, on the other hand, in adopting a maxim I am motivated
solely by the form of the maxim, its conformity to the principle of universal law, then I have acted morally. It is only on
this basis that pure reason can be practical, and my actions
have that autonomous character which stems from a self-
imposed law.

For Kant, action of any kind is always directed towards
an end or material, which is an object of the faculty of desire
(*KPV* 34, p. 34). He therefore never denies that moral actions

---

29. And one must not forget that it is the dogmatic assertion that there
is no God which is completely antithetical to rational moral action. Kant says
that the belief that God's existence is possible is the minimum for rational
moral action. See Wood, p. 31.

are directed towards ends. Nevertheless, when I act morally I choose my maxim not on the basis of my desire for a certain end, but because the maxim conforms to universal law as such. But Kant, far from holding that moral acts have no end, explicitly says that the moral law systematically defines an end as the object of pure practical reason (*KPV* 63, p. 65).

Kant says that the objects of practical reason in general are the good and the evil (*KPV* 58, p. 60). However, he distinguishes between good and evil proper (*das Gute* and *das Böse*) and what he calls well-being and woe (*das Wohl* and *das Übel*) (*KPV* 59, pp. 61-62). Well-being and woe have to do with our happiness; they indicate a relationship between an object and our desires as a sensible being. Thus, to say of an object that it is good in this sense is to relate it to our own condition as a sensible being. Good and evil in the strict sense, however, have to do with actions themselves, and the manner of acting, i.e., the condition of the will.

> If something is to be, or is held to be, absolutely good or evil in all respects and without qualification, it could not be a thing but only the manner of acting, i.e., it could be only the maxim of the will, and consequently the acting person himself as a good or evil man. (*KPV* 60, p. 62)

This good is virtue of course, and it is said by Kant to be the highest good, in the sense of the Supreme Good, the good which is good unconditionally and which is the condition of all other goodness (*KPV* 110, p. 114). It is therefore the object of pure practical reason, and Beck is not in error in asserting that the good will has itself as object.[30] However, Kant nowhere says that the supreme good is the sole and entire object of pure practical reason.

> But these truths do not imply that virtue is the entire and perfect good as the object of the faculty of desire of rational finite beings. For this happiness is also required and indeed not merely in the partial eyes of a person who makes himself his end but even in the judgment of an impartial reason, which impartially regards persons in the world as ends-in-themselves. (*KPV* 110, p. 114)

---

30. Beck, *A Commentary*, p. 134.

Happiness is included in the concept of the highest good if this term be taken to mean not just the supreme good, but the complete or perfect good, that whole which is no part of a larger whole of the same type (*KPV* 110, p. 114). And it is the highest good in this sense which Kant says is the unconditional totality of the object of pure practical reason. Kant thus views the highest good as having two parts, virtue and happiness, which he argues cannot be identical nor connected analytically (*KPV* 113, p. 117).

Of course these two elements are not "co-equal." Their relationship is that of "ground and consequence" or "condition and conditioned," since virtue is always good without qualification, while "happiness, though something always pleasant to him who possesses it, is not of itself absolutely good in every respect but always presupposes conduct in accordance with the moral law as its condition" (*KPV* 111, p. 115). Kant stresses that though the highest good, in the sense of the complete good, is the necessary object of pure, practical reason, it is not, except in a special sense, the determining ground of the pure will. Kant has already argued in the Analytic of the *Critique of Practical Reason* that the attempt to derive the moral law from an object which is assumed or asserted to be good results in heteronomy and the subversion of the moral principle. Rather the moral law must be defined first and recognized as the sole determining ground of the pure will. The highest good can be said to be the determining ground of moral action only in the technical sense that one of its elements — the moral law as the object of virtue — is the determining ground of the pure moral will (*KPV* 113-114, pp. 109-110).

Lewis White Beck, therefore, in his *Commentary* on the second *Critique* is correct in his assertion that the highest good is not the determining ground of pure will, and he recognizes that Kant repeatedly affirms this. However, Beck claims that Kant's answer is "not so clear and unequivocal as one might wish."[31] As evidence he presents the two paragraphs at the end of chapter one of the Dialectic (109-110, pp.

[margin, handwritten: impossible]

---

31. *Ibid.*, p. 242.

113-114), which we have just discussed, where Kant asserts that only the moral law is the determining ground of the moral will, and that therefore the highest good can be said to determine the will only in the sense that one of its components does. According to Beck this is hedging on Kant's part.

> This [the two paragraphs referred to] is certainly an inept way of making one point twice; it means that the highest good is not an independent determining ground of the will in addition to or in place of one of its components. It cannot be supplementary to it and leave the purity of will undefiled; but Kant is unwilling to draw this conclusion in its full force.[32]

Beck is certainly right on the essential point here, namely that the "highest good is not an independent determining ground of the will in addition to or in place of one of its components." But I fail to see any indication that Kant is unwilling to draw this conclusion in its full force. For at the conclusion of this very paragraph Kant resolutely affirms that the moral law, which is of course included and thought of as part of the highest good, and *no other object* determines the will, and cautions that this order of concepts should not be lost sight of (*KPV* 110, p. 114).

The point that Kant is making here seems inept to Beck because he does not fully appreciate the unity of the concept of the highest good, admittedly composed as it is of disparate elements. It seems unnatural to him to speak of this concept as a determining ground in virtue of one of its components because he conceives of those two components as merely thrown together. Kant does claim that virtue and happiness are not analytically linked, and that therefore goodness is in a sense heterogeneous. But he nonetheless believes that these two types of goodness can — and must — be united synthetically to form a *single* concept of the highest good, the object of pure practical reason.

In what sense is the highest good the object of pure practical reason? Beck claims that there is no "command of reason" to seek the highest good as such, but only one of its

---

32. *Ibid.*, p. 243.

components — namely virtue. The command to seek the highest good is only my duty to fulfill the categorical imperative. "For suppose I do all in my power — which is all any moral decree can demand of me — to promote the highest good, what am I to do? Simply act out of respect for the law, which I already knew."[33] Beck therefore concludes that all the moral consequences of the highest good, both as motive and as object of the pure will, are drawn from one of its members, the supreme good or virtue. He insists that "the object of pure practical reason is not an effect of action, but the action itself; the good will has itself as object."[34]

But even if we grant, as we surely must, that there is a sense in which the object of the virtuous man's will is virtue itself, surely the good will does not have *only* itself as object. Such a doctrine would seemingly entail that moral action is unconcerned with achieving real results in the world. Kant's moral philosophy is frequently caricatured along these lines because of his belief that the moral worth of an action lies in the intention and hence cannot be measured by the results obtained. But this is very far from the view that the moral man is unconcerned as to whether he actually achieves good results. A good will is not, Kant says, a mere wish, but "the straining of every means so far as they are in our control" (*Gw* 4, 394, p. 62).

Allen Wood has given a definitive criticism, in my opinion, of the view that the good will has only itself as object.[35] His arguments do not depend on the melancholy, all-too-human fact that men seem generally to be incapable of duty for duty's sake, but are drawn from the necessary conditions of finite, rational volition. First, it simply must be noted that all maxims have a matter as well as a form; in addition to conforming to a universal law, they posit a specific end. The fact that I adopt the maxim in virtue of the form alone in no way modifies the fact that in adopting the maxim I neces-

---

33. *Ibid.*, p. 244.

34. *Ibid.*, p. 134.

35. The following remarks rely heavily on Wood's *Kant's Moral Religion*, pp. 40-67.

sarily adopt the matter of the maxim as well; I make the end
my own end. And it is quite clear that this matter cannot be
identical with the form. The mere desire to be moral could
not in itself determine a specific action, though it could be the
motive for a specific action which is determined. It is clear
that Kant holds that the categorical imperative presupposes
that man is a being with needs and ends.

It is this situation which Paton attempts to describe in
the distinction he makes between the purely formal maxim of
morality — the categorical imperative or formal law as such
— and the material maxims of specific actions.[36] Material
maxims, such as "When I borrow money, I will repay it
within the time agreed," and "When life offers me more pain
than pleasure, I will take my life" posit for man specific ends
in specific circumstances. The moral man must act on material maxims, but he chooses his material maxims by asking
himself if the maxim in question is just an arbitrary principle, an exception, or whether it is rather a principle *through*
which he can express his commitment to act only on those
principles valid for a rational agent as such. The formal
maxim of morality does not act in a vacuum; it selects from a
variety of proposed material maxims.[37]

Wood makes this same point by noting Kant's reply to a
criticism of Garve, where Kant plainly asserts that duty consists in the *limitation* of our natural needs and ends by the
moral law.[38] It is plain that real human needs, both of the
agent and of others, are more than just compatible with morality. They are systematically included within the ends
which I must adopt, if my will is pure, that is, determined by
the moral law as such. "The *final end* for all moral striving,
therefore, which it is my duty to adopt, is the unconditional
totality of all those ends which constitute the material of
maxims whose form is legislative."[39]

---

36. H. J. Paton, *The Categorical Imperative* (London: Hutchinson, 1965),
pp. 134-139.

37. *Ibid.*, p. 136.

38. Wood, p. 56.

39. *Ibid.*, p. 92.

If Kant's concept of the highest good is to be questioned, it will not be in virtue of the fact that happiness is included within the concept. Few philosophers would disagree with the thesis that happiness is at least a conditioned or qualified good, a state or an ideal which is at least good on some occasions. Criticism should rather center on the failure to include other conditioned goods explicitly (though it could be argued that they are included implicitly) such as knowledge, beauty, and the like. Fortunately, whether one wishes to argue that happiness is, as Kant seemed to believe, the ideal which reason forms of the highest "natural good" or not, the structure of Kant's argument for theism remains intact. If the concept of the highest good is reformulated, the argument can be reformulated accordingly. The thrust of the argument is essentially that without belief in God there is an absurdity in the situation I find myself in as a rational, moral agent, a contradiction between what I am in duty bound to strive for and what I can rationally hope to accomplish. I am unconditionally obligated to strive for ends in a world which is fundamentally alien to those ends and by means (moral action) which are diverse from the laws by which results in the world are achieved. Or in Kant's own words, there is "an open contradiction" between "a final end within, that is set before them (men) as a duty, and a nature without, that has no final end, though in it the former end is to be actualized" (KU 458, p. 129). The meaning of the postulate of God's existence, then is, in the words of Karl Barth, "the presupposition of the truth of the ultimate unity of nature and freedom, of that which is with that which must be, and thus of duty and desire."[40]

It can be easily seen, I think, that the absurdity or contradiction here, at least as I have expressed it, is not a logical contradiction. It seems rather more like a violation of a kind of insight as to how things ought to be in a world with rational, moral agents. Looked at detachedly, as if it were simply another argument like the cosmological argu-

---

40. Karl Barth, *Protestant Thought from Rousseau to Ritschl*, trans. Brian Cozens (New York: Harper and Row, 1959), p. 161.

ment, it seems to rest on considerations which are almost esthetic in character. There is some sort of discrepancy between the belief that there exist moral beings who are themselves under an unconditional obligation to achieve ends in the natural order, and who are themselves part of that natural order, and the belief that the natural order is fundamentally alien to and indifferent to morality.

But we must remember that Kant's argument is not to be viewed as a detached argument. It is an argument which is said to be sufficient subjectively and for moral persons only. The significance of this cannot be underestimated. We must remember that for Kant *action* is itself rational and *presupposes a belief that the end is ultimately attainable.* There is thus a kind of practical absurdity in acting morally, adopting the highest good as my end, if I believe that the highest good is incapable of being fulfilled.

However, I should not wish to deny that the force of Kant's argument ultimately stems from a kind of *insight,* an insight that if I am truly a moral being, then the world of which I am a part and in which I must act must be a moral world, even if all appearances are to the contrary. That this insight is vague and imprecise does not of course entail that it is illusory. Kant himself seems to recognize that the inference he is appealing to is not, at least in its origin, a strictly logical inference.

> This moral proof is not in any sense a newly discovered argument, but at the most an old one in a new form. For its germ was lying in the mind of man when his reason first quickened into life, and it grew and ever developed with the progressive culture of that faculty. (*KU* 458, p. 128)

This natural insight is simply the insight that there is something for which man is bound to strive, which is wholly discordant with what nature from one perspective seems to offer as a possibility. This discrepancy can only be reconciled by viewing nature itself from a different perspective, by regarding it as grounded in a Moral Person. We must not forget that the idea of an ultimate ground or condition of the natural order has already been presented to man as a natural or believable concept. And even more relevant, the interpretation of nature in terms of purpose or ends, has also been shown to be a natural way of viewing nature, and even more than that, a scientifically necessary and fruitful methodological procedure. The importance which Kant himself placed on these "common insights of mankind" should not be underestimated. It could even be argued that Kant saw the whole of his philosophy as a defense and elucidation of these natural inferences or insights. He explicitly says of the insight which underlies the moral argument, in a passage reminiscent of Plato's slave-boy, that "if we care to try the experiment we shall find that it [the moral argument] can be elicited in its completeness from anyone without his ever having been instructed in it" (*Rel*, p. 170).

Kant's own arguments, especially the dialectic of the second *Critique*, can best be viewed as attempts to make the nature of this discrepancy or contradiction more precise. And because he viewed happiness as the highest natural good, and therefore an important component of the highest good in the sense of the perfect good, most of his formulations seem to center around the concept of rewards or a correlation of virtue and happiness. This is unfortunate and has given rise to Schopenhauer's picture of virtue, her work completed, stealthily holding out her hand for a reward.

However, it is not difficult to understand why Kant so often formulated his argument in this form. The highest good is not for Kant, as we have seen, just a lump of goods thrown together. It is a systematic ideal; goods are included or excluded on the basis of a principle, their conformity to the categorical imperative. Thus happiness, for Kant, to be truly good must be conditioned by virtue. The happiness of an evil or depraved man itself may well be regarded as positively depraved. Yet Kant felt that happiness *is* a natural end, an end which all men strive for by nature. Clearly then, happiness will be among the natural goods which, when conditioned by moral worth, the virtuous man must strive for. Indeed in Kant's opinion happiness is the systematic totality of those natural goods. There is therefore nothing stealthy about Kant's thesis that the virtuous man has as his end a world where men are both virtuous and happy, and happy to the extent that they are virtuous. According to Kant the desire that all men (including oneself) be virtuous, and happy on the condition of being virtuous, far from being a selfish or arbitrary whim, is what any rational man would desire. Therefore the fact that moral action does not necessarily or even generally lead towards this end, the fact that virtuous action may even lead to misery both for the agent and for others, constitutes a kind of absurdity, and even tempts men to regard their obligation as a mere ideal incapable of any real fulfillment.

That Kant has formulated his argument along these lines does not mean that it could not be formulated differently. As a matter of fact, if the inference to God from morality is the sort of natural inference Kant says it is, we should expect the argument to be formulable in other ways. Kant himself seems to feel that there are a variety of factors which lead one from moral self-knowledge to religious faith. Many of these he throws out almost casually.

For example, in *Religion Within the Limits of Reason Alone* Kant suggests that belief in God is required by the social character of our situation as morally obligated beings. God is seen as the presupposition of the practical idea of an ethical commonwealth (*Rel*, p. 89). The highest good is there seen as a social goal, which can only be achieved by a social organization which could only be rooted in and founded by God himself.

Later on in the *Religion* Kant suggests that the discovery in man of the capacity for virtue, and the awakening of human consciousness to its true nature, itself leads one to the belief in a Creator. The recognition of the dignity of humanity, which a man must respect and which he recognizes as man's true destiny, itself "exalts the soul" and leads to the concept of a Holy Legislator of virtue as world-ruler (*Rel*, 171). Kant here is even less clear as to just how this "leading" arises, but it would seem that he is asserting that without the concept of God, man himself, viewed as a moral being, is a kind of inexplicable oddity. When he properly understands who he is, man recognizes that his being stems from a Moral Purpose greater than his own will.

Of course it may be objected that we are certainly pre-judging the case by calling what Kant is appealing to an insight or inference. Why not call it a prejudice? Or perhaps a blik? What this challenge makes clear is that Kant's view of the relationship of moral experience to religious faith involves one in a metaphysical interpretation of the human situation. If it is conceded that such metaphysical interpretations can never be definitely verified by any determinate experience, and that no linear proof or argument could establish the truth of such a position, then it might well be asked how such a view can ever be justified. As a preliminary hint, we might suggest that Kant's own procedure suggests a possibility, namely the capacity of a metaphysical position to unify and illuminate very diverse areas of our experience. It is in this respect that what we called the harmonious dove-tailing of theoretical and practical reason becomes significant. But such considerations go beyond the subjective justification of belief.

It must not be forgotten that Kant seemed to regard the teleological proof, and to a lesser extent the cosmological proof of God's existence, as natural inferences as well. We have argued that these proofs, while they fail as apodictic demonstrations, do succeed in articulating a possible, believable metaphysical view of the world. Perhaps Kant's moral argument can be viewed as an articulation of another metaphysical insight. The essential difference between them is of course that the latter insight is rooted in the fact that I must *act*; hence neutrality or suspension of judgment is itself irrational. But it might be argued that the inferences in both the theoretical and practical sphere can be rejected. The ultimate disharmony between the moral law and nature might just be a fact, however repugnant to our reason. The crucial question to ask the critic in this case is "Why should we think that such an absurd condition is a fact?" The critics' answers to this question, including those answers which involve the assertion that "the world is all that is the case," necessarily become metaphysical positions themselves, again leaving us with the question, "How is a metaphysical belief justified?" We shall attempt to argue in the last chapter that whatever

weak response.

justification is possible of a metaphysical belief will at least
be of the same logical type as the considerations Kant advances. That is, the success of a scheme will be judged by its
ability to integrate and illuminate man's knowledge of the
world and himself, including his knowledge of himself as a
choosing and acting creature, complete with needs, obligations, and ends.

Perhaps it is the concept of an end which best illustrates
the sort of unity and coherence which belief in God provided
the critical philosophy. Kant affirms the methodological
value and necessity of conceiving natural objects in terms of
purpose, and as we have noted, seems to suggest that the
physico-theological argument, which takes its starting point
from ends or purposes in nature and argues to a designer or
purposive being as the ground of nature, has a degree of
plausibility. However, it could not definitively establish the
existence of an all-powerful, moral being as the creator of the
universe. Still, although the maxim of seeking to discover
final causes is subjectively valid only, Kant says darkly that
reason wakens some suspicion or that "nature gives a hint"
that final causes might be objectively valid as well (*KU* 390,
p. 41).

However, from the moral standpoint the situation
changes dramatically. Kant declares that morality requires
man to conceive himself as an end in itself, and he argues that
man must form his view of nature from this perspective (*KU*
442-445, pp. 108-112). Once the concept of a final end is
firmly in hand, man's attention and interest are directed in a
new way to the beauty and ends of nature. The belief that
there is an ultimate unity between nature and freedom transforms man's view of the world. The beauty and ends in nature, though they could not give rise to the view that the
ground of nature is purposive and that the final purpose is
man himself, are admirably calculated to strengthen that idea
(*KU* 459, p. 129). The examples of finality which man discovers in nature, which connect mechanism with mind or purpose, provide analogies or illustrations of the relationship
which practical reason believes must characterize the whole
of the phenomenal and noumenal realms (*KU* 479, p. 155).

Thus the insight that moral action and the world in which moral action takes place are not alien to each other is confirmed by our experience of nature itself.

Kant's practical approach to theism represents a systematic, unified argument. From the standpoint of theoretical reason, he has argued that, though knowledge of God's existence or non-existence is both impossible and undesirable, the idea of God is a concept the reality of which reason must necessarily consider a possibility. The idea of a necessary being as the Supreme Condition of the world's existence is certainly a believable and cogent metaphysical interpretation of reality, even if it cannot be scientifically verified or logically demonstrated. It is a concept in which man has a rational interest. From the standpoint of practical reason, Kant has argued that the concept of God as a Moral Person is a postulate of rational, moral action. Here the rational interest which man has in God's existence takes the form of a necessary belief. Finally, Kant has united these two interests through the key concept of an end. The purposiveness which as scientists we must presuppose in our investigation of nature and which we as ordinary humans find there, is systematized and justified when we look at nature as the arena for moral endeavor. The perspective which we as moral beings must adopt, whereby men are viewed as intrinsically valuable (ends in themselves), is confirmed by the manifold examples of benign purpose and providence which we discover in nature.

3

Kierkegaard: Belief
As Existentially Necessary

KANT AND KIERKEGAARD

DESPITE THE DIFFERENCES IN STYLE AND CONTENT, A comparison of Søren Kierkegaard and Immanuel Kant reveals many striking parallels and ultimately leads to the discovery of a deep common ground. There is present in Kierkegaard a basic distinction between objectivity and subjectivity, with a stress on the limitations of the former and the priority of the latter with respect to deciding big religious questions. This tying of religion to feelings and morality certainly does suggest a pattern essentially parallel to Kant, as Jerry Gill has noted.[1] Perhaps this affinity between Kierkegaard and Kant is due to a common affinity with Socrates. Socrates affirmed that he had no time for astronomy, as Kierkegaard was fond of recalling, because he didn't know who he really was, a god or a monster.[2] This task of finding out who he was constituted his chief end, a higher kind of knowledge than knowledge of the stars. Kant, despite all his respect for science and learning, ultimately agrees with Socrates that ethical self-awareness is man's *highest* end, and that lacking this, a man is less than a man, no matter how vast his scientific knowledge.

This position is essentially Kierkegaard's as well, though Kierkegaard's insight into the nature of that self-knowledge differs in some respects from Kant. Kierkegaard's denigration of systems and his nasty comments about the natural

---

1. See Jerry Gill, "Kant, Kierkegaard, and Religious Knowledge," *Philosophy and Phenomenological Research,* 27 (December, 1967), 188-204.

2. See, for example, *PF,* p. 46. Reference is to *Phaedrus,* 229E.

sciences and about "the professor" are misleading in some respects. For he actually had a great respect for scholars and scholarship. What he fought so passionately was the idolatrous identification of objective thought with man's highest end. Hence his fondness for the passage where Socrates declares he doesn't know who he is. This obligation to attain Socratic self-knowledge was the rock on which the speculative project foundered. Kierkegaard constantly strives to show that, contrary to the view that ethical and religious self-knowledge constitute a kind of childish or immediate simplicity, this self-knowledge or simplicity is only attained, if at all, through a constant, life-long struggle.

For both Kant and Kierkegaard religious faith does not stem directly from theoretical or objective reason. Kant affirms that though the noumenal world cannot be *known,* it is yet something that in *action* I become a part of and know myself as a member of. Similarly in Kierkegaard, the eternal is something which I cannot know abstractly, but which I achieve in action. The true self, the eternal self, cannot be grasped via Cartesian reflection, but only in ethical and religious decisiveness (*Post,* pp. 280-289).

So for Kierkegaard and Kant man is constantly seen as under an obligation to seek the highest good, or man's highest end, which is to be achieved via a process of subjective reflection. For both thinkers this obligation necessitates religious faith, and not merely as a means to attaining this highest end. The ethical-religious mode of existence is ultimately seen as a constituent, even the determining constituent of that highest end.

Kierkegaard's view of the nature of man's highest end differs from Kant in some important respects, however. We shall see that this difference has significant implications both for the content and the quality of the religious faith and mode of existence which Kierkegaard wishes to urge on his readers. The most significant difference concerns the ultimate religious object. For Kierkegaard, the essential religious question does not concern merely God's existence, even when God is conceived not merely as first cause, but as a moral and practical postulate. The decisive question revolves around the *God*

in time, the incarnation.[3] Thus, though Kierkegaard does consider the validity of religion in general, he is more concerned
with the validity of a particular historical religion, namely
Christianity.

We should perhaps pause here to consider the objection
that this sort of consideration of Kierkegaard represents a
fundamental distortion. Nothing is more evident than that
Kierkegaard had a hearty contempt for apologetics and defenses of religious belief, at least with respect to Christianity.
And yet we seem to be interpreting him as offering just that
— a subjective defense of religious belief. In reply we can
only say that though Kierkegaard certainly does not offer us a
theoretical defense of the truth or probable truth of Christianity, he does offer us an account of the logic of the decision
to become a believer in Christianity. Certainly, Kierkegaard
admits, even insists, that this logic is an insane one from a
certain perspective.[4] But nevertheless the overall thrust of
his literature is to build a convincing case for the appropriateness, even necessity, of this insane logic, in view of the
human situation. Thus, although Kierkegaard does not give us
an objective argument for the truth of Christianity, it is possible — to me it seems inescapable — to read his literature as
giving a kind of justification of subjective *belief.* If anyone
should object that this is just not Kierkegaard, I retreat to the
view that this is a meaningful position which I discovered in
Kierkegaard's writings. The view itself is more important
than the question of whether Kierkegaard would claim it.

OBJECTIVE AND SUBJECTIVE THOUGHT

The presupposition of what we have termed the practical
approach to religious belief lies in a distinction between two

---

3. Of course Kant is also concerned with far more than mere belief in
God. In *Religion Within the Limits of Reason Alone* he gives a full account of
the necessity for elements of the Christian religion, such as the incarnation,
conversion, and the church, reinterpreted as means for the attainment of a
personal and social moral order. But the difference remains that for Kierkegaard the *historicity* of the incarnation has decisive religious significance.

4. See Merold Westphal, "Kierkegaard and the Logic of Insanity," *Religious Studies,* 7 (September, 1971), 193-211.

types of thinking, which was illustrated well by Kant's conception of theoretical and practical reason. Both theoretical and practical reason are rational activities; reason is always reason. The distinction concerns the types of questions or problems which the mind is attacking. This can be well described in terms of the notion of a perspective or stance which the mind occupies.

This notion of perspective or standpoints is the key to a proper interpretation of Kierkegaard. His pronouncements on faith, despair, sin, and the like (particularly in the pseudonymous works) cannot be understood unless one takes care to determine from what standpoint the matter is being viewed. In the course of his literature he characterizes a large number of perspectives which we might characterize as polar, or mutually exclusive. Among these would be the poetic/ethical, temporal/eternal, speculative/existential, abstract/concrete, objective/subjective, Christian/worldly, spiritual/unspiritual, truth/untruth. If one is willing to take Kierkegaard's view of himself as reliable, his personal standpoint from first to last was the standpoint of a religious author (*PV*, p. 5). And though it is accurate to see in his literature a series of standpoints which seem progressively closer to that religious stance, it is nonetheless true that in the final analysis there are only two perspectives, *one* either-or. The religious, the existential, the eternal, the subjective, and the ethical are attempts to describe, in ways which are more or less adequate, one mode of thought which stands in sharp contrast to the poetic, the speculative, the objective, and impersonal, all of which represent life-views regarded by Kierkegaard as decidedly un-Christian. "There is an either-or: either God/or . . . the rest is indifferent" (*ChD*, p. 333).

Perhaps the characterization of perspective which comes closest to the Kantian distinction of theoretical and practical reason is the distinction which Kierkegaard makes between objective or abstract thought and subjective thinking:

> While abstract thought seeks to understand the concrete abstractly, the subjective thinker has conversely to understand the abstract concretely. Abstract thought turns from concrete men to consider man in general; the subjective thinker seeks to

understand the abstract determination of being human in terms
of this particular existing human being. (*Post*, p. 315)[5]

Objective or abstract thought for Kierkegaard goes away
from the personal and ethical dimensions of existence. The
subjective thinker seeks an understanding of what it means
to be human that will be reflected in his own existence. The
objective thinker is the man who relates himself externally to
his thought. Though he may occupy himself with such ethical
questions as "What is the nature of the good life?" and "What
is the nature of moral obligation?" he asks these questions
from the wrong standpoint, the standpoint of neutrality or
non-involvement. He does not recognize the importance of
these question to himself as an individual, and he does not
recognize that he is called upon to make choices which involve taking a stand on these questions. He does not achieve
the passionate concern which is the mark that one understands a question existentially. "Abstract thought is disinterested, but for an existing individual, existence is the highest interest" (*Post*, p. 278). "To think about existential problems in such a way as to leave out the passion is tantamount
to not thinking about them at all, since it is to forget the point,
which is that the thinker is himself an existing individual"
(*Post*, p. 313).

Notice carefully that the distinction Kierkegaard draws
is not merely the distinction between an attempt to understand a datum abstractly or universally, and an attempt to
understand a datum *in concreto*. This is a very popular interpretation of the distinction between an objective, scientific understanding of something and an existential grasp of an

---

5. I am well aware of the difficulties posed by attributing to Kierkegaard
the ideas of the pseudonymous authors. It is my conviction that the passages
which will be appealed to in this chapter represent Kierkegaard's own
deepest convictions, and that this can be verified by a close examination of
Kierkegaard's non-pseudonymous writings and his *Journals and Papers*. To
argue this is impossible, however, in an essay of this type, as it would require
detailed discussion of each of the books and pseudonyms, particularly the
Fragments and the *Postscript*. If a reader does not agree with my conviction
that these two books essentially embody Kierkegaard's own convictions, then
I ask him to read this essay as an exploration of an important argument found
in Kierkegaard's writing, and disregard my references to the Dane himself.

object, but it is not what Kierkegaard has in mind. The distinction between objective thought and subjective thought is not that one is concerned with the abstract while the other is concerned with the concrete. Both deal with abstractions. It rather lies in the relationship of the abstract thought to the thinker. The objective thinker seeks to understand a concrete actuality abstractly by subsuming it under objective concepts; the subjective thinker seeks to understand an abstract concept in relationship to his own concrete existence as a particular human being.

Louis Mackey gives a helpful account of this distinction when he comments on Kierkegaard's treatment of thought and action.[6] Thought is the translation of an actuality into a possibility (existence into essence), while action is the transformation of a possibility into an actuality (essence to existence). Mackey's distinction between thought and action is closely related to the distinction between objective and subjective thought which we have in mind. Subjective thinking for Kierkegaard *is* a certain type of action, just as practical reason for Kant is a certain type of willing. To say that it *is* action, however, is not to say that it is *not* thought. (Mackey's terminology is not very helpful here.) Just as for Kant, practical reason is the willing of actions in accordance with principles, so for Kierkegaard to think subjectively is to *conceive* of certain sorts of possibilities with a view towards actualizing them. It follows then that subjective thought may, indeed must, have an objective content; what is distinctive is the relationship of the thinker to that content. To begin to consider the relationship of the thinker to the content of a possibility with a view towards actualizing it is to think about what one ought to *do*.

The object of thought for Kierkegaard is always an abstraction, a possibility. However, as Paul Holmer notes,[7] it is a mistake to think that the translation into possibility fal-

6. "Kierkegaard and the Problem of Existential Philosophy," *The Review of Metaphysics,* 9 (March and June, 1956), 417-418.

7. "On Understanding Kierkegaard," *A Kierkegaard Critique,* ed. Howard Johnson and Niels Thulstrup (New York: Harper and Row, 1962), p. 44.

sifies the actual, or that Kierkegaard believed that it did.
Rather as Holmer says, it was Kierkegaard's genius to recognize that the situation of the thinker himself could be
conceptualized — that the possible modes of existence could
be recognized, described, and communicated. If thought falsified its object, this would obviously be impossible. These
modes of existence Kierkegaard conceives as universal and
objective in content. However, what he desired to do was not
merely to describe these modes of existence in an objective
way; what he wished to do was to communicate them in such
a way that his readers would consider them subjectively, that
is, with an understanding that these are possibilities which
confront them as individuals for rejection or actualization.

Kierkegaard has taken Kant's two kinds of thinking and
pushed them even further. On the one hand, there is objective scholarship, science, and philosophical speculation —
impersonal, objective, detached. The *individual,* however, is
faced with another kind of problem. Am I a human being?
Have I attained the eternal happiness which constitutes my
highest end? With regard to this question another type of
reflection is required — personal, subjective, passionately
concerned.

At this point an objection will surely arise. Is the dichot-
omy which Kierkegaard seems to be drawing legitimate? Is
objective, honest scholarship incompatible with ethical and
religious self-understanding? Is the lofty place of neutral,
unbiased scholarship always an attempt to escape the necessity for personal decisions? Obviously, the answer is no, and I
believe Kierkegaard would agree wholeheartedly (at least in
his best moments). The question is not whether objective
scholarship has a legitimate place in the total context of
human activity. The either-or concerns the question as to
what I conceive to be man's *highest* end, the over-arching,
ordering principle which gives unity and coherence to my
life.

> All honor to the pursuits of science, and all honor to everyone
> who assists in driving the cattle away from the sacred precincts
> of scholarship. But the ethical is and remains the highest task
> for every human being. One may ask even of the devotee of

science that he should acquire an ethical understanding of himself before he devotes himself to scholarship, and that he should continue to understand himself ethically while immersed in his labors. (*Post,* p. 136)

Just as Kant asserted the primacy of practical reason over theoretical reason, so Kierkegaard is asserting the primacy of subjective, existential thinking over objective, abstract thought. It is when abstract, objective thought is absolutized as man's highest end that there occurs an either-or, either the subjective or the objective. It is this scientistic perspective which views objective knowledge as the be-all and end-all of existence which Kierkegaard is referring to when he rejects the perspective of objective thought. There is no either-or between the subjective and objective *per se;* the either-or concerns the manner in which a man will make his most basic decisions.

We thus see that Kierkegaard's protest against objective thought on behalf of existence is not an attack on thought *per se.* It is a protest against the Hegelian notion of speculative thought. It is an assertion that existence involves more than the knowing of particulars in terms of abstract possibilities; existence is the process of actualizing abstract possibilities in the form of concrete particulars. Among the acts which are potentially actualizable are acts of *knowing,* but existence is not reducible to those acts. Still, existence is far from thoughtless; when a man exists in the fullest sense his life is permeated by reflection.

The distinction which Kierkegaard is drawing is broader than the Kantian distinction. Kant distinguished two types of thinking, two applications of reason, and two corresponding approaches to religious truth. Kierkegaard is distinguishing two views of man's highest end *qua* man, each of which represents what we might call an absolutization of a kind of thinking. When each type of thinking is viewed, not merely as one human activity among others, but as the source or embodiment of the essentially human, which is to be preferred? Shall we choose to become speculative, to make the objective scientific acquisition of knowledge the highest end of life, and escape all questions about what I as an individual am to become?[8] (Even the question as to whether I am to become a scientist?) Or shall I strive to become the individual, the subjective thinker who does not merely know the truth in an external fashion, but who constantly asks himself about his relationship to the truth?

This is sufficient, I think, to attain a preliminary understanding of what Kierkegaard means by objective and subjective thought. We must now examine the manner in which these different types of reflection deal with religious questions. We must first, however, enter a caution. The distinction between objective and subjective thought which Kierkegaard is drawing is legitimate only when the objective is absolutized as Kierkegaard thought Hegel had done. In existence objective and subjective thinking are quite intimately related.[9] Not only is it the case that knowing is something that one decides to do, but often what one decides to do is determined by what one knows or understands. And this concerns not only the "what" but the "how" of decision-making; a man ought to seek all the knowledge of a situation he can get and he ought to seek it as objectively as possible. This is a subjective duty. Kierkegaard often seems to lose sight of this intimate relationship, and we shall appeal to it later to question the autonomy of purely "subjective" defenses of religious belief.

THE FAILURE OF THE OBJECTIVE APPROACH

Given this preliminary distinction between objectivity and subjectivity, we can proceed to examine Kierkegaard's subjective justification of religious belief. We will first consider his contention that a purely theoretical, objective ap-

8. It is clear that Kierkegaard's opposition to "objective" approaches to existence would include modern positivistic scientisms as well as Hegelian metaphysics. Kierkegaard in several places indicates a fear that natural science is a threat to existence, or that "physics may supplant ethics." See Gregor Malantschuk, *Kierkegaard's Thought* (Princeton: Princeton University Press, 1971), pp. 141-142.

9. Gregor Malantschuk maintains that Kierkegaard fully realized that there is no objectivity without some subjectivity and no subjectivity without some objectivity. See *ibid.,* p. 140.

proach to religious truth is inadequate. Kierkegaard and Kant both agree that objective reason is inadequate in this way. Kant argued that the theistic proofs and arguments failed to attain knowledge, which required apodictic certainty, and he believed that they were therefore without much value *in themselves*. In the field of theoretical reason, no conclusions which were not certain were of any value. The valuable conclusions of theoretical reason were negative: no knowledge is possible. Kierkegaard basically agrees with these conclusions.

However, Kierkegaard seems to have two criticisms of the objective approach, which at first glance do not seem to be compatible. First, he agrees with Kant that objective thought is powerless to produce certainty and must be judged by that failure. There is an incommensurability between the evidence supplied by historical research, for example, and the decision to become a Christian which the proponent of the objective approach wishes to base on such evidence. The historical evidence attains at most a certain level of probability. The decision which I must make on the other hand carries with it an infinite risk — eternal happiness or eternal damnation may be the result. No amount of probability could be sufficient to base such a decision upon.

The second objection which Kierkegaard seems to have is that the objective approach seeks certainty, but faith requires uncertainty. Faith requires that a man be out over the deep, over seventy thousand fathoms. The attempt to take away this uncertainty is an attempt to do away with faith. Thus the objective approach is damned coming and going — for failing to attain certainty, and for trying to attain it.

However, this apparent inconsistency is only apparent. We must remember that Kierkegaard is here not expounding his own view, but criticizing another approach. For purposes of such criticism, it is not uncommon for a thinker to concede an assumption which he does not really accept, in order to show the deficiency of a position on its own terms. This is in no way incompatible with the thinker's simultaneously putting forward another criticism which is external in nature. What Kierkegaard has done is exactly this. First, conceding the rationalist interpretation of religion put forward by the proponents of the objective approach, he proceeds to examine the knowledge claims put forward as security on behalf of religion. Here he maintains that the type of evidence attainable is inadequate to provide certainty for the conclusions which the religious believer wishes to reach. Next he proceeds to argue that the search for this type of security is misguided in principle. Even if it were attained, it would never amount to "the certainty of faith," and would even be a hindrance to the attainment of faith. There is a parallel here to Kant, who criticizes theoretical reason for failing to obtain knowledge, but also contends that such scientific knowledge of God would be as great a calamity as possible. Let us proceed to examine these two criticisms in detail.

Kierkegaard's rejection of any claim to establish objectively the truth of Christianity must be treated with care, as it has led to much misunderstanding. His arguments are integrally related to certain well-thought-out but nonetheless debatable epistemological views. It is important to note that what he wishes to establish is not that Christianity cannot be known to be true, but only that it cannot be known to be true in a particular way. We shall examine his views on a variety of topics: first, the theistic proofs, followed by his view of empirical knowledge in general, his account of the nature of historical knowledge in particular, and finally, his account of the particular historical claims which are accepted as supportive of Christianity.

Kierkegaard's views on the theistic arguments are not well-developed. He was obviously not much interested in traditional rationalists such as Wolff, who seemed an unimportant threat in comparison with the Hegelian project of incorporating Christianity into a free-wheeling speculative system. However, he does give some attention to this area in the *Fragments* and his comments are important.

In general we may say that Kierkegaard believed that these theistic proofs, as speculative arguments of reason, involved a hidden premise — a non-neutral starting point.[10]

---

10. Kierkegaard is not merely reiterating Mill's claim that no demon-

> The idea of demonstrating that this unknown something (the God) exists, could scarcely suggest itself to the Reason. For if the God does not exist it would of course be impossible to prove it; and if he does exist it would be folly to attempt it. For at the very outset, in beginning my proof I would have presupposed it, not as doubtful but as certain (a presupposition is never doubtful for the very reason that it is a presupposition), since otherwise I would not begin, readily understanding that the whole would be impossible if he did not exist. (*PF*, p. 49)

It is certain that any purely a priori argument will fail to establish God's existence because it is impossible, by developing the purely logical consequences of a concept, to show that a being really exists. This is of course a familiar criticism of the ontological argument.

> Thus I always reason from existence, not toward existence, whether I move in the sphere of palpable fact or in the realm of thought. I do not, for example, prove that a stone exists, but that some existing thing is a stone. (*PF*, p. 50)

Spinoza, who Kierkegaard believed had developed the ontological argument in its purest form, has given us a profound tautology in saying that God's essence (the idea of a perfect Being) involves existence. It is a profound tautology because Spinoza profoundly plumbed the depths of the God-idea, but it is a tautology nonetheless because Spinoza explains perfection in terms of degree of being and degree of being in terms of perfection of *esse*. Kierkegaard charges that Spinoza's profundity hides an unclear conception of being. "What is lacking here is a distinction between ideal being and factual being." Factual existence is said to be subject to Hamlet's dialectic: "to be or not to be." When we are speaking of factual being, the doctrine of degrees of being is meaningless. Therefore to tell us that the concept of God is the concept of a being which exists in the fullest degree does not escape the realm of essence. The difficulty, says Kierkegaard, is assuring

---

strative argument can reach a conclusion not already contained in the premises. His point is that the arguments are deceptive — they hide or conceal their true assumptions.

ourselves that such a being exists factually (*PF*, pp. 51-52, note).[11]

As to the question of proving God from his works, Kierkegaard again holds that God's existence is a presupposition of the proof. The various features of the world which have suggested proofs, such as its contingency, purposiveness, goodness, are not "manifest upon the very face of things" (*PF*, p. 52). The natural order is subject to doubt and a variety of interpretations. In beginning such a proof, I stake myself to a certain ideal interpretation of nature, and this ideal interpretation is equivalent to a confidence in God's existence (*PF*, pp. 52-53). For example, one does not prove God's existence by seeing purpose in nature. Rather it is the idea of a moral, purposive God which makes possible the coherent interpretation of the world as purposive (*PF*, p. 54).[12]

Kierkegaard would be equally critical of the claims for certainty put forward by more empirical types of objective approaches such as arguments from religious experience. In the light of the traditional quest for certainty any attempt to gain knowledge of God can at most lead to some degree of probability because all objective human knowledge is at most probable.

> The study of Greek scepticism is much to be recommended. There one may learn thoroughly what it will always require time and exercise and discipline to understand ... that the certainty of sense perception, to say nothing of historical certainty, is uncertainty, is only an approximation. (*Post*, p. 38)

It follows therefore that the man who wishes to eliminate

---

11. It may well be that Kierkegaard is question-begging here. Spinoza no doubt did not wish to maintain that God existed factually in Kierkegaard's sense, and would no doubt reject the whole distinction. Perhaps Kierkegaard's essential criticism is that it is factual existence that is the real issue in the controversy over proofs of God. People don't want to know if God exists in some special sense; they wish to know if he exists in the same sense that a tree exists (though they admit that the sort of existence God has differs). Whether this notion of "factual existence" is itself clear is another matter.

12. Cf. Kant, *KU* 477, p. 153, where a similar argument is given.

the uncertainty from religious belief is bumping his head against a brick wall.

> I will remind myself that the wisest man that ever lived, and the most shallow that ever lived, would get equally near to the truth when it is a question of vouching for the next instant, and when it is a question of explaining the least occurrence, get equally near to a perhaps, and the more passionately a man raves against this perhaps, the nearer he comes only to losing his mind. For no mortal ever broke through, ever penetrated — yea, not even the prisoner confined within walls seven yards thick, bound hand and foot, and nailed to the floor, is so bound as every mortal is by these bonds constructed of nothing but this perhaps. (*ChD,* p. 264)

The notion of "perhaps" is more apt than the notion of probability as a description of the relationship of the individual to objective religious knowledge because it is notoriously difficult to give any clear meaning to the notion of probability when dealing with theistic proofs or with the weight of experiential evidence for religious truth. From Kierkegaard's perspective the objective approach leads a man only to the position where he can say, "Perhaps it is true."[13] It is not surprising that this is so, because empirical knowledge is knowledge of existence, of factual being. Because existence is becoming, lacks finality and closure, and includes a brute element of fact (which Kierkegaard calls "coming into existence"), so also must knowledge of existence be tentative, be an *anticipation* of the conformity of thought and being which exists only for God (*Post,* pp. 107, 170; *PF,* pp. 89-106). Everything that we call empirical knowledge must therefore include belief, which Kierkegaard sees as an act of the will.

With regard to the providing of an historical basis for the truth of a particular religion, the attempt of course involves one in all the difficulties which attach to empirical knowledge in general, plus the additional factor that a successor must rely on the testimony of some contemporary of the event. But the particular attempt to prove the truth of Christianity via an appeal to the miracles found in the Bible, the

---

13. However, we shall later disagree with Kierkegaard about the importance of this achievement of objective thought.

resurrection of Jesus, and the like, faces even greater difficulties. The problem lies with what I shall call "estimating a probability factor." In looking at historical records we do not simply ask ourselves whether a witness is trustworthy and then decide whether to accept his testimony. We look at the testimony itself as one of the factors which determines our decision as to whether a witness is reliable. The main point of Hume's essay on miracles is that (according to Hume) the likelihood of a miracle occurring is always less than the likelihood that the witness to a miracle is unreliable.[14] Certain events seem so inherently unlikely that we would have to be very convinced of the reliability of an account to accept them as actual occurrences. At least the two factors — the likelihood of an event and the trustworthiness of a witness — can be shown to reciprocally influence each other. An alcoholic who reported seeing a Martian in the Bowery in New York would probably not get much of a hearing; a reporter for the *New York Times* who gave the same report would no doubt cause a stir. On the other hand, an alcoholic who reported finding a body in a high-crime area of New York would certainly get a serious hearing. But a *New York Times* reporter who reported having seen a gorilla 5,000 feet tall would very likely be asked if he had not been hitting the bottle a little too frequently.

With regard to the New Testament miracles, and specifically with regard to the incarnation, Kierkegaard believes that this problem of determining the likelihood of the events in question is a bar to anything like objective certainty. Kierkegaard believes that the incarnation is from the point of view of "human understanding," an absurdity, a "contradiction."

> The absurd is — that the eternal truth has come into being in time, that God has come into being, has been born, has grown up, and so forth, precisely like any other individual human being, quite indistinguishable from other individuals. (*Post,* p. 188)

---

14. Whether Hume was right or wrong here is not essential.

The situation for which the Biblical miracles are adduced as proof is one which seems inherently improbable.

> The *situation* is inseparable from the God-Man, the situation that an individual man who stands beside you is that God-man. . . . There is neither in heaven, nor on earth, nor in the depths, nor in the aberration of the most fantastic thinking, the possibility of a (humanly speaking) more insane combination. (*TC*, p. 84)

A good case has been made that by asserting the incarnation is a paradox, Kierkegaard does not mean to say it is a logical contradiction.[15] Indeed he specifically denies in at least two places that the incarnation is such a logical contradiction (*PF*, p. 127 and *TC*, p. 125). We might rather view the incarnation as an extreme case, perhaps even a limiting case, of an historical situation to which we would give a low estimate of probability for its occurrence. Kierkegaard himself speaks in very similar terms:

> The idea in whatever concrete form it may be understood, of attaching a demonstration of probability to the improbable (to prove — that it is probable? but in that case the concept is altered: to prove that it is improbable? but in that case it is a contradiction to use probability for the purpose) is so stupid when seriously conceived, that it would seem impossible for it to be entertained. (*PF*, p. 118, note)

We shall deal with the paradox of the incarnation more extensively in our consideration of the subjective approach to Christianity. The question as to why the incarnation is a paradox and why the existing individual nevertheless has an interest in it is crucial. The importance of the paradox in this context is negative; like a Kantian antinomy it marks the boundary of objective thought and stands guard against any attempt of prove objectively the truth or probability of Christianity. Kierkegaard affirms in the strongest terms that to believe in Christ is always to believe "against the understanding."

---

15. See Alastair McKinnon, "Kierkegaard: Paradox and Irrationalism," *Essays in Kierkegaard*, ed. Jerry H. Gill (Minneapolis: Burgess Publishing Co., 1968), pp. 102-112. Also Westphal, "Logic of Insanity," pp. 207-211.

THE SUBJECTIVE THINKER:
KIERKEGAARD'S METHODOLOGY

Put in terms of the general structure outlined in chapter one, our exposition of Kierkegaard has now accomplished, or at least attempted to accomplish, two things. We have first delineated two ways of rationally approaching the question of religious truth, and then attempted to show that one of those approaches, the objective approach, must inevitably fail to come to grips with the decisive issues. We must now consider Kierkegaard's attempt to show the impossibility of neutrality and his attempt to explicate the subjective factors which can and ought to lead a man to faith.

To think subjectively is to think about what things I ought to do, what kind of life I shall lead, what sort of person I shall be. In Kierkegaard's vocabulary these questions are summed up in the question, "How shall I exist?" (which presupposes the more fundamental question, "Shall I exist at all?"). Kant held that the man who begins to reflect in this manner will ultimately be led to theistic belief *via* a rational-moral-psychological imperative: "In order to be a fully rational, moral being one must believe in God." We shall interpret Kierkegaard's defense of Christian belief as stemming from a similar imperative: "In order to become a human being in the fullest sense, one must become a Christian." There are two important differences from Kant. First, what man is under an obligation to actualize is his potential as a whole person, and that is conceived to involve freedom and love, passion and creativity, as well as thought and moral decisiveness. Secondly, the mode of actualizing that potentiality is not merely the purely rational religion which Kant deduces from man's situation as a moral being in the world. It is a particular historical religion which presents itself to individuals as possessing divine authority.

Before looking at the case which Kierkegaard constructs for his view that the most adequate fulfillment of one's humanness comes through Christian faith, it would be well to clear up a possible misconception concerning the concept of humanness. Kierkegaard at times uses the term "human" disparagingly: human wisdom, human desire, the merely human, and so on. On the other hand, he also speaks of Christianity as the fulfillment of what it means to be a human being. In this context, he at times uses "becoming a person" or "becoming an individual" as almost the equivalent of "becoming a Christian." He nonetheless declares that Christianity is dying from self. He asserts that, humanly speaking, Christianity is suffering and madness. What then is the true relationship of Christianity to humanness?

I believe that this problem can be resolved if we recognize that Kierkegaard talks of man at times in a normative, at times in a factual sense. In speaking disparagingly of the human condition, Kierkegaard is using the term "man" descriptively — he is telling us what man actually *is*, how he actually thinks. When, however, he says with Nietzsche, "let us be men, let us become what we are," he is using the term normatively — let us become what God intended us to be.

A second preliminary matter concerns the method which Kierkegaard follows. The question as to how to go about determining "what it means to be a human being in the fullest sense" (or any such value question) is notoriously difficult. Abraham Maslow, in *Toward a Psychology of Being,* proposes that we answer this sort of question by selecting those persons who seem to have achieved the essentially human, self-actualization, and observing them.[16] However, this procedure is open to the obvious objection that one's preconceived notions govern the selection of those men in the first place. For a critic who holds a different view of the ideal human, whatever observable traits the selected group of self-actualizers possess will have a double-edge. One could read the results of such empirical observation as *"These* are the traits which self-actualizers seem to have in common." But they could equally be read as, "Since these particular men have *these* traits, it follows that our original selection process was faulty and biased; they do not represent people who have actualized human potential maximally." Basic disagreements over the value, for example, of the work ethic could hardly be

---

16. (2nd ed., New York: Van Nostrand Reinhold Co., 1968), pp. 3-8.

resolved in such an empirical manner, without presupposing some ultimate values as criteria for judging.

The point is that there does not seem to be *any* objective, scientific way of answering such a question as "What does it mean to truly be a person?"[17] Those who would dismiss such a question as meaningless merely because of this fact are appealing to the a priori principle that all significant questions are scientific questions, a principle which I consider a mere prejudice. Of course such a question may be unanswerable; it probably is not finally resolvable, but that does not entail that it is meaningless. It is certainly meaningful because it is seriously asked by many people, philosophers as well as non-philosophers. It is a genuine human concern, and neither philosophy nor science have the authority to arbitrarily rule out such questions.

Now Kierkegaard would fully agree that such a question is not a "scientific" question. It is exactly for this reason that it can be seen as a kind of starting point for his way of thinking. Recognizing fully that such a question cannot be answered objectively, Kierkegaard proceeds along these lines. He gives us in his literature a series of conceptual pictures (including actual characterizations via the use of pseudonyms and fictional creations) of what he calls stages or spheres of existence, which we might today describe as alternative life-styles based on different value-systems. Kierkegaard regards them as qualitatively different ways of life that are describable in terms of the basic concepts or categories which they presuppose. These different spheres are not to be seen as absolutely different in content. In passing from the esthetic to the ethical way of life, for example, it is not the case that all the joy of living is extinguished. Though the life-style is radically new, there is a sense in which the esthetic reappears, transformed and shorn of its absoluteness.

What is his point in giving us these conceptual pictures? Some have interpreted Kierkegaard as giving us no help in deciding between these different modes of existence. He

---

17. This of course has serious implications for any religion which rests its case on the answer to such a question.

merely presents us with the alternatives. Because we have no rational grounds for choosing between them, the choice is personal and arbitrary (subjective in a different sense from Kierkegaard's). And it is true that Kierkegaard himself, through much, but not all, of his writings, claims to avoid direct communication of the truth, that is, directly saying the religious and specifically the Christian sphere of existence is the highest, is the truth. However, if we are to accept his account of the matter, he is from first to last a religious author, and the whole of his writing is directly related to the problem of "becoming a Christian" (*PV*, pp. 5-6). And this position can certainly be well supported by the writings themselves. Even disregarding the later direct communication, there is plainly present in the pseudonymous works what one might term an existential dialectic, an attempt to help the reader out of the poetic and the speculative towards the direction of "becoming an individual."

Of course Kierkegaard makes no pretense of making the choice for another individual; by the nature of the case no mere man can make another into an individual. In making another dependent on one's own efforts, one would rather be taking him in the opposite direction. But this does not mean that Kierkegaard does not give the individual any help in choosing between these alternatives. The help which he offers is increased self-understanding. In painting these conceptual pictures he is holding up a mirror, attempting to get men to recognize the true character of their own existence. Kierkegaard believes firmly that when a man begins to understand himself in this fashion, it becomes at least possible that he will begin to progress towards becoming an individual. This existential dialectic is an ideal account of the development of that essentially human quality that he termed "inwardness." He wishes to help the individual to become subjective.[18] For we must remember that he sees man as lying under an obligation — the obligation to become what he truly

---

18. When Kierkegaard says that truth is subjectivity, it is in this sense, i.e., ontologically speaking, subjectivity is the truth, that mode of existence which deserves the name true.

is, in traditional terms to actualize his essence.[19] This human ideal is not, however, merely rational thought or poetic feeling or imagination, or even ethical decisiveness, taken alone. The task is the task of simultaneously developing all of one's human potentiality—thought, feeling, imagination, and will (*Post*, p. 311). It is Kierkegaard's thesis that this development of inwardness is fully actualized only in that mode of existence which is made possible by becoming religious, and even more specifically, by becoming a Christian.

So to discern the nature of inwardness it is perhaps best to look first at the highest sphere of existence, where it is most fully developed and can therefore most plainly be seen.

> All religiousness consists in inwardness. . . . People as they are for the most part . . . make sacred promises, they resolve . . . tomorrow, etc., but what is really the decisive point, *to be entirely present to themselves in self-concern,* is something with which they are totally unacquainted. (*AR*, p. 155)

This confirms but expands Kierkegaard's point in *The Sickness unto Death* where he says consciousness of self is the decisive criterion of self. Being self-conscious is all important, but self-consciousness in this sense is by no means an intellectual relationship which all men possess as a matter of course. It is a relationship involving not only knowledge (true self-awareness which most people do not possess), but those elements of personality which we describe in terms of will, passion, and emotion. The man who is conscious of his self is the man who wills to be himself, who is passionately concerned about the self he is, passionately concerned to become the self he ought to be.

Of course this description of inwardness or subjectivity comes close to the formula Kierkegaard gives us for faith: "Faith is: that the self in being itself and in willing to be itself is grounded transparently in God" (*SD*, p. 213). The important addition is of course "is grounded transparently in God."

---

19. Kierkegaard definitely believes in the "universally human," an ideal for man which is in a sense "given." Therefore he is not an "existentialist" in Sartre's sense at all. However, he believes that the universally human is only achieved, paradoxically enough, by becoming "the individual," which is therefore higher than the universal, though not opposed to it.

Why is religious faith seen by Kierkegaard as the highest form of subjectivity? Why does he say as he does in *The Sickness Unto Death,* "the more conception of God, the more self?"

We have already noted the impossibility of objectively establishing the truth of any "ideal image of man." Recognizing this, Kierkegaard proceeds in Socratic fashion to confront his reader directly. Rather than presenting objective 'arguments that the Christian picture of man is correct, he proceeds indirectly to present us with those conceptual pictures of existence which he calls stages, so as to develop these possibilities with as much clarity and depth as possible. The presupposition is not that the choice between these different ways of life is arbitrary, but rather that if a man truly understands himself and his existence, he will see the truth. The truth will show itself to him. Kierkegaard is assuming that either (1) the truth is already within man, in which case he has the potential for recognizing it if properly presented, or (2) the condition for understanding the truth will be given to a man if he truly desires to understand himself.[20]

What grounds does he have for making such an assumption? First, there does not seem to be any viable alternative. Shall we abandon the sphere of ultimate choices (what sort of life to live?) to irrational whim? Or shall we declare that a mindless acceptance of whatever cultural values and lifestyle one has imbibed is the path men ought to follow? Or alternatively shall we put forward a pseudo-scientific theory which seeks to conclude how man ought to behave from empirical generalizations as to how he does behave? Or should we deduce our ideal image of man from a dogmatic, unfounded political ideology? I submit that Kierkegaard's approach, which relies on the assumption that a "man of good will" will recognize the truth about himself and his existence if his self-understanding is sufficiently developed and if the alternatives are clearly understood, is far better. How are these alternatives to be clarified? Perhaps it is by seeking to

---

. 20. The first of these alternatives represents the Socratic position; the second that of Christianity.

develop each possible answer to the fullest extent possible and asking whether, when viewed as a comprehensive picture of the human ideal, this way of life does justice to all that I know about myself.

The second point in favor of Kierkegaard's assumption stems from this way of proceeding. He believes that if we view the alternatives clearly, an existential dialectic *does* stand out. The choices which confront a man do not "stand on the same level." Kierkegaard believes, for example, that the unsatisfactory character of what he terms "the esthetic view of life" soon becomes evident, even from the viewpoint of the esthete himself, when this view of life is absolutized. Kierkegaard attempts to show that the esthetic life, the view of life which holds that one ought to make each moment of one's existence as pleasurable and enjoyable as possible, ultimately leads directly to a contradictory emotion which he calls despair. And he believes that this dialectical pathos, this contradiction in man's emotional being, is what might lead a man to recognize that there is more to being a man than enjoyable moments, no matter how refined or tasteful the esthetic life may be.

This oversimplified account of Kierkegaard's picture of the esthetic way of life is merely intended to illustrate the value of Kierkegaard's procedure. Even if his particular account of the matter is faulty, one-sided, incomplete, one can well appreciate Kierkegaard's conception of the problem which he thought every man ought to face, and his method of attacking the problem. However, this equally serves as a reminder that no exposition of Kierkegaard's thought can possibly replace the individual encounter of the reader with the living portraits of existence which Kierkegaard has left us.

THE DIALECTIC OF THE SUBJECTIVE THINKER: BECOMING A PERSON

Though we can by no means recreate these existence-spheres in all their fulness and concreteness, we must nevertheless try to recount the essential features of "the development of a self." Only by this means can we truly understand the situation of the existing thinker confronted by the paradox of the incarnation and the ground of his choice.

The Ethical

Kierkegaard's notion of the self can be seen as taking its departure from Kant's emphasis on "the good will." Kant had affirmed that the noumenal self could not be known through speculative reason, but that I know myself as a free moral agent in moral action, the essence of which is rooted in "a good will." Kierkegaard's notion of the self bears a close resemblance to this Kantian idea, though perhaps Kierkegaard's notion is fuller than this. The development of moral character is for him essential to becoming human, but it is not the *whole* of the matter.

In any case it is ethical resolve which Kierkegaard sees as the most important feature of a man who has "willed to be his self" or "begun to be his self" or "become a self." (I do not believe these different expressions hide any significant differences in meaning.) It is the ethical which Kierkegaard sees as the bulwark against the "speculative" interpretation of existence. (Man's highest end is to acquire objective knowledge). And it is to the ethical level of existence that he hopes to rouse the esthetic man, who attempts to build his existence around the category of the satisfying *moment*. It is absolutely essential to see the importance which the ethical occupies in Kierkegaard's thought. The relationship of the ethical to the religious is by no means analogous to the relationship between the esthetic and the ethical. The connection between becoming ethical and becoming an individual is an essential one, a relationship which is by no means lost when an individual becomes religious. Kierkegaard makes this abundantly clear in the *Postscript* (pp. 261, 347-348 for example). Even at what was practically the end of his literature, Kierkegaard could write: "For what is it to be or to will to be the single individual? It is to have and to will to have a conscience" (JY, p. 109).

In Kierkegaard's opinion the decisive characteristic of human life, that characteristic which gives to each individual a decisive significance, is the capacity to choose and decisively will an end. The more will a man has, the more self (*SD*, p. 162), and conversely the man who completely lacks any ethical decisiveness really has no self; he is not *existing*, not engaged in decisively willing and actualizing various possibilities. In this emphasis on willing, Kierkegaard echoes Kant's depreciation of results:

> The most cleverly calculated and daring plan for transforming the world is subject to the principle that it becomes great or not by virtue of the result. But the simple and loyal resolution of an obscure human being embodies the principle that the plan itself is higher than any result, that its greatness is not dependent upon the result. And this is surely a more blessed privilege than being the greatest man in the world and a slave of the result, whether the result be success or failure. (*Post*, p. 357)

Such a view of human life is certainly humane: it is on the basis of this view that Kierkegaard believes every individual's life possesses infinite significance. The ethical perspective does not ask a man whether he was fortunate or lucky, whether he was born rich or poor, whether he was crippled by illness or in robust health; it asks only whether he has truly willed *one thing*—the good. It is the ethical in this sense that marks the beginning (and, as we shall see, in a way the culmination also) of the development of self. The ethical man is the man who has begun to realize what it is to truly be a man; here he recognizes his own infinite importance. It is the ethical perspective which drives us to affirm that man's highest end is "becoming subjective."

This identification of existence with ethical striving will ultimately give us our answer to the problem of why the individual cannot remain indifferent to religious questions, despite the lack of objective certitude. Kierkegaard is affirming with Kant the primacy of the practical. No man can escape the sphere of the subjective without escaping existence altogether; to exist is to strive, to choose, *to be interested.* Objective thought is itself a legitimate (necessary in fact) actualization of one's subjectivity, but to attempt to escape from the realm of decisions and actions altogether represents a kind of insanity. For would not such a project represent a *choice?*

We must clearly see that when Kierkegaard tells us that the task of the existing thinker is to become "the individual," he does not mean us to take individuality merely in the sense of non-conformity, and certainly not in the twentieth-century sense of eccentricity or oddness (though the ethical man may well be thought eccentric and quite possibly will be a non-conformist with regard to certain characteristics). Ethics is concerned with the universal; the task is the same for every man.

> To wish to live as a particular human being (which is what everyone undoubtedly is), relying upon a difference is the weakness of cowardice; to will to live as a particular human being (which everyone undoubtedly is) in the same sense as is open to every other human being, is the ethical victory over life and all its illusions. (*Post,* p. 319)

What are the characteristics of this ethical person? We have already spoken of the quality of inwardness, which is practically a synonym for what Kierkegaard means by subjectivity. In the context of ethics he says inwardness may be regarded as *seriousness,* that attitude of self-concern which characterizes the self who has begun to exist, who is attempting to understand the significance of his death, of the social relationships which envelop him, of worldly ambitions and goods, and relate to all of these things in an ethical way. Seriousness does not consist in busyness about temporal affairs, such as livelihood, place-finding, and the like. Nor does it consist in a presumptuousness which denies the reality of our everyday existence or takes it as a dream. Seriousness is the humble resolution to express the ideal in everyday life (*TC,* p. 188).

However, perhaps the most significant characteristic of the ideal which the ethical person sets before himself and attempts to embody in his existence is that of continuity. Kierkegaard has a tremendous sense of the importance of what modern psychologists term "personal integration." He recognizes that the self is not to be conceived as a static substance, that existence is the realm of striving, of the essen-

tially incomplete (*Post,* p. 110). But he sees that in the midst
of the constant change which characterizes human existence
there must be something solid, something about a man which
endures. In modern terms, for a man to function in the midst
of a changing world, to successfully meet new situations and
challenges, he must have a sense of identity, a concept of who
he is:

> In so far as existence consists in movement there must be some-
> thing which can give continuity to the movement and hold it
> together, for otherwise there is no movement. Just as the asser-
> tion that everything is true means that nothing is true, so the
> assertion that everything is in motion means there is no motion.
> ... The difficulty facing an existing individual is how to give
> his life the continuity without which everything simply van-
> ishes. (*Post,* p. 277)

It is this problem which engaged Kierkegaard even in so
early a work as *Either-or.* In Volume I we get a picture of a
man who lives his life under the category of the "moment,"
and his existence is merely a collection of moments. In a
significant sense he has failed to *exist,* failed to become a
human being, because his life has no continuity in time,
which is of course the realm of existence. Judge William, in
contrast, through an enduring ethical commitment (mar-
riage) has learned something about what it means to be a
human being.

Religiousness A

Without minimizing the importance of the ethical, Kierkegaard emphatically asserts that the task of becoming human
requires more than what is usually designated as an "ethical
life," particularly if that phrase be taken in a conventional
way — to be a patriotic citizen, faithful husband, loyal
worker, etc. Actually Kierkegaard uses the term "ethical" in
several different senses. The first is the ethical viewed as a
stage on the way to the religious. Even within this sphere
there are important differences, which we will note,[21] but
even when most fully developed, the ethical way of life, taken

---

21. See below, pp. 103-104.

alone, is essentially incomplete. Kierkegaard also speaks of the ethical in a new sense, the sense in which it is an essential aspect of religious existence. Here the ethical is both preserved and transformed. The difference between the two ethics is that the first is a science "which can strictly be called ideal" while the second "begins with the real" (*CD*, p. 18). I believe Kierkegaard delineates this new ethic in *Works of Love*. But before this new ethic can become a reality, there is a sense in which the ethical must be transcended: a man must become religious. This transition to the religious has two elements: the recognition of guilt and the recognition of the absolute character of the requirement which is laid on man. These are the two factors which produce an immanent God-relationship.

It is not enough, says Kierkegaard, to affirm that man's significance lies in a decisive willing of the ethical. We must recognize that this requirement which is laid upon every man is an ideal. The real problem does not even emerge until we go beyond the mere proclamation of the ideal and consider the pervasive fact of man's inability to attain this ideal.

> As soon as sin makes its appearance, ethics come to grief precisely upon repentance; for repentance is the highest ethical expression, but precisely as such it is the deepest ethical self-contradiction. (*FT*, p. 108)

Ethics points to the ideal as a task. Furthermore, from the point of view of ethics it must be assumed that the individual is in possession of the conditions necessary to perform this task[22] (*CD*, p. 15). But to the subjective thinker who has some understanding of his own mode of existence, this leads precisely to a contradiction (or in Kantian terminology an antinomy) because he knows that he in fact lacks the necessary conditions. This antinomy is resolvable only through a religious existence.

> When the individual by his guilt has gone outside the universal he can return to it only by virtue of having come as the individual into an absolute relationship with the absolute. (*FT*, p. 108).

---

22. Cf. Kant's thesis that "ought implies can."

The problem is not the validity of the ethical requirement; if a man is not acutely ethically developed the true
religious problem does not even arise. The problem concerns
the means of achieving the requirement of ethics. The difference between the ethical and religious standpoints is that for
ethics the whole of existence is locked up in the requirement
itself, while the religious standpoint affirms that in addition
to the requirement the condition for its fulfillment must be
provided. The religious address reflects "the way to the good"
(*Post,* p. 383). And with that providing of the condition "the
whole of life and of existence begins afresh (repetition), not
through an immanent continuity with the foregoing . . . but
by a transcendent fact which separates the repetition from
the first existence by . . . a cleft" (*CD,* p. 16, note).[23]

It is of course Kierkegaard's belief that man is not in
possession of the condition; still, the highest conception of
"what it means to be a man" is "that every individual is
capable of a God relationship, in which consists his essential
humanity, and for the sake of which every earthly establish-
ment and order may and must at times be opposed" (*TC,*
p. 92).

The religious is higher than the ethical because it makes
it possible for a man to actualize all those characteristics
which we described as constituting the authentic self from
the ethical standpoint. It is through a God-relationship that
the self achieves the continuity and unity, the seriousness
and inwardness which characterize the subjective thinker.
The religious calls on a man to enter more deeply into the
complexities of existence; it attempts to push him further
towards the goal of truly becoming a human being by educat-
ing him as to the true nature of guilt and suffering. For the
profoundest truth about human existence is that becoming a
person is not something which is a direct increment of the
natural life of man; it constitutes a new life (*FSE,* p. 96). It is
the most ethically developed man who realizes the necessity

---

23. Kierkegaard is here describing the religious in its most fully developed sense, and does not yet clearly distinguish between religion in general and Christianity.

of a discontinuity — of a break with the "natural man" — most acutely.

What is the nature of this religious mode of existence? Precisely how does it enable a man to truly become himself? In the *Concluding Unscientific Postscript,* Kierkegaard develops two conceptions of the religious, religiousness A, which is the religion of "immanence," and religiousness B, the specifically Christian sphere which he designates as the "dialectical." However, it would be a mistake to regard these two different spheres as mutually exclusive, competing religions. The intimate tie which we found when we examined the relationship of the religious to the ethical characterizes the relationship of religiousness A to religiousness B even more strongly. That is, religiousness A must be seen as a stage in the development of religiousness B, and a stage which is not left behind but incorporated into the highest stage as an essential moment. As Kierkegaard says, "it is only on paper that one finishes the first state, and then has nothing further to do with it" (*Post,* p. 436).

We have already taken note of Kierkegaard's statement in *Fear and Trembling* that the individual who has "gone outside the universal" can return to it only by coming as an individual into an "absolute relationship with the absolute." This is simply his philosophical expression for the necessity of a personal relationship with God, a relationship which is not exhausted by my recognition of ethical duties.

Kierkegaard is not completely clear as to the relationship of the ethical to the religious. He at times takes the ethical in a deficient sense, in which it means that view of life which takes for granted a collection of duties and tasks, all of which have some validity. Even within the distinctively ethical sphere, the ethical way of life can, however, take on a concern which is infinite in character, a concern which is focused on oneself. The religious believer differs from the ethicist in having an infinite concern in the reality of *another,* that is, God (*Post,* pp. 287-288). For religiousness A this concern is still within the arena of immanence; thus the distinction between the highly developed ethicist and religiousness A is not sharp and intermediate cases are possible.

How is the transition made from the ethical to religiousness A? We have already noted the importance of a recognition of one's ethical failings. What makes that recognition
religious is the simultaneous recognition of the true nature of
the absolute requirement. In the religious thinker, the absolute standard of rightness which undergirds his ethical consciousness is now recognized as a distinct reality, an absolute
telos. This recognition resolves the notion of ethical duties (or
even of an absolute duty towards oneself) into the conception
of an absolute duty towards God. Religiousness B goes further and actually conceives the object of a man's infinite concern to be the God who has existed in time (*Post,* p. 288).
Clearly the religious in any form represents a break with the
ordinary human conception of what it means to be ethical,
which does not even recognize an absolute standard.

Far from admitting that I have achieved all I can as a man
by being a relatively good family man, relatively good citizen,
relatively honest, and so on, the religious affirms that one
thing is needful, and that one thing is absolute in character.
In a sense the recognition of guilt and the recognition of the
necessity of an absolute duty towards God are simultaneous.
And it is precisely such an absolute duty which transcends
the common human conception of an ethical life.

> The most humane doctrine about what it means to be a man is
> that every individual is capable of a God-relationship, in which
> consists his essential humanity, and for the sake of which every
> earthly establishment and order may and must at times by op-
> posed. The established order wishes to crush this God-
> relationship, to abolish this ideal, and to become itself the stan-
> dard of goodness, righteous. (*TC,* p. 92)

The recognition of this absolute duty is the attainment of
a "God-relationship" in an individual and personal sense,
and it is this which constitutes the religious. Of course this
emphasis on the individual and personal character of the
God-relationship in no way smacks of exclusivism; the truly
religious man acknowledges that every man has an equal approach to God (*Post,* p. 456). Nor does this emphasis on a
personal God-relationship annul the ethical. To the contrary,
it bears an essential relationship to the ethical; not only in

the sense that it is an awareness of one's ethical deficiencies which leads one into the religious, but also because ultimately the distinguishing mark of the religious, one might even say its fulfillment, is ethical action (*Post,* p. 456).

The phrase "an absolute relationship to the absolute" is more than philosophical jargon, however. It constitutes part of Kierkegaard's determination of the notion of a God-relationship which he explicates in the *Concluding Unscientific Postscript.* The religious formula for the task which confronts a man is to achieve simultaneously an absolute relationship to the absolute *telos* and a relative relation to relative ends.

What is this absolute *telos?* Kierkegaard describes it as achieving an eternal happiness, the absolute good which confronts every man as a problem. One should not be misled by this phrase into the belief that Kierkegaard has perverted the ethical stance via the intrusion of gross hedonism.

The concept of an eternal happiness in Kierkgaard bears at least some analogy to Kant's notion of the highest good, and it in no way involves an abandonment of the notion that duty must be done for duty's sake. An eternal happiness is not a happiness which is describable in terms of any particular ends or pleasures. It is not to be desired because it is a state of happiness. Rather it is to be desired because it is man's highest end. It is a state of happiness because it also constitutes man's highest fulfillment . An eternal happiness, though it is itself man's highest end, is not itself merely a collection of finite ends such as happiness and knowledge at all. It is perhaps a mistake to describe it as desirable at all, because to attempt to characterize it in esthetic categories is to miss the point entirely. "An eternal happiness as the absolute good has the remarkable trait of *being definable solely in terms of the mode of acquisition. . . .* There is nothing to be said of an eternal happiness except that it is the good which is attained by venturing everything absolutely" (*Post,* p. 382).[24] At times Kierkegaard identifies the absolute *telos* (God) with an eter-

---

24. Note the parallel with Kant, who asserted that the highest good is defined by the moral law.

nal happiness, but strictly speaking an eternal happiness for man consists in being related to the absolute *telos*.

How do we know there is a highest good or absolute *telos* in this sense which constitutes a man's eternal happiness? One might say it is perfectly rational to venture everything if there is indeed such a good, but it hardly seems rational or prudent to make such an absolute commitment without such assurance. This objection precisely misses the point. "If what I hope to gain by venturing is itself certain, I do not risk or venture, but make an exchange" (*Post*, p. 380).

Venturing all — making an absolute commitment of oneself—is not at all a matter of what is prudent. The objection has no more place than the question "How do we know the highest good exists? would have for Kant. Strictly speaking, for Kant we don't *know* the highest good *exists;* we recognize that the moral law requires us to seek to actualize it. Similarly for Kierkegaard, the real question is "Do you recognize that a man truly becomes himself when he has experienced his capacity for absolutely willing the good?" What is the absolute good which he wills? The proper object of such an absolute commitment is defined by the nature of the commitment itself — it is and can be no particular good — it is the absolute good itself. The condition of being related to that absolute good which is an eternal happiness is to be desired for its own sake. In Kantian terms, the good will has itself as object.[25]

A question might be raised as to why this attainment of an absolute relationship to the absolute deserves to be called "religious." On what grounds can Kierkegaard maintain that this relationship is a *God-relationship?* The answer to this question reveals an important and interesting feature of Kierkegaard's approach, one which I do not think is generally appreciated. Kierkegaard wishes to maintain that through a process of subjective reflection, a man is inevitably led to consider himself in the light of his relationship to God (*JY*, p. 122). There is implicit in his approach a strong Augustin-

---

25. Though again as in the case of Kant, it does not have *solely* itself as object. The absolute commitment to the absolute requires and expresses itself through a relative commitment to relative ends.

ian theme. In coming to understand his own inadequacies and his obligation to "venture all" or "make an absolute commitment," a man is measuring himself by an infinite standard. If the commitment which a man is required to make is truly absolute, then there can be only one appropiate object of that commitment— what Kierkegaard calls the absolute *telos*. In an Augustianian way Kierkegaard wishes to identify this absolute end to which I must relate myself, with God. In a culture which has been informed by revelation, it is natural for man to identify the absolute *telos* with the God of Judaic-Christian belief, but I believe Kierkegaard holds that our awareness of this absolute *telos* is not dependent on that revelation.

Thus, contrary to popular ideas about Kierkegaard, we can regard his view here as in the tradition of those who believe man has — or at least potentially has — a direct or intuitive awareness of God. It is only on this condition that religiousness A— which is not a religion based on revelation but a religion of immanence— is possible at all. Whether one should call this awareness of God "innate" is debatable. In any case, Kierkegaard clearly believes that this awareness is only present or actual in the man who has reached a certain stage of personal development—the man who has achieved that recognition of guilt which constitutes the highest form of the ethical as well as the defeat of the ethical life considered in isolation.

It is only on the thesis that there is something like an intuitive awareness of God that Kierkegaard's statements on theistic proofs make sense. He states "to prove the existence of one who is *present* is the most shameless affront." The fact that one attempts a proof only shows that one has "permitted oneself to ignore him" (*Post,* p. 485). Kierkegaard is critical of proofs because they remove God's existence from this subjective process which leads one to the awareness. They attempt to make God's existence objectively compelling, but to attempt to do that is precisely to abandon the process by which one actually receives assurance. As a matter of fact, doubts about God's existence arise only when one attempts to prove it objectively. The objective proofs actually create criticism and doubt because they attempt to ground our awareness of God in something other than the process of self-reflection which actually leads to knowledge.

> With what industrious zeal, with what sacrifice of time, of diligence, of writing materials, the speculative philosophers in our time have labored to get a strong and complete proof of the existence of God. But in the same degree that the excellence of the proof increases, certitude seems to decrease. (CD, p. 125. Also see FSE, p. 88)

In sharp contrast to these speculative attempts, Kierkegaard recommends the inward approach. "The speaker may privately have a rendezvous with the Deity, who is present as soon as the uncertainty of all things is thought infinitely" (PF, p. 80). And in a passage even more strikingly reminiscent of Augustine:

> He (God) is in the creation, and present everywhere in it, but directly he is not there; and only when the individual turns to his inner self, and hence only in the inwardness of self-activity, does he have his attention aroused, and is enabled to see God. (Post, p. 218)

If God's existence had to be proved, we would be in trouble because, Kierkegaard argues, we always reason *from* existence, never *to* it. What I in fact do is show that my awareness of a certain unknown X is in fact an awareness of God (PF, pp. 47-49). One who really is aware of God can see him everywhere — in nature, in human love, and so on. God is not seen by all people because so many lack spiritual development.

> If one does not strain his spiritual powers in their spirituality simply by choosing the inward direction, he discovers nothing at all, or he does not discover in the deeper sense that God is. ... In the human spirit as such there lies a selfishness which must be snapped if the God-relationship is to be won in truth. (WL, p. 332)

It is this snapping of selfishness, dying to *self*, or immediacy with which religiousness A is primarily concerned. It is this personal transformation which much be achieved if the God-relationship is to be "won in truth," that is, if the individual is to become absolutely related to the absolute *telos* and relatively related to relative ends. This area of personal inward transformation is far from being a purely rational process; it is a transformation in the whole person, particularly his attitudes and emotions; it represents the achievement of religious pathos.

This is what Kierkegaard is referring to when he speaks of renunciation and suffering as the characteristics of religiousness A. The individual cannot just begin in a straightforward manner to relate himself absolutely to the absolute and relatively to the relative. No, the problem is that in his immediacy each individual is absolutely committed to relative ends (*Post,* p. 412). Our lives are built around fame, money, friends, pleasure. Kierkegaard does not deny that any of these are goods *per se;* the problem is that if our life is lived solely in these finite categories, we never realize the deeper significance of human existence—never become what a man is potentially. And all men are captured by these finite goals. So our tendency is to mediate; we seek to make the absolute *telos* simply another end among many; being religious becomes simply one more thing that a man is, along with being a citizen, family man, tradesman, and the like.

> Mediation is a rebellion of the relative ends against the majesty of the absolute, an attempt to bring the absolute down to the level of everything else, an attack upon the dignity of human life. (*Post,* p. 375)

So the individual must begin with an act of renunciation, a kind of dying away to natural or worldly goods. This is what is necessary if the individual is truly to venture all. This dying away is a painful process, so much so that Kierkegaard says the essential expression for religiousness A is suffering. From the viewpoint of the finite — the perspective of shrewdness, worldly wisdom, and calculation — becoming religious in this sense is foolishness, even insanity.

> The essential existential pathos in relation to an eternal happiness is acquired at so great a cost that it must from the finite point of view be regarded as simple madness to purchase it. (*Post,* p. 346)

What this suffering really amounts to existentially is a real-

ization that "the individual can do absolutely nothing of himself but is as nothing before God" (*Post,* p. 412).

Before writing this off as the neurotic expression of
chronic melancholia, we ought to examine carefully the pervasive nature of such sentiments in the general religious experience of mankind. Kierkegaard's analyses correspond
closely with some of William James's observations in *The
Varieties of Religious Experience.* James argues that the religious man who needs to be twice-born has in some way a more
profound understanding of the realities of the human condition than the healthy-minded once-born types because he has
encountered and faced the reality of evil and suffering. All of
the great religious traditions begin with a diagnosis of some
flaw in man or existence which prevents man from becoming
what he was meant to be. And James points out the overwhelming number of cases in which, to obtain salvation, an
individual must come to a place where he simply gives up —
recognizes his own inability to transform himself into the
person he ought to be — and in that very recognition begins to
achieve not only a sense of reconciliation with that recalci-
trant self, but also a new confidence and vitality in the
achievement of his true goals. "Self-surrender has been and
always must be regarded as the vital turning-point of the
religious life" (*Var,* p. 210). Kierkegaard would quarrel only
with James's view that self-surrender can be accomplished in
a single act. It is for Kierkegaard a process — a constant
striving.

This religious suffering is not masochistic (*Post,* p. 414).
Renunciation is not to be conceived as an end in itself; it is
the means whereby a man frees himself from the tyranny of
the relative and realizes his true dignity and worth.

By making the absolute venture, an individual does not
just become "one more thing" — religious as well as miserly,
patriotic, benevolent, and so on. "In making the absolute venture he becomes another individual" (*Post,* p. 378). He does
not cease to be a human being, nor does he wish to withdraw
from the world to enter a cloister. "He still lives in the finite,
but he does not have his life in the finite" (*Post,* p. 367). He
has grounded his self in transcendence, and he has therefore

gained the capacity to give up anything and everything relative for the sake of the absolute *telos.*

We have noted that from the perspective of prudence and worldly wisdom this seems a kind of insanity. Yet, in another sense, not to make this venture is even more truly insane.[26] For if Kierkegaard is right in asserting man has a capacity for an absolute, total commitment, and if indeed each of us does choose a highest good around which our lives are ordered and built, the choice of a particular relative end can only lead to fragmentation of the self.

> The tortured self-contradiction of worldly passion arises from the attempt to sustain an *absolute* relationship to a relative *telos.* Avarice, vanity, envy, and so forth, are thus essentially forms of madness; for it is precisely the most general expression for madness that the individual has an absolute relationship to what is relative. (*Post,* p. 378)

This is the message of *Purity of Heart.* If the self is to achieve the unification and integration it must possess to be a self, it must be able to truly "will one thing," that is, order its values around one highest value. That value, if it is truly to be one thing, can only be "the Good" (*PH,* p. 55).

The mark or criterion of the religious person is his absolute devotion and commitment to God, a commitment which requires of him that he recognize that he can do nothing without God, but with God he can do something (*Post,* pp. 434-437). The religious man is the man who strives to bring the God-idea into relationship with every thing he does; he must recognize his absolute dependence upon God. We can perhaps distinguish three possible attitudes of the self toward the self. First, I can look upon myself as pure facticity, as a product of a brute mechanical world. Here I am posited completely by an Other which allows no possibility of freedom. Or secondly, I can regard myself as not posited by anything external to myself; in this instance I create myself and my freedom is absolute. Or I can regard myself as posited by

---

26. It is evident that Kierkegaard believes that both the religious and the worldly thinker can and must characterize each other's views as "insane." This, as Westphal notes, forces us to ask "Who is mad after all and who decides?" See Westphal, "Logic of Insanity," pp. 193-195.

an Other (God), but in such a way that I am free to choose myself or fail to become myself. It is this sort of freedom which Kierkegaard believes man to possess and it is this recognition — that the self is grounded in a transcendence — which is expressed existentially in the formula "Without God I can do nothing, with God I can do something." The religious represents the defeat of pride.

While the essential expression of the religious is suffering in the sense we have described, the decisive expression of the religious is guilt. The task of self-understanding in a sense goes backward. The religious thinker knows his task is to be related absolutely to the absolute and relatively to the relative. But the individual is in the condition of being suffocated by the relative. Hence, the absolute venture is impossible unless one "dies to immediacy." But as the thinker truly begins this task of putting the God-idea into relationship with every finite end, he discovers that this too is impossible. Hence the decisive expression for the religious thinker is his recognition that he is *guilty*. The recognition which Kierkegaard describes as being both the highest development of and the end of the ethical way of life is also the culmination of the religion of immanence.[27] It is almost as if the whole of religiousness A constitutes an attempt by the individual to understand himself as guilty in a progressively deeper sense. From the ethical thinker who conceived his guilt merely in terms of his failure to will and do those specific ends he recognized as obligatory has come the religious thinker who perceives the need to relate himself absolutely to an absolute *telos,* but who also recognizes his inability fully to achieve the existential transformation of dying to immediacy which makes that relationship possible.

Guilt in the sense that Kierkegaard is attempting to describe is not to be confused with mere guilt-feelings, feelings of inferiority, and the like which are sometimes today designated by that name. Though guilt is an emotion, or at least is recognized in an emotion, guilt as the religious thinker con-

---

27. Kierkegaard maintains in the *Postscript* that in the fullest sense the concept of *sin* is acquired only in religiousness B.

ceives it is not comparative or quantitative. It is not merely a matter of recognizing that I am inferior to some other person whom I regard as a good person. Guilt is a descriptive or qualitative category; it describes my true condition, which I become aware of when I bring my existence into relationship with the conception of God (*Post,* p. 472). Insofar as a man does bring himself into an immanent relationship to God, it must take the form of this "dis-relationship." The incompatibility of God and man which guilt expresses is "the first deep plunge into existence, and at the same time it is the expression for the fact that an exister is related to an eternal happiness" (*Post,* p. 473). This guilt is not mere feeling; it expresses itself existentially in repentance, in action. But the individual is nonetheless unable, says Kierkegaard, to overcome his guilt by himself; the more religiously developed he is, the more he will recognize how far away from a God-relationship he is. And it is precisely this recognition that is the sign that he does indeed have a God-relationship of sorts, the only immanent relation possible.

Religiousness B

When the individual has reached this stage, he is ready to encounter the dialectical, which distinguishes religiousness B. The dialectical refers to the specific form which Christianity gives to religion, that form which Kierkegaard referred to in the *Postscript* as religiousness B. With the introduction of the dialectical we are back to the point from which we began this discussion of the stages along life's way. In criticizing the objective approach, Kierkegaard had tried to argue that objective rational inquiry, whether taking the form of rational proof or historical argument, reaches an impasse in attempting to discern the truth of Christianity. Christianity, when rightly understood, presents man with a paradox which, objectively, he cannot deal with. Whether he chooses to believe or to be offended, the choice will not be the result of objective rational inquiry. Rather, the choice has to be seen as a self-revelation — as grounded in one's own character. Let us assume that an individual has progressed along the road to becoming a human being so far as to see the following: (1) an

eternal happiness is man's highest end; (2) the eternal happiness for an individual human being is a God-relationship
(maintaining an absolute relation to the absolute *telos* and a
relative relationship to relative ends); (3) this can be existentially achieved only via our renunciation of all finite ends; (4)
the individual is incapable of achieving this state; therefore (5) his God-relationship takes the form of guilt (*Post,*
p. 495). Such a man is then ready for what Kierkegaard terms
the "desperate categories" of Christianity. To "give up one's
understanding" — to embrace something that cannot be
understood — is indeed a desperate remedy. What Kierkegaard is trying to get his reader to see is that a desperate
remedy is exactly what is necessary because man's situation
is indeed desperate. If Kierkegaard is to be criticized, it
should not be on the grounds that he is an irrationalist, re-
pudiating reason. No, if he is to be criticized, it must be on the
basis of charging him with a faulty analysis of the human
situation. Given his analysis of man's situation, becoming a
Christian is in a sense the most rational thing a man can do,
because Christianity offers a reasonable solution to the overwhelming human problem — how to become a person in the
fullest sense.

So before an individual can be in the situation in which
he can become a Christian, he must be ethically and religiously developed. This development is a development of
inwardness, a development of what a man is capable of
passionately feeling, thinking, doing. Kierkegaard describes
religiousness A as the pathetic factor, the pathos which is in a
sense the foundation of one's becoming a Christian. But there
is no question that Christianity itself is something quite
distinctive.

> But to be thus profoundly moved is a very indefinite expression
> for something so concrete as Christian awakening or conver-
> sion. . . . To be shaken (pretty much in the sense that one speaks
> of shaking a person to make him wake up) is the more universal
> foundation of all religiousness; the experience of being shaken,
> of being deeply moved, the coming into being of subjectivity in
> the inwardness of emotion, the pious pagan and the pious Jew
> have in common with the Christian. Upon this common basis
> . . . the difference must be erected. (*AR,* p. 163)

The difference which must be erected is that Christianity posits specific *conditions* for the attainment of an eternal happiness, dialectical conditions which must be "mixed together with religiousness A to produce a new pathos" (*Post*, pp. 493-494).

Kierkegaard has said that by making the absolute venture, an individual becomes "another individual" (*Post*, p. 378). However, it is, as we have seen, precisely this that the individual is unable to do by his own resources. The problem is that an individual must become another individual; if, however, he could accomplish this *himself*, he would not truly be a *new* individual, but rather a modification of his old self. If the individual is related to God immanently, if he is relying upon an eternal determinant within himself, then he has not yet been brought to the place where he sees the need for a *total* transformation of himself which is effected not by himself but by God.

> The exister must have lost continuity with himself, must have become another (not different from himself within himself), and then, by receiving the condition from the Deity, he must have become a new creature. (*Post*, p. 510)

If a man is relying on what we might call his innate knowledge of God, relating himself to God through *recollection*, then the *breach* with the old man, the re-birth which Kierkegaard calls "repetition" is not possible. In order for the individual to be reborn as an individual, the eternal must encounter him in a particular historical form.

> But the breach, in which lies the paradoxical accentuation, cannot occur in the relationship between an exister and the eternal, because the eternal embraces the exister on all sides, and therefore the disrelationship or incompatibility remains within immanence. If the breach is to be effected, the eternal must determine and define itself as temporal, as in time, as historical. (*Post*, p. 474)

In the *Philosophical Fragments*, Kierkegaard argued that *if* the Moment in time is to have decisive significance, if there is another alternative to the Socratic view that the Truth is within man, then that alternative could only be the paradox of "the God in time." In the *Postscript*, via his analysis of subjectivity, he attempts to bring his reader to the place of seeing the *necessity* of the paradox of this God in time. The subjective thinker is now ready to be presented with the claims of Christianity.

> So when the eternal happiness as the absolute *telos* has become for him absolutely the only comfort, and when accordingly his relationship to it is reduced to its minimum through the attainment of existential depth, by reason of the fact that guilt-consciousness is the repelling relationship and would constantly take this *telos* away from him, and yet this minimum and this possibility are absolutely more than everything else to him, then is the appropriate time to begin with the dialectical. (*Post*, p. 497)

Thus the existential thinker is brought to the point of "making the leap," of embracing the paradox. However, Camus' picture of Kierkegaard, driven by despair and desperation into a leap to the religious, presents the matter in a misleading way. True, the categories of Christianity are desperate categories. Certainly the religious is the sphere of objective uncertainty and of subjectivity and passion, and hence of leaps. Clearly the religious thinker does pass from the bankruptcy of his own resources to the healing power of the God in time, manifesting love towards him. However, this transition, though against the understanding, in the most important sense is far from irrational. It presupposes and is in one sense the culmination of a process of personal development, the attainment of an increased self-understanding. And though salvation is found ultimately by embracing the paradox which is the ultimate limit of human understanding, it is via the human understanding that Kierkegaard seeks to get us to see the appropriateness, or rather the *necessity*, of the paradox. As he says in somewhat abstract language in the *Fragments*, there is present in all thinking the desire to discover the limits of thought itself, so that reason itself "desires its own downfall" (*PF*, p. 47). The incarnation marks precisely this limit to thought, the place where a man must recognize the complete inability of his thought to carry him further; it marks the point of decision.

The paradox of the incarnation is twofold. First, there is

the paradox that a man must base his *eternal happiness* on an historical event which, like all other historical events, can never be more than approximately certain. Secondly, there is the further paradox that this historical event could become an historical event only by going against its own nature (*Post*, p. 513). This twofold paradox constitutes the possibility of offense; to believe, a man must give up his understanding.

We must, however, explore this matter of the paradox and the offense a little further. First, as Kierkegaard plainly says and as we have noted earlier,[28] the paradox is not a *logical* self-contradiction. It is not a case of affirming A and Not-A which would "cancel the two terms and bring the sign to naught." The contradiction is qualitative; it involves a putting together into one term what seem to be, from a human standpoint, the most dissimilar elements possible, God and man. And such a combination is not a logical contradiction; thought is free to occupy itself with the paradox as "the strangest possible proposal" (*PF*, p. 127; *TC*, p. 125).[29] "There is neither in heaven, nor on earth, nor in the depths, nor in the aberration of the most fantastic thinking, the possibility of a (humanly speaking) more insane combination" (*TC*, p. 84).

This situation constitutes the possibility of *offense*, which is not itself a logical conclusion, but a passion, the opposite passion to faith.

> If one would learn to understand offense, let him study human envy. ... The narrow-mindedness of the natural man cannot welcome for itself the extra-ordinary which God has intended for him; so he is offended.[30] (*SD*, p. 217)

Though Kierkegaard affirms that Christianity is absurd from the viewpoint of the human understanding, it is clear

---

28. See above, pp. 88-89.

29. In addition to the articles by Westphal and MacKinnon previously cited in this context, see N. H. Søe, "Kierkegaard's Doctrine of the Paradox," *A Kierkegaard Critique*, ed. Johnson and Thulstrup, pp. 207-208, for a clear discussion of Kierkegaard's notion, and an argument that the incarnation was not for Kierkegaard a rational contradiction.

30. Kierkegaard describes the psychological origin of offense at length in *Training in Christianity*.

that his use of terms like "human understanding" and "human reason" is tendentious, to say the least. "Human understanding" in his sense is far from what we should term "rationality" itself.

> When a man so lives that he recognizes no higher standard for his life than that provided by the understanding, his whole life is relativity, labor for a relative end; he undertakes nothing unless the understanding, by the aid of probability, can somehow make clear to him the profit and loss and give answer to the question, why and wherefore. It is different with the absolute. At the first glance the understanding ascertains that this is madness. . . . If I subject myself to suffering, says the understanding . . . then I want to know what profit I can get out of it. (*TC*, p. 118)

In Kierkegaard's opinion not only is human reason limited by finiteness, such that some religious truths are above reason, but what is called "reason" is partly a matter of historical conditioning, and the use of the term represents an attempt to deify certain decidedly un-Christian attitudes and fundamental assumptions of the established order.[31] The transition from the encounter with the paradox to offense is not strictly a logical or rational conclusion, but a psychological reaction which attempts to justify itself via calling the paradox madness. It is not the case, Kierkegaard feels, that the unbeliever is rationally led to conclude that Christianity is untrue, while the believer repudiates his rationality and affirms Christianity to be true anyway. Rather the unbeliever concludes that Chrisitanity is untrue as the result of fundamental attitudes which Kierkegaard believes are pervasive aspects of human thought but are far from rationally inescapable.

At times Kierkegaard speaks less tendentiously of reason and his meaning becomes clearer.

> A true sentence of Hugo de St. Victor (Halferrich: *Mystik,* Vol. 1. 368):
>> 'In things which are above reason faith is not really supported by reason, because reason cannot grasp what faith believes; but there is also a something here as a result of which reason is determined, or which determines reason to honour faith which it cannot perfectly understand.'

---

31. Westphal, "Logic of Insanity," p. 197.

> This is what I explained (e.g. in the *Final Postscript*); not
> every absurdity is "the absurd" or the paradox. The effect of
> reason is in fact to know the paradox negatively — but not
> more. (*Jour*, p. 180)

Kierkegaard here approves the statement that there is "something which determines reason to honour faith," and he could
have added that there is also a something which may determine reason to dishonour or be offended by the requirement
of faith. But in neither case is the something reason itself;
reason can deal honestly with the paradox only by recognizing that the paradox lies beyond its limits. What attitude a
man should have towards the paradox is not thereby
established.

What does determine a man's response? Clearly, it is
man's existential self-awareness — his awareness of his own
limitations and the limitations of reason itself. Kierkegaard's
admonition to "give up one's understanding" is not an
embracement of irrationalism.[32] True, reason must recognize
its own limitations; the understanding must yield itself. But
the crucial point is that reason is itself capable of recognizing
its limitations. A *paradox* (and Kierkegaard clearly believes
there are other paradoxes — the incarnation being the absolute paradox) serves as a boundary, a limit to the pretension
of human reason, in much the same way in which Kant's
antinomies provided evidence that reason had exceeded its
proper function.

> There is only one mistake in Kant's theory of radical evil. He
> does not make it clear that the inexplicable, the paradox, is a
> category of its own. Everything depends on that. Until now,
> people have always expressed themselves in the following way:
> the knowledge that one cannot understand this or the other
> thing does not satisfy science, the aim of which is to under-
> stand. Here is the mistake; people ought to say the very oppo-

---

32. For an account of Kierkegaard's view of faith and reason which sees
him as developing his ideas in the direction of a traditional Thomistic view
see Cornelio Fabro, "Faith and Reason in Kierkegaard's Dialectic," *A Kierkegaard Critique*, ed. Johnson and Thulstrup, pp. 156-206. This essay includes a useful collation of some texts which favor a non-irrationalist interpretation. In the same volume James Collins, "Faith and Reflection in
Kierkegaard" supports a similar interpretation.

site: if human science refuses to understand that there is something which it cannot understand, or better still, that there is
something about which it clearly understands that it cannot
understand it — then all is confusion. For it is the duty of the
human understanding to understand that there are things
which it cannot understand, and what those things are. (*Jour*,
p. 117)

Though reason must give itself up, be submerged, it is
not a matter of committing intellectual suicide. Reason is not
annihilated by the paradox; one might rather say that reason
finds its true fulfillment through this submergence, at least in
the sense that it is precisely what reason itself desires (*PF*,
p. 59). Faith is that happy passion in which *reason sets itself
aside,* and a man is presented with the paradox (*PF*, p. 73). It
is possible for a man to come to understand (by use of his
understanding) that his highest end is not understanding,
and that understanding cannot finally make him what he
ought to be. The paradox marks a boundary — the boundary
of objective thought. The response of a man to the incarnation
reveals his self, and the nature of the self determines his
choice. Kierkegaard believes there are only two options, faith
and offense. Faith is the passion in which reason and the
paradox encounter each other happily in the Moment (*PF*,
p. 73). Offense is unhappy love, disguised admiration.

To the man who conceives his highest good to be an eternal happiness which consists in a relationship to an absolute
telos, and who recognizes his actual situation to be one of
estrangement from the absolute *telos,* the encounter with the
paradox may indeed be happy. Though to a man who lacks
this perspective the paradox may appear insane or absurd,
the main thrust of Kierkegaard's literature is to explore the
logic of the choice to believe in the paradox so as to drive
home to the individual thinker the appropriateness, even
necessity, of such a choice. Despite his distaste for reason, I
am driven to viewing Kierkegaard's account as an attempt to
show that such a choice is subjectively rational.

CONCLUSION: FAITH AS A MODE OF EXISTENCE

In viewing Kierkegaard as giving us a subjective justification of Christian belief, it is important to note again the intimate connection which holds between belief and action. Kant held that a man was morally obligated to act in such a way as to seek to achieve a certain end, and he could not rationally believe that that end was impossible of fulfillment; hence he must believe in the conditions for its fulfillment. Similarly for Kierkegaard, what I recognize first is not that I ought to accept certain doctrines. Rather I recognize that I have an obligation to become something which I am not and cannot become on my own; hence I must believe in the objective reality of the condition of becoming what I ought to be. Kierkegaard holds that this belief in the reality of the paradox establishes a relationship to the paradox which makes possible this transformation. But to see how this is possible we must see belief here as more than assent; it is primarily a mode of existence, which does, however, embody certain conceptual beliefs.

Christianity then is that mode of existence which posits that a man's eternal happiness depends upon his relationship with a particular historical event — the God in time. The particular character of that relationship Kierkegaard has discussed at great length in *Training in Christianity, Judge for Yourself,* and *For Self-Examination.* The task is that of becoming *contemporary* with Christ, a task which is no easier or harder for men today than it was for those actual historical contemporaries, some of whom said, "I will follow thee, but first I must. . . ." It would be the height of misunderstanding merely to regard Christianity as religiousness A plus a collection of historical beliefs upon which salvation is dependent. The whole emphasis falls on the character of the individual's relationship to those historical events. Christianity is a mode of existing, a kind of inwardness of subjectivity. Nor does this mean it is something exclusively inward, because it expresses itself concretely as *action.* It is not a doctrine that needs to be abstractly, speculatively understood, but a doctrine that has to be realized in existence, and "is understood by understanding that the task is to exist in it" (*Post,* p. 339). The paradox is not merely the object of belief; Christ is the Pattern and to believe is to accept him as the Pattern.

Being a Christian is determined not by the what of
Christianity but the how of the Christian. Nevertheless, it
would be a great mistake to regard Christianity as content-
less, because this personal mode of existence which is the
how of the Christian can correspond to only one thing — the
absolute paradox (*Post,* p. 540). A Christian must indeed believe something definite, but the real problem is for him to be
quite definite that *he* believes. To direct one's attention exclusively to the doctrines is to go in the opposite direction
from faith. But nevertheless the doctrines themselves are
quite objective and necessary.

> But verily, as little as God lets a species of fish remain in a
> particular sea unless the plant also grows there which is its
> nutriment, just so little shall God leave in ignorance of what
> he must believe the man who truly was concerned. . . . The
> thing sought is in the seeking which seeks it, faith in the
> concern at not having faith; love, in the concern at not loving.
> The need brings with it the nutriment. . . not *by itself*. . . but
> by virtue of God's ordinance. (*ChD,* pp. 248-249)

This Christian inwardness or subjectivity is a mode of
existence to be distinguished from every other, including the
ethical and religious in the broader sense; however, it must
not be regarded as *excluding* these, but as incorporating their
truth, in almost Hegelian fashion. For example, the religious is
certainly ethical in the highest sense of that word:

> God is not a part of existence in such a way that he demands his
> sphere for himself; he demands everything, but as you bring it
> you immediately receive. . . an endorsement designating where
> it should be forwarded, for God demands nothing for himself,
> although he demands everything from you. (*WL,* p. 159)

Thus we see Kierkegaard has attempted to shift our attention away from the objective problem of the truth of
Christianity, the pursuance of which only leads the honest
thinker to skeptical conclusions, to the subjective problem
"Ought I to become a Christian?" The attempt itself is
paradoxical because normally before asking whether we
ought to believe something, we first seek to know whether it
is true. Kant argued that if a man wishes to be moral, to
accept the validity of the moral law, he is subjectively ration-

ally obligated to believe in God. Kierkegaard has transformed and broadened the sphere of the subjective. Instead of saying, "if you want to be moral," Kierkegaard says, "if you want to become a human being in the fullest sense of the term, with all that this includes, then believe, not merely in God, but in the God in time." For Kant the belief in God which is rationally necessitated is a practical faith, a belief in God as moral ruler and moral legislator which is a necessary accompaniment to rational moral action. For Kierkegaard the belief in God which is truly significant is belief in God as Savior, as the Being who recreates me and saves me from the despair and alienation which I perceive as my true condition, and it is a belief which expresses itself in the practical acceptance of the Savior as the Pattern. Neither thinker perceives religious truth as included in, or the culmination of, a scientific or theoretical system.

Kierkegaard clearly admits that a person can understand what Christianity is without being a Christian. What is denied is that a person can know what it is to *be* a Christian without being one (*Post*, p. 332). Objectively, existence has the strange quality of presenting truth and deception as two equal possibilities, so that the choice reveals the truth that is in you. Objectivity in the sense of fairness, honesty, openness to the truth is absolutely necessary. But true fairness will not exclude a priori the possibility that the truth itself will transcend the limits of human reason. How then can it be attained? In the same way as Kant said freedom is attained — not through theoretical insight but in action. So Kierkegaard concludes that an honest, penetrating analysis of the human situation leads one to Christianity.

> Who could have conceived this conclusion? And yet no other conclusion is conceivable — and neither is this. When everything has come to a standstill, when thought is brought to a halt, when speech becomes mute, when the explanation in bewilderment seeks the way home — then there must be a thunderstorm. Who can understand this? And yet who can find out any other conclusion. (*Rep*, p. 117)

4

James: Belief as Pragmatically Justified

INTRODUCTION: JAMES AS A SUBJECTIVE THINKER

WILLIAM JAMES SHARES WITH KIERKEGAARD THE CONviction that the moral life which is characterized by earnestness and adherence to duty is not the profoundest level of existence, though James also shared with him a deep respect for that way of life. James agrees with Kierkegaard that the ideal of personality which we ought to seek includes needs, concerns, attitudes, and beliefs which go beyond the moral sphere and which have traditionally been characterized as religious. The religious sphere for James has a uniqueness which it does not have for Kant. James is, however, much closer to Kant than Kierkegaard in the emphasis he places on the connection of religious belief with practical action. For Kant religious belief was grounded in the necessity for moral action, and the object of that belief was primarily God conceived as Moral Ruler. The other doctrines of religion, such as our belief in the Son of God, conceived as a man who perfectly exemplifies a life in accordance with duty, are essentially related to our fundamental moral obligation. Kant sees God as desiring moral obedience — not worship or priestly rites. Kierkegaard, though second to none in his insistence that religious faith be expressed in action, nevertheless clearly affirms that a God-relationship is an absolute good which is to be valued for its own sake. James consistently takes the middle road. With Kierkegaard he recognizes the uniqueness and importance of religious beliefs, attitudes, concerns, and emotions, but he affirms clearly that the value, and even the truth, of religion must be judged in terms of the concrete experiences which it

124

makes possible and the specific actions which it enjoins towards believers.

> The whole defence of religious faith hinges upon action. If the action required or inspired by the religious hypothesis is in no way different from that dictated by the naturalistic hypothesis, then religious faith is a pure superfluity. ... (*WB*, pp. 29-30, note)

In any case James clearly fits the general model, which we found exemplified in Kant and Kierkegaard, of a thinker who tries to give a subjective justification of religious belief. All of the following theses are clearly indicated in "The Will to Believe": (1) From a purely "theoretical" point of view (James would say "intellectual" or "scientific") the truth of religion cannot be either demonstrated or refuted, although religion has a high degree of plausibility to many. (2) Despite this absence of *compelling* intellectual evidence, one cannot suspend judgment about key religious questions. (3) In such a situation a person is rationally justified in holding to those religious beliefs which are life-enhancing, that is, those which make possible the integration of personality and effective action in accordance with the highest range of human purposes. (4) When judged by these criteria, theistic religions are superior to agnostic and pantheistic religious perspectives.

In considering James's defense of religious belief, it is imperative to distinguish carefully three different aspects of James's case. There is first his abstract description of a possible situation in which the "will to believe" becomes the "right to believe." In his essay "The Will to Believe" James gives us what we might call a formal description of the logic of a situation where one is epistemologically justified in allowing one's beliefs to be influenced by subjective considerations. We must carefully consider the question of whether James's views here are epistemologically sound.

Separate from this question is the question of the relevance of the model James sketches. Be it ever so logically sound, James's argument that in certain highly-qualified cases one is justified in making a commitment which out-runs the purely intellectual evidence has little importance if it turns out that the situation he describes is never actually exemplified in human experience. We must remember Antony Flew's warning that what sounds initially like a bold, even shocking thesis may little by little suffer "the death of a thousand qualifications." James believes that the epistemological situation he describes is neither unique nor even unusual, even in the non-religious realm, but we must seek to determine if this is really so. Particularly we must ask if there are religious hypotheses which satisfy the conditions James specifies.

Finally, even if James's views on both of the preceding points are sound, the question must still be asked as to whether the vague variety of meliorism that James called "piecemeal supernaturalism" is worthy of belief. This is an important question to ask. Just raising it undercuts one fundamental misunderstanding of James's position. One might be inclined to interpret James as follows: "If James is correct, then there can be no question of judging religious perspectives to be more or less rationally adequate. Each individual will be free to believe what satisfies his own psychological proclivities, and the fact that James found supernaturalism appealing is of no logical interest to anyone else."

It must be admitted that James invited such an interpretation through his emphasis on tolerance; he emphatically rejected any religious perspective (including agnosticism) which required harsh judgment on those who differ. In an area characterized by so much uncertainty, he strongly defended the freedom of the individual to choose and hold his own religious beliefs, however idiosyncratic those beliefs may be. However, we shall see that we must distinguish the question of the logical justification of a belief from the matter of personal freedom and tolerance concerning questions where the final truth has not been attained.

If we make this distinction we shall see that James rests his case for theism, not on his own personal idiosyncrasies, but on general features of human nature as such. What he wishes to argue is that theism is the brand of religion which is most compatible with those abilities, propensities, and needs which are most fundamentally human, if you wish, *essential*. Thus, the considerations he advances purport to be of significance to other men than himself. Of course the question as to what aspects of man are essential is itself a value question, one that James feels cannot be answered by the intellect alone. He is therefore in a sense affirming that God satisfies his *own* deepest needs when he testifies to his belief. Nevertheless, insofar as James's ideas are to be significant to us, we must take him to be saying that he believes that these needs and capacities, so deeply felt by him, represent genuine aspects of human nature in general at its best and highest level.

RELIGIOUS QUESTIONS AS CONSTITUTING LIVING, THEORETICAL OPTIONS

In analyzing James's argument that in some cases the "will to believe" is the "right to believe," we must be very careful not to unconsciously focus our discussion on the viability of any particular religious perspective. This is in sharp contrast to Kierkegaard, who does not devote much attention to the viability of religion in general and would no doubt have considered any such defense to be a waste of time. James believes that one can point out certain general features in the logic of believing which are relevant and important when it comes to assessing a particular perspective. James himself believes that the negative reactions felt by many persons to his view are the result of their moving away from "the abstract logical point of view" and considering instead some particular religious hypothesis which for them is no longer a viable candidate for belief (WB, p. 29).

Therefore, the very first condition which James notes that a religious hypothesis must have to be *worthy* of belief is that it be one which it is *possible* to believe. The religious hypothesis must be a living hypothesis. James defines a living hypothesis in admittedly psychological terms. "A live hypothesis is one which appeals as a real possibility to him to whom it is proposed" (WB, p. 2). "Credible" might pass as a synonym for "live" in this context. James's notion certainly has an affinity with the concept of "believability" which was explored earlier in connection with Kant.[1] An "option" James defines as a choice between two hypotheses, a living option being a choice between two living hypotheses.

These distinctions are of course noted by almost every commentator of James. Nevertheless, although James introduces them briefly and does not dwell on them in any detail, we must not fail to see how crucial they are nor how much is packed into these notions. James wishes to discuss the logic of believing. One might term "The Will to Believe" an essay which sketches for us a decision theory. To get right to his topic he attempts to short-circuit what is for most philosophers of religion the most vital area of discussion. He does not discuss the logical status of theistic proofs, nor the evidential value of mystical experience. (Though he does deal with these issues elsewhere.) The question he is seeking to answer is as follows: "Given that religious and non-religious beliefs constitute mutually exclusive hypotheses with each possessing some degree of credibility, is an act of personal commitment irrational? If not, what sorts of considerations determine such commitments, and what sorts of considerations *ought* to determine such commitments?" It is a typically Jamesian procedure to begin by asking "Is it believable?" instead of "Is it true?" No doubt it is precisely this psychological point of departure which makes many of James's critics (and friends) uncomfortable.

Perhaps some of this anxiety will be removed by an examination of the notion of the credibility or liveness. Strictly speaking, to say of some hypothesis H that H is credible is to say only that for some person N, H is appealing. N finds H believable, though N may not in fact believe H. Ultimately, James is going to argue that N has the *right* to believe H, given that certain other conditions are met. Here the critic's uneasiness begins to multiply by leaps and bounds. James's theory seems to be opening the door to an incredible host of absurdities, because for just about any H, no matter how absurd, some N can be found for whom H is credible. We can perhaps even make the stronger claim that for practically

---

1. See above, pp. 38-50.

any H, no matter how absurd, some N can be found who actually believes H, and for whom, therefore, H is certainly believable. If James carries through and actually shows that, given certain conditions, N has a *right* to believe H or is justified in believing H, unless these conditions are highly restrictive, this seemingly commits us to holding that many people are rationally justified in believing things which are so absurd as to be almost certainly false. Clearly some of the things some people believe *are* almost certainly false, but we should not wish to hold that they are (generally) rationally justified in believing these things.

Now there is of course nothing paradoxical about the thesis that some rationally justified beliefs are false. It is not difficult to point to cases in the history of science where warranted beliefs did indeed turn out to be false. What seems suspicious in James's view is the notion that in some cases a belief in a hypothesis, which judged by some objective standard is *unsupported by evidence* and is clearly or very probably false, is nevertheless rationally justified. However, this suspicion is, in my opinion, totally unfounded. It arises from an ambiguity in the concept of justification.

An analogous problem arises in ethics. It seems a truism to say that a man ought to do what he sincerely believes is right. Yet it seems certain that in some cases what a person believes to be right may be, objectively considered, wrong. When it is the case that the person commits the objectively wrong act in the sincere belief that it is right, and if his wrong evaluation of the act is not the result of any previous moral lapses, then subjectively speaking (and with certain other qualifications perhaps), it is correct to say he was morally justified in acting as he did. This is in no way incompatible with judging the act itself to be objectively morally reprehensible. Nor does our judging the man to be morally blameless in this instance relieve him of the task of improving his defective understanding of the true status of his act. One of his moral duties would be to take advantage of any opportunity to add to his limited knowledge or improve his moral sensitivity.

The analogy to belief here is very close. Granted a situation which calls for a judgment, it seems obvious that a person ought to accept what he sincerely believes to be true, or most likely true. Certainly in some cases things which people sincerely believe either to be true or more likely true than any other view, are in fact false, perhaps even obviously false to someone who has more information or mental ability. In some of these cases, the person who holds the false view may be blameworthy because he has failed to exercise reasonable diligence in his search for relevant evidence. But surely in some cases we must accept the fact that persons are subjectively justified in accepting views which those who have had the opportunity to acquire more evidence might regard as highly unfounded. In saying that a person would be epistemologically blameless in such a situation, we would again not be excusing him from his obligation continually to reconsider his views as he attempts to gain more information and evidence. Thus by distinguishing between objective and subjective justification we can assert without paradox that some persons are subjectively justified in holding views which are objectively considered extremely flimsy. Thus in an area as uncertain as religion, it is not surprising that James should hold that many people are justified in holding beliefs which are regarded as flimsy by others with more knowledge. After all, many people are denied the opportunity for an education through no fault of their own. But this in no way precludes the assertion that people ought to give up or modify such beliefs as they acquire more knowledge. For all beliefs it remains the case that "we ought to believe what is true." James's exploration of the logic of believing in no way minimizes our "duty to truth."

It is the connection of belief with truth which makes James's psychological starting point philosophically significant. It is plausible to regard "N believes P" as an elided form of "N believes P is true" or "probably true," or "more likely to be true than the alternatives." "N believes P" is compatible with "P is false," but it is surely incompatible with "N believes P to be false." In asserting that believability is one of the characteristics any religious hypothesis must possess to be worthy of belief, James has said nothing about the question as to what sorts of hypotheses *ought* to seem credible to us. But it does not follow from this that he has no views on this matter.

As we noted earlier in our discussion of Kant, the concept of believability is a mixed logical/psychological notion. James himself was deeply aware of the role which such not-completely-rational factors as temperament, culture, and up-bringing have on the formation of belief. But he recognized just as strongly the stubborn connection of belief to the facts.

> Between the coercions of the sensible order and those of the ideal order, our mind is thus wedged tightly. Our ideas must agree with realities, be such realities concrete or abstract, be they facts or be they principles, under penalty of endless inconsistency and frustration. (*Prag,* p. 210)

In some cases, clearly enough then, to say of a hypothesis that it is living is to say of it that it is tied up in some way with the tissue of experiences and principles which a person appeals to when he is called on to justify his beliefs. And it is fully consonant with James's thesis to say that insofar as it is possible, each thinker *ought* to try to make the credibility of hypotheses a function of such rational factors, and seek to minimize the influence of more subjective factors on the formation of his beliefs.

Of course it is impossible to do this completely, partly because what a person considers to be rational evidence is at least in part a function of such subjective factors, as we shall argue later. This fact lends support to James's view. Specifically it is what led him to the thesis that we must see that our preferences, desires and values are not merely regrettable necessities, but have a legitimate role to play in the search for truth.

Let us look specifically at the question of God's existence. Some thinkers are convinced that God exists on the basis of such considerations as logical proofs, religious experiences, or perhaps purported revelations. For many others who do not actually believe, these considerations make religious belief a living option in James's sense. Others see these considerations as totally worthless. The question as to who is right is of course important. It really amounts to this: for an intellectually honest modern thinker, is belief in God a living option?

Of course we cannot settle here the question of the evidential value of theistic proofs, religious experience, and claims to divine revelation. It may well be true that religious beliefs ought not to be living hypotheses today and that they remain so only because of prejudice, fear, emotional needs, and the like. If this is the case, then James's model is for us moot and irrelevant. It may still of course be a piece of sound philosophy, for the truth of a hypothesis is not invalidated by one of the conditions of the hypothesis being missing. But I do not believe that this is the case. The best evidence for this is simply the continued philosophical dialogue on these issues between men of good will.

Thus we must take James to be presupposing that some religious hypotheses are indeed credible because of their intellectual appeal. James himself no doubt found the truth of religion credible partly as an explanation of the amazing personality transformations which he observed as the result of religious experience. But we can take "The Will to Believe" as applying to anyone who finds religious belief credible, on whatever grounds. It is perhaps unfortunate that James did not clearly state that the factors which go into making a belief a live hypothesis are not all equally desirable. John King-Farlow suggests that James's talk of liveness is not meant to deny that there are honest criteria for judging whether assessments of credibility are reasonable. James's subjective-sounding talk is a reflection of James's belief that even "liberal empiricists of a reasonable temper are sometimes likely to reach differing conclusions about different faiths, systems, and ideals."[2] James certainly has a deep appreciation for the role which subjective and non-rational factors play in generating beliefs, even those beliefs we regard as most secure. No careful commentator can deny, however, that James has an even deeper appreciation of the value of minimizing, *insofar as it is possible,* the role of such factors, especially

---

2. John King-Farlow, "Rational Commitment and 'The Will to Believe'," *Sophia*, 8 (1969), 6.

insofar as those factors are idiosyncratic, and substituting objective, scientific procedures. The difficulty is that in the case of religious hypotheses James believed that *at present* the possibility of completely removing such subjective factors was practically nil.

It is for this reason that the choice between a religious and non-religious hypothesis may be a living option. If religion had no intellectual appeal, there would be no question of the "will to believe." If its intellectual appeal were overwhelming, there would likewise be no issue worthy of notice. James is thus treading a fine line and will be open to attack from two quarters, both from those who find the evidence compelling and from those who find it completely lacking. However, it is undeniable that to some, James's view of the status of religious knowledge seems correct; to them, some religious hypotheses present themselves as living options. As it is quite possible that these thinkers' view of the matter is the most dispassionate and reasonable, a discussion such as James's essay, concerning the *logic* of choosing between such options, certainly possesses philosophical significance.

It follows from this that at least one of the common criticisms of James, which is that even if we were justified in believing what we wish to believe, we would be unable to because our wills are powerless to produce belief, is beside the point. Not only is it false to say that will is always powerless to produce belief, but James is only discussing religion insofar as it does make a powerful appeal to our intellect. That religion makes such an appeal to many is undeniable. James himself clearly held that there were empirical facts which tended to confirm religious world-views, though James felt there were also facts which went against the religious view. Hence he concluded that "the facts of natural experience are ambiguous." Nevertheless, even within the sphere of ordinary experience religion is not without some intellectual appeal. And James felt that the consideration of specifically religious experience added much more weight to the intellectual argument for religion (RF, pp. 197-201). It follows that the liveness of religious hypotheses is not purely a function of emotional and idiosyncratic factors.

Despite this presumption that to some thinkers, at least, religious questions constitute living options, we must equally emphasize the extent to which James's view of religion tends towards agnosticism. The evidence adduced on behalf of religion by philosophers, whether rational or experiential in nature (including the evidence presented by James himself), seems clearly inadequate to James if judged by theoretical or scientific standards. And James does tie knowledge to these scientific canons. James does not himself argue for this theoretical agnosticism in great detail. He does give a masterful critique of the truth-value of mystical states in chapters sixteen and seventeen of *The Varieties of Religious Experience*. And in chapter eighteen of that book he gives some sketchy and not very powerful criticisms of philosophical theology. Nevertheless, his agnosticism is definite and is perhaps best viewed as founded on the whole modern discussion of religion, ranging from Hume's attack on natural theology to modern critical attacks on the Bible.

Thus James's portrait of the psychology of belief is complex. On the one hand, he sees religious doctrines as perhaps supported by some evidence, at least to the degree that they are believable to rational persons. But, on the other hand, he sees these same rational persons are capable of sitting back dispassionately and recognizing the inconclusive character of that evidence, judged by scientific standards.

It is here that we meet the distinction in James which corresponds most closely with the Kantian distinction between theoretical and practical reason, and the Kierkegaardian distinction between objective and subjective thought. In "The Sentiment of Rationality" James characterizes rationality in terms of its subjective marks, namely, the psychological state of satisfaction, contentment, and rest that accompanies a rational solution to a problem (SR, p. 63). This psychological state occurs when we arrive at conceptions which satisfy certain demands which we place upon our beliefs and theories. Chief among these demands are the "logical demands" of our "theoretic rationality," among which James lists clearness (faithful intimacy to concrete fact) and simplicity (theoretical elegance). But these demands do not exhaust our rationality according to James, just as theoretical reason for Kant and objective thought for Kierkegaard do not exhaust our cognitive life. Beliefs (James, following Hume, says "ideas") can also be rational in a practical sense, even if they lack the conclusive logical marks of rationality, insofar as they "banish uncertainty from the future" and serve to free our "active impulses" (SR, pp. 75-77). These demands can never supersede the logical demands, but they are not on that account unimportant.

> Of two conceptions equally fit to satisfy the logical demand, that one which awakens the active impulses, or satisfies other aesthetic demands better than the other, will be accounted the more rational, and will deservedly prevail. (SR, pp. 75-76)

Thus James's procedure is a following-up of Kant's lead in the first *Critique,* in the section of the Transcendental Dialectic entitled "The Interest of Reason in These Conflicts." Kant here proposed that even if neither of the antinomic claims amounts to knowledge, we can still ask what human interest each claim represents. James's procedure is similar but he attaches more importance to these interests than does Kant; specifically, James believes they may be the key determinants of beliefs which are rational. This is the background to James's defense of faith in "The Will to Believe," which can now be seen, not as an attempt to justify wishful belief, but as an attempt to specify or restrict those conditions in which our practical interests have a right to produce belief.

UNDERCUTTING PHILOSOPHICAL AGNOSTICISM

The most usual response to a thinker like James, who maintains that the choice between religious belief and non-religious belief cannot be decisively made on purely intellectual grounds, is to argue that the proper rational response is suspension of judgment. James has attempted to meet this objection by introducing two additional qualifications: the situation he is considering is one in which the option involved is both forced and momentous.

A forced option is defined as "a dilemma based on a complete logical disjunction" (WB, p. 3). Forced options always have the form "A or not A," not "A or B." The choice between believing in materialism or believing in theism is not a forced option; I may believe a third option or simply have no opinion at all between the two. The choice between believing in theism or not believing in theism is, however, a forced alternative. There is no possibility of getting outside the alternatives. It must be admitted, however, that James himself for the most part tended to state his dilemma in the logical form of "A or B," materialism vs. theism, spiritualism vs. naturalism, perhaps because it seemed to him that those who reject theism do so to espouse one of these other views.

Taken alone, without James's other condition, this notion of a forced option does not seem very significant. Every single theory or proposition imaginable is part of such a forced option, yet there are multitudes of propositions about which we have no settled convictions, nor do we think it important to have any. Though strictly speaking all these may be cases of "either believe this truth or go without it," there are many propositions and theories which, even if true, we would not consider lack of belief in them worth troubling ourselves about. Though in such cases our laziness amounts to "choosing not to believe A," we have not actually made a conscious decision one way or another, and many would perhaps consider this to be the equivalent of "suspension of judgment." One can hardly force someone whose opinion is unsettled to come to some conclusions by putting the question to him in the form of a logical disjunction.

Thus it seems to me that the other qualification James introduces here is crucial. The option posed must be momentous. To be momentous, an option must present a unique opportunity to gain some significant good, and the decision must be one which cannot be reversed without doing some "vital harm" (WB, p. 4). James is therefore going to consider religious convictions which purport to offer man some great vital good. It follows that if one of these religious belief-systems be true, then all of us who have failed to believe it will have lost that good. The nature of that good may vary greatly, an exception being that it ought not to be conceived solely in terms of a reward after death, but must in some way be connected with life here and now. Presumably, a reward after death is a good which could possibly be acquired through death-bed repentance, thus making a decision not to believe reversible at a later time. So we must interpret the vital unique good which religion offers as being at least in part a function of one's present, continuing religious commitment. As James says in "The Will to Believe," one of the tenets of religion is that a person who believes is better off now. Of course the decision to believe or not to believe is still reversible in the sense that a person can change his mind. But the person who waits until late in life to believe has presumably irretrievably lost those benefits which religion could have provided in his earlier life, while the person who overthrows his religious faith similarly excludes himself from those goods from then on.

What sort of unique good is it which religion purports to offer? For James there are a cluster of goods which revolve chiefly around the notion of integration of personality. In the *Varieties of Religious Experience* James gives case after case of the functions religion may have in transforming a personality, re-orienting a person's identity and sense of values, enabling him to overcome negative feelings such as depression and guilt, and replacing them with inner peace and moral earnestness. In other essays James looks at the function of religion in answering the question of the meaning of life and in giving us an assurance that the universe is not fundamentally alien to such distinctive personal goods as moral action. We cannot here decide whether any religion does do all or any of these things, or whether or not religion alone can supply these goods most adequately. Nor do we have to as yet. It is enough to note that it is one of the tenets of religion that religion does supply man with these goods, and that they are of an important and momentous nature. It follows from this, not that religion is true, but only that religious questions are significant and momentous. To determine the truth of religion, one criterion which will indeed be of interest will be, "How well does a religion accomplish what it purports to accomplish?" But what we can conclude so far is that religious questions do present themselves in terms of forced, momentous options. The thinker who dismisses the questions or can come to no decision misses the possible positive benefits of religion just as surely as if he had rejected religion decisively.

This is particularly so in view of the connection James emphasizes between belief and action. If it is emphasized that James views all rational questions as practical questions, the extent to which he views practical questions as rational questions must be equally emphasized. Following Peirce he holds that a belief is a rule for action, and following Kant (and Peirce) he holds that an action is the embodiment of a belief: "Since belief is measured by action, he who forbids us to believe religion to be true, necessarily also forbids us to act as we should if we did believe it to be true" (WB, p. 29, note).

If James is right in this account of the relationship between belief and action, and if religious beliefs do entail actions which differ from those which are entailed by nonreligious beliefs (if this is not so, James does not think religion is worth considering), it will follow that a man who lives in the world and performs actions *cannot* merely remain neutral.

> It is often practically impossible to distinguish doubt from dogmatic negation. If I refuse to stop a murder because I am in doubt whether it be not justifiable homicide, I am virtually abetting the crime. . . . He who commands himself not to be credulous of God, of duty, of freedom, of immortality, may again and again be indistinguishable from him who dogmatically denies them. Skepticism in moral matters is an active ally of immorality. Who is not for is against. The universe will have no neutrals in these questions. In theory as in practice, dodge or hedge, or talk as we like about a wise skepticism, we are really doing volunteer military service for one side or another. (SR, p. 109)

THEISM'S PRACTICAL CONSEQUENCES

We have pointed out that one essential tenet of many religious systems is the belief that a person may lose some vital good if he does not believe. If the religion is true, then this claim will also be true, which means the issues involved may indeed be momentous; and if the religious system has that degree of intellectual appeal or experiential support which makes it a living option, and if the choice to believe or not to believe be forced, then that religion obviously deserves more careful consideration. For James that type of religion vaguely designated "theistic" satisfied those conditions. For James, theism signified little more than a view situated somewhere between materialism and idealistic monism. He wished to hold that the natural order is not the whole of reality, that behind that natural order there is a super-human being (or beings), who is nevertheless in some ways dependent upon human cooperation to accomplish his aims. The more specific the belief, the more James termed it an "over-belief," less susceptible of rational support.

Of course, if religions do claim to entail momentous consequences, it follows from this that one of the criteria which we may use in evaluating a religion will be whether or not its claims to make possible some important good are sound. Though this admittedly is a difficult area to judge, to show that a religion cannot make good on its promises would be a serious criticism indeed. It would be particularly serious from James's perspective if it could be shown that religious beliefs about the world, *even if granted to be true,* would make no important differences in men's practical activities. We must therefore explore the connections which James adduces between belief in God and practical action in more detail. It is by no means as obvious to us today as it was to James that metaphysical beliefs have such practical bearings.

For James the practical meaning of alternative conceptions is of course the difference which they make "in concrete fact and in conduct consequent upon that fact" (*Prag,* p. 50). It would be a grave mistake to leave out the difference in "concrete fact," and speak merely of the "difference in conduct imposed by that fact," though James himself seems to do this at times. If we ignore the "difference in concrete fact," it makes it appear that the difference in conduct is solely a product of the *believing.*

Such noted critics of James as A. O. Lovejoy have

charged that James himself is confused on this issue.[3] In effect Lovejoy says James gives (at least) two theories of meaning which are incompatible. On the one theory an assertion is meaningful if any sensible effects would follow from its truth, and its meaning is equivalent to those effects or consequences. This would be a narrow, positivistic theory which would eliminate much of traditional metaphysics. But Lovejoy says James also holds that any assertion is meaningful if any effects would follow from *believing* that assertion and (even) that the meaning of the assertion would be equivalent to those consequences. This would in effect make just about any assertion that any person ever believed meaningful.

There is a weakness here in James's published writings, especially *Pragmatism,* as James himself admitted.[4] However, it is possible to show that this confusion of the "effects of the truth of a belief" with the "effects of believing" is not essential to James's position and, on a sympathetic interpretation, is not present at all, except in the form of a careless statement. In a recent article Robert G. Meyers has argued that James's theory of meaning identifies the meaning of an assertion with its "sensible effects" and not at all with the effects of believing the assertion.[5] Meyers is essentially right here, though it would be an overstatement to claim that the meaning of a belief has no relation to conduct. James does believe that the meaning of a belief is essentially related to our conduct; belief for him is a "rule for action." In one sense, of course, it is the act of believing something which causally determines our conduct. And in special cases James did believe that the act of believing something could contribute to its becoming true.[6] Nevertheless belief is determined — and

3. See A. O. Lovejoy, "The Thirteen Pragmatisms," *Journal of Philosophy, Psychology, and Scientific Method,* 5 (1908), 5-12, 29-39; reprinted in *The Thirteen Pragmatisms and Other Essays* (Baltimore: Johns Hopkins Press, 1963), pp. 3-10.

4. See R. B. Perry, *The Thought and Character of William James* (Boston: Little, Brown and Co., 1935), II, 481.

5. "Meaning and Metaphysics in James," *Philosophy and Phenomenological Research,* 31 (March, 1971), 369-380.

6. These cases all involve future events which could not have been "there" beforehand.

ought to be determined — by what is the case. And for James "what is the case" is tied up with "the future course of events." Thus even so abstract a belief as "the validity of the moral ought is tied up with the innermost nature of things" implies something quite definite about the future course of events.

> The notion of God . . . guarantees an ideal order that shall be permanently preserved. A world with a God in it to say the last word, may indeed burn up or freeze, but we then think of Him as still mindful of the old ideals and sure to bring them elsewhere to fruition; so that, where He is, tragedy is only provisional and partial, and shipwreck and dissolution not the absolutely final things. (*Prag*, p. 106)

Thus materialism means the denial that the moral order is eternal, theism the affirmation that it is. The essential locus of meaning is the future course of events, even with regard to metaphysical doctrines. And James believes that such notions, though not practically verifiable in anyone's lifetime, are nevertheless conceivably confirmable.[7] So the difference which theism and materialism make is not merely a difference related to *believing* one or the other to be true; it is a difference which follows from the *truth* of one or the other. However, though conceivably verifiable, the verification could not occur in a particular man's lifetime. Nevertheless, what one believes to be the truth (about the future course of events) will have a decisive effect on one's behavior *now*, undercutting the viability of a position of neutrality.

The Consequences of Religious Belief for Theists in General

What practical difference in conduct does religious belief make? James gives two different but entirely compatible accounts of the nature of this difference. First, James seems

---

7. In several essays James seems to allude to a notion of verification that bears some analogy to Hick's notion of "eschatological verification." See John Hick, *Faith and Knowledge* (Ithaca: Cornell University Press, 1957), pp. 145-163.

to feel that a man's most basic *beliefs* about the nature of reality as a whole, taken at its most fundamental level, have a great impact on his actions (or ought to have such an impact) regardless of whether his beliefs be religious or non-religious, and if religious, regardless of whether he is a practicing member of a particular faith. Thus, for James, the mere question as to whether to believe in God has momentous practical bearings, regardless of whether the believer is a practicing Christian, Jew, or whatever. This is necessarily so because the question of God is not just a question about the existence of another being; it is a question concerning the nature of the universe, not only taken as a whole, but taken as its individual parts as well. As soon as we begin asking questions such as "What is the nature of the real?" and allowing our answers to determine our attitude and actions towards the world of which we are a part, we are in the realm where the existence of God is an important question. And James believes that all men do implicitly have such beliefs insofar as they regard certain attitudes and actions as natural or fitting.

> However vaguely a philosopher may define the ultimate universal datum, he cannot be said to leave it unknown to us so long as he in the slightest degree pretends that our emotional or active attitude toward it should be of one sort rather than another. He who says "life is real, life is earnest," however much he may speak of the fundamental mysteriousness of things, gives a distinct definition to that mysteriousness by ascribing to it the right to claim from us the particular mood called seriousness. . . . The same is true of him who says that all is vanity. (SR, p. 86)

The notion that whatever the nature of the fundamental reality, the character of that reality has the right to make certain claims on us, is perhaps foreign to much of modern philosophy, which has so strongly stressed the distinction between questions of fact and questions of value, and strictly divorced metaphysics from ethics. However, we can recognize the distinction between fact and value without denying that fact and value are related in various ways. To say of some N that it is X is not to say that it ought to be X. But if we wish to inquire as to what N ought to be, the question of what sort of thing N actually is will clearly be relevant. It seems to me that this relevance increases insofar as our questions about the nature of N go in the direction of asking not about N's present accidental features, but "What is N really or essentially? What really makes N to be the kind of thing which it is?" As one moves in the direction of asking about N's essence (a metaphysical rather than a scientific question), the answers have an increasing bearing on the question as to what a *good* N should be.

Now even if it were admitted that such relationships between questions of fact and questions of value hold, that essences form middle terms between facts and values, some would still object to James's connecting of metaphysics to attitudes and actions. For it could be argued that though questions about the nature of *particular* beings or kinds of beings do have value-implications, questions about the nature of reality in general or as a whole do not. It could be argued that such notions as "reality as a whole," and the "ultimate datum" are meaningless. Though particular beings may be said to have essences, it is meaningless to speak of the essence of reality as such.

The notion of essence, when applied to reality as a whole, is no doubt a metaphor and a misleading one at that. Nevertheless, I think James's assertion that men do have beliefs about the character of reality as a whole is correct, and I believe his thesis that such beliefs have a bearing on human actions and attitudes can be plausibly defended as well. For example, if theism is true, it follows that one of the essential aspects of every finite being is a continuing dependence on God's creative activity. If true, this might perhaps entail that certain prideful attitudes which ignore or minimize this dependence should be eschewed. Thus anyone who denies God's existence implicitly denies this property to everything which exists, and thus is agreeing that beliefs about the character of reality as a whole are meaningful.

Every variety of physicalism or materialism embodies beliefs about the character of reality as a whole. Even such a sophisticated thesis as "Nothing exists which is not amenable to or explainable by the methods of empirical science" em-

bodies such beliefs. However one views "the methods of empirical science," one is still saying that every thing which
exists is the kind of thing which is amenable to those
methods; the more those methods are specified, the more
specific one's beliefs about the nature of the real. Even if one
says with Herbert Feigl that "the basic *laws* of the universe are the *physical* ones," it is not entirely correct to maintain as Feigl does that this does not commit him "in the least
as to the nature of the *reality* whose regularities are formulated in the physical laws.[8] Clearly that reality will be the
type of reality whose regularities are formulated in terms of
physical laws, and I should not think that this conception,
though admittedly vague, is entirely without content.

James certainly regarded such beliefs as entailing important practical consequences:

> The mention of material substance naturally suggests the
> doctrine of "materialism," but philosophical materialism is not
> necessarily knit up with belief in "matter," as a metaphysical
> principle. One may deny matter in that sense, as strongly as
> Berkeley did, one may be a phenomenalist like Huxley, and yet
> one may still be a materialist in the wider sense, of explaining
> higher phenomena by lower ones, and leaving the destinies of
> the world at the mercy of its blinder parts and forces. (*Prag,* pp.
> 92-93)

But even if it be granted that one can speak meaningfully
of reality as a whole, one might claim that difficulties in
James's view are still present. For why ought our beliefs
about reality as a whole to determine our actions and attitudes? Is the notion that "reality as a whole" can make a
claim on a person intelligible or plausible at all? Even if it be
granted (as it surely must be) that our beliefs about what is
the case do determine such actions and attitudes, is it not in
every case *specific* beliefs about *specific* matters of fact which
make a difference? The answer to this charge is simply to
point out that beliefs about the character of "reality as a
whole" or "the ultimate datum" have implications for our
beliefs about particular beings or kinds of beings. Though I

---

8. Herbert Feigl, "Mind-body, *not* a Pseudo-Problem" in *The Mind-Brain
Identity Theory,* ed. C. V. Borst (London: The Macmillan Co., 1970), p. 40.

should not wish to say that "God exists" is equivalent in meaning to a series of propositions about particular beings, it certainly does entail such a series of propositions. Indeed, if such beliefs about "reality as a whole" are not to be utterly vacuous as well as vague, they must entail such specific propositions.

Despite these considerations, it is practically certain that many thinkers would question whether the notion of ultimate reality making a claim on our attitudes and actions is anything more than misguided personification. However, the belief that human conduct and attitudes ought somehow to be in line with or in harmony with the innermost nature of things runs very deep in the history of western thought, prominent not only in Platonic and Christian thought, but in Stoicism, Spinoza, and such thinkers as Nietzsche as well. It is also foundational in such Eastern traditions as Confucianism and Taoism. Some such belief clearly underlies James's account. Does reality make such a claim on us?

I submit that one cannot answer this question without first deciding as to what is the nature of the reality in question. It is clear that certain types of things, most notably persons, are capable of making a claim on us. Impersonal sorts of things, on the other hand, we would not ordinarily regard as having the ability to impose obligations on us. Obligation is a relationship between persons. It follows from this that if one believes that a personal being is the ultimate reality upon whom all things in the universe (including oneself) are most intimately dependent, it is logical to regard this reality as possibly imposing on us certain obligations or claims. On the other hand, if ultimately all things, including persons, are the product of impersonal, physical causes, it would be equally logical to discount the notion of ultimate reality as making any claim on us. (Though perhaps particular persons could still make such claims on us.) Thus, I am sympathetic with Ronald Hepburn who argues that in the absence of God, the universe is not necessarily to be seen as positively unfriendly or heartless. One should not replace belief in a benign deity with belief in a malevolent God. For Hepburn there are a variety of possible imaginative slants on the universe which

are possible for the unbeliever.[9] I believe Hepburn is right
here and that it is wrong to argue that materialism logically
entails some particular kind of life or set of attitudes, particularly not some morally repugnant way of life. If the world is
as materialists say, then reality simply makes no claims upon
us at all.

But for James this is just the point. To say that the fundamental nature of reality is such as to make *no* claims on my
attitudes and actions is to say something very significant
about reality which may have a tremendous impact on my
attitudes and actions. For James the question of the ultimate
nature of things has a tremendous bearing not just on the
question, "How ought I to live?" but on the question "What is
the status of this 'ought'?" The radical question of life is the
question as to whether this be "at bottom a moral or an unmoral universe" (SR, p. 103). By that he means "Is the
judgement of *better* or *worse,* or *ought* as intimately pertinent
to phenomena as the simple judgement *is* or *is not?*" The
materialist cannot maintain that his moral notions are rooted
in the very character of things; there is a discontinuity between the fundamental nature of things and the personal
arena where moral judgments are felt to be appropriate. It
follows from this, argues James, that the moral judgments
possess an ultimacy or authority on some metaphysical accounts that they do not possess on other views. "He who
believes this to be a radically moral universe must hold the
moral order to rest either on an absolute and ultimate *should,*
or on a series of *shoulds* all the way down" (SR, p. 104). The
person who denies this, says James, when his moral interests
clash with the facts of this world is (logically) free to seek
harmony by attempting to tone down his real feelings. "The
absolute moralist, on the other hand, when his interests clash
with the world, is not free to gain harmony by sacrificing the
ideal interests." Resistance, poverty, even martyrdom may be
his lot (SR, p. 104). Thus the issue at stake for James is not
"What sort of claim does reality make on us?" but "Is the

9. *Christianity and Paradox* (New York: Pegasus, 1968), pp. 181, 200.

fundamental nature of reality such as to be capable of making a claim on us?"

The non-theist may of course reply that one's obligations to persons still remain, regardless of whether ultimate reality be personal in nature. If one admits that moral obligations may be constituted by the mere existence of persons in relationship, then from the moral point of view, one's obligations to persons would hold, regardless of one's beliefs about the character of reality as a whole. James would certainly agree with this reasoning; he strongly supports the notion that persons (and perhaps even other creatures) constitute moral imperatives simply by their presence.

> Take any demand, however slight, which any creature, however weak, may make. Ought it not, for its own sole sake, to be satisfied? If not, prove why not. The only possible kind of proof you could adduce would be the exhibition of another creature who should make a demand that ran the other way. (MPML, p. 195)

One does not have to agree with this assertion to agree with one thing that it entails, namely, that obligations are not constituted by divine fiat, but are a consequence of the existence of persons in community. Why then does James believe that theism crucially affects our moral beliefs?

Part of the answer is his belief, mentioned earlier, that theism gives grounds for hoping that one's moral efforts will not be ultimately wasted, pointless, and forgotten. The final outcome of man's efforts is not a futile nothingness. But equally important is the whole question of the *status* of persons in the universe and the status of those ways of looking at the universe which are distinctively personal, including the moral point of view. From this personal standpoint, the existence of persons in community does in itself obligate men in certain ways. But what is the status of this standpoint? Must I accept the personal standpoint as ultimately valid or am I free, when I wish strongly, to characterize this standpoint and the moral judgments which stem from it as themselves mere matters of fact, to be explained as the result of evolutionary cultural and sociological dynamics? (SR, p. 103).

It is precisely the ultimacy of personality which is at

stake. James holds that some supposedly scientific views of reality tend to deny that persons and personal actions are a necessary condition of any events and assert that our world in its own essential and innermost nature is a strictly impersonal world (WPR, p. 327). For an example of a current view we may cite such philosophers as D. M. Armstrong. In an essay defending the mind-brain identity theory, Armstrong argues for the view "that we can give a complete account of man *in purely physico-chemical terms.*" Armstrong implicitly admits that such a metaphysic will have moral and religious implications when he asserts that scientists who reject such a view do so for "philosophical, moral, and religious reasons."[10] Armstrong's fellow identity theorist J. J. C. Smart agrees with this metaphysical view when he asserts that such an important ethical conception as "love" can be analyzed as either bodily behavior or as an internal physical state which causes such behavior.[11]

In *The Varieties of Religious Experience* James refers to such reductive accounts of the ontological status of persons as "the survival theory." Following Comte, such thinkers view explanations of events which require such personal categories as choice, will, and value as anachronisms (*Var,* pp. 490-498). James's reply is essentially the same as Kierkegaard's. Such scientific theorizing is itself the product of an *individual,* who feels and wills, as well as thinks. However adequate the conceptual theories science presents us may be, they are nonetheless theories about reality, while the existence of an individual person *is* a reality in the completest sense of the term.

> The cosmic objects, so far as the experience yields them, are but ideal pictures of something whose existence we do not inwardly possess but only point at outwardly, while the inner state is our very existence itself; its reality and that of our experience are one. (*Var,* p. 499)

James's point here is not to defend mind-body dualism.

10. "The Nature of Mind," in *The Mind-Brain Theory,* ed. C. V. Borst, p. 67.

11. "Materialism," *ibid.,* p. 160.

The same point could have been made in non-dualistic language. The point is the ultimacy of the concept of a person, conceived as a unified complex of feelings, wantings, cognitions, and the like. The ontological status of persons is crucial because it is linked to a belief in the reality and ultimacy of moral obligation and because *we are persons* and we do have a concern for the ultimate meaning and destiny of our existence as persons. Thus for James the question as to whether there are dimensions of the human person which are not reducible to physical events or patterns of events is crucial, and he sees this question as intimately linked to the question of the nature of the universe of which man is a part and product.

There is of course no good reason why non-theists or materialists may not simply ignore the non-ultimacy of the personal standpoint. But for a thinker like James, for whom "differences of fact" even at the most distant level ought to be taken into account in adopting courses of action, the question as to whether this be "at bottom a moral or unmoral universe" will remain the "radical question of life." We may not be able to say yet whether a personalistic metaphysic will ultimately be rationally confirmed, but our beliefs concerning these questions have momentous consequences for our behavior here and now.

The Consequences of Religious Belief for Religious Devotees

So far the discussion of the momentous practical differences which are at stake in dealing with theistic religious questions has been tied up with the theoretical or metaphysical aspect of religion: What difference in conduct does belief in God impose on us? But James also felt that religion makes a difference at a still more practical level. For if religion or some form of religion be true, certain distinctive types of experience and ways of living open up to a man. A person may not only believe that the world-picture presented by theism (or some other type of essentially religious world view) is true, he may also adopt a style of life which revolves around those truths. If religion be true, this way of life is the highest possible for a man, and the man who is an unbeliever cuts himself off from that way of life — surely a momentous difference. "If there is a God, it is not likely that he is confined solely to making differences in the world's latter end; he probably makes differences all along" (PCPR, p. 355).

The sorts of differences which James believed God could be making all along become apparent in *The Varieties of Religious Experience* where, in his discussion of the twice-born type, James gives a close look at the phenomenon of religious conversion. James views conversion as a reorientation and integration of the personality, and he is struck both by the pervasiveness of such happenings and by their effectiveness in transforming a personality for good. The fruits of saintliness, though of course open to perversion and extremism, he sees as, on the whole, beneficial. These fruits include an immense sense of well-being and freedom, a shift toward loving and harmonious affections, and the achievement of emotional and personal strength (*Var,* pp. 272-273). The value of these is unquestionable, James thinks, and they are for the believer the product of his self-surrender and the active working of God in his life.

Here a skeptic will surely call a halt. Even if it were granted that religious conversions generally do have such beneficial consequences, it is surely unwarranted to attribute these effects to the working of the deity. Surely it is possible to explain these events and their consequences in purely psychological terms. James partially agrees with this objection. He himself is inclined to argue that conversion is best explained psychologically by the hypothesis of subliminal or subconscious ideas which suddenly break out and grip a man. But this psychological explanation of the mechanism involved does not settle the question of the ultimate source of these transformations. As to the ultimate cause, the answers "God" and "the nervous system" still seem possible.[12] Bringing in the subconscious simply raises the question of the nature and origin of the human subconscious, viewed as a "deep structure" of the person. In James's view it is plausible to

_____

12. And for a theist who believes God created the nervous system these are not incompatible either.

regard the notion of the subconscious as that region of the person which is in intimate contact with a "something more," a greater Self.

James does not claim that these considerations are scientifically conclusive in any way. They at most make *plausible* a life characterized by "conversations with the unseen, voices and visions, responses to prayer, changes of heart, deliverances from fear, inflowings of help, assurances of support, whenever persons set their own internal attitude in certain appropriate ways" (PCPR, p. 357). Whether all of these are distinctive aspects of the religious way of life or not, at least some of them (answers to prayer, for example) are clearly impossible if religion be false. And the goods they make possible possess genuine human significance. We can agree then with James's assertion that in cases where questions of religious truth come in the form of forced, momentous options, choices must be made. And more specifically, the question as to whether or not theism be true is a forced option with momentous options, whether one becomes a religious believer or even if one merely concludes that the theistic world-picture is essentially true. And for those who accept James's analysis of the situation, our vital human interests are definitely on the side of religion.

THE LEGITIMACY OF BELIEVING

It is now time to face squarely the most frequently-heard criticism of James—namely, that his justification of religious belief amounts to wish-fulfillment, a defense of the man who projects his needs and fantasies on the universe. For example, Dickinson Miller claims that James simply confuses what is valuable with what is probable.[13] This criticism is not altogether unfounded, and James's reply to it is rather astonishing. It consists simply in maintaining steadfastly that, in certain cases, to say a belief is held (in part) because it satisfies certain human needs is not to criticize the belief but to commend it.

---

13. "James's Doctrine of 'The Right to Believe'," *Philosophical Review*, 51 (November, 1942), 546.

> I have said, and now repeat it, that not only as a matter of fact
> do we find our passional nature influencing us in our opinions,
> but that there are some options between opinions in which this
> influence must be regarded both as an inevitable and as a lawful
> determination of our choice. (WB, p. 19)

We must first recognize that in many cases the idea of a
person's subjective preferences determining his beliefs about
some matter of fact would be evidence of a pathological loss of
touch with reality. Self-delusion is of course common and
probably present in every man to some extent. Nevertheless,
this melancholy fact does not make what is a sign of sickness
to be anything other than a sign of sickness. And even in cases
where we should not say it is positively sick, the person who
believes he will get the good job merely because he wants it
very badly is certainly not an example to be emulated. We
might not brand him immoral as W. K. Clifford does, but we
nonetheless regard him as lacking somewhat in a critical faculty he ought to possess and make use of. As a psychologist
James was aware of the possibility of subjective preferences
distorting our judgments.

However, we must be equally wary of another sort of
distortion which desires, fears, and the like may occasion. If
some believe things merely because they wish to believe,
others refuse to believe for the opposite reason, or even, in
pathological cases, allow their beliefs to be determined by
their worst fears. Either as the result of fear or disappointment, or perhaps masochistic enjoyment, some people
"know" things are as bad as they can possibly be. As Wittgenstein notes in another context: "There is a strong tendency to
say: 'We can't get round the fact that this dream is really such
and such.' It may be the fact that this explanation is extremely repellant that drives you to adopt it."[14]

This error, if anything, is perhaps more insidious than the
former and is less warned of perhaps only because we usually
value "the avoidance of error" above "the finding of truth."
For James these two values are not co-extensive; if a man

---

14. Ludwig Wittgenstein, *Lectures and Conversations on Aesthetics,
Psychology and Religious Belief*, ed. Cyril Barrett (Berkeley: University of
California Press, 1967), p. 24.

fears error in a neurotic fashion, it may well prevent him from taking the risks which would lead him to the truth (WB, pp. 18-19). Even at the level of purely subjective wishes and desires then, the fact that we wish very much to believe something should not in itself make us shy away, though perhaps it ought to awaken in us a sense of caution.

However, James's defense of religious belief does not really revolve around what we should ordinarily call mere wishes and desires at all, but rather around what I should like to call the satisfaction of legitimate human interests. The thrust of his defense of religious belief is not to maintain that we have a right to maintain certain irrational beliefs if it is in our interest to do so, but rather to maintain that certain beliefs are rational partly because they satisfy certain distinctive human interests. This defense rests on a re-interpretation of the nature of rationality itself and a new focus on the relationships between rational inquiry and human needs and values. The "will to believe" is not simply an eccentricity on James's part; the argument there is integrally related to James's pragmatism.

This does not entail, however, that to accept the argument James gives in favor of theism, one must accept a "pragmatist theory of truth," whatever that theory be taken to be. What must be broadened to justify religious faith is not the concept of truth but the concept of reason. And the exposition of Kant and Kierkegaard which we have given should make the direction which James is following clear.

Kant distinguished between theoretical and practical reason, but it is clear that there are not two kinds of reason in Kant; rather the one reason has two different employments. He has not introduced a new, special kind of reason; he has broadened the notion of rationality by showing how reason is exercised by men in *actions* and *choices*. Men not only reason about what is the case, but about what ought to be the case; the latter kind of reasoning is reasoning about what ought to be done, and therefore about what *I* as a rational being ought to do. What is significant for James is Kant's revolutionary thesis of the primacy of practical reason: "All interests are ultimately practical." The standpoint of theoretical reason can never displace the practical standpoint because theoretical inquiry is itself a human activity. Knowing is itself something that man does, something that he in fact ought to do. It follows that man cannot ultimately interpret reality in a way that makes unintelligible his own reality as a practical being. The theoretical standpoint is a standpoint; theoretical knowledge is a value which satisfies a human interest. To say this is not to degrade or minimize the theoretical; the interest is not a personal or idiosyncratic desire, but a universal, legitimate human need.

The notion of a "broadened concept of reason" clearly illuminates the Kierkegaardian position as well, if we regard as polemical overstatements Kierkegaard's diatribes against "the objective." In several places Kierkegaard makes it clear that he has no quarrel with scientific inquiry *per se;* his protest is not against objectivity as such but against the notion that objective knowledge or speculative understanding constitutes a man's highest end. That it was a legitimate end he did not deny, though perhaps in his zeal to defend the "primacy of the subjective" against the Hegelians he comes close to doing that at times. As he says in *Repetition,* speculative metaphysics arises from a human *interest;* man wishes to know and understand his world. However, it seemed to Kierkegaard that the whole impact of speculative metaphysics was to deny the importance of interests — to view man as a disinterested knower. Whether this view of Hegel and the spirit of the age be accurate or not, Kierkegaard felt compelled to protest that objective knowing is an activity of persons who exist, and whose existence is not reducible to that knowing. Hence speculative metaphysics, viewed as the project of interpreting reality and all its elements, including persons, in terms of the objective categories of disinterested knowledge, "founders upon the very interest that gave rise to it" (*Rep,* p. 53). It is the fact that objectivity is itself the result of an interest which makes the attempt to abolish subjectivity comical in Kierkegaard's eyes. His protest here does not logically preclude all metaphysics. The interest which gives rise to metaphysics (presumably the "desire to understand the whole") is a legitimate interest. But if metaphysics does seek to understand the *whole*, it surely must not ignore the importance of *interests*, and devour the hand which feeds it. The interests involved in metaphysical inquiry are the interests of individuals who exist and who necessarily take an interest in their existence.

However, the structures of existence in this sense are clearly universal structures. Thus Kierkegaard in arguing for the primacy of subjectivity is not arguing the primacy of irrationality. He is arguing that objective knowledge can never replace self-understanding and self-knowledge, that objective inquiry is one activity of a self. Questions about the nature of that self and what sort of activities it ought to engage in are fundamental. Only in the context of subjective reflection does objective reflection find its proper function and meaning. If we do not limit the term "reason" to theoretical or objective inquiry but include within it all aspects of "reflection," it is legitimate to view Kierkegaard as broadening the conception of reason and rationality rather than attacking reason, so as to deal with fundamental questions which must be faced.

It is in this context that James's statements about rationality and religious belief begin to make sense. We pointed out earlier that James's notion of rationality involves more than the purely theoretical or logical demands which we place upon our conception. Beliefs may also be rational in a practical sense.

> I had supposed it to be a matter of common observation that, of two competing views of the universe which in all other respects are equal, but of which the first denies some vital human need while the second satisfies it, the second will be favored by sane men for the simple reason that it makes the world seem more rational. (*MT*, p. xxxiii)

In so early a work as the *Principles of Psychology* we find James adumbrating the view of thinking and scientific inquiry which makes such a puzzling statement meaningful. Thinking is from the outset selective, and this is even more true of scientific thought. From the chaos of fragmentary impressions man produces an "abstract system of hypothetical data and laws" (*Prin*, p. 634). Scientific understanding, far from being the result of copying experience, is the result of a most energetic reorganization of that experience.

> The most persistent outer relations which science believes in are never matters of experience at all, but have to be disengaged from under experience by a process of elimination, that is, by ignoring conditions which are always present. The *elementary* laws of mechanics, physics, and chemistry are all of this sort. (*Prin,* p. 636)

Such hoary principles as causality and uniformity of nature are even better examples of principles which are not so much derivations from experience as demands placed upon experience. The significance of all this is that this transformation of the world of impressions into the world of conception is a transformation effected *for the sake of certain interests.*

> Destroy the volitional nature, the definite subjective purposes, preferences, fondnesses for certain effects, form, orders, and not the slightest motive would remain for the brute order of our experience to be remodelled at all. (RAT, pp. 117-118)

James is not saying that scientific conceptions are subjective in the sense of constituting a *ding für mich* which can never reveal a reality which is a *ding an sich.* The marvelous thing, he says, is that this remodelling of experience by our volitional nature is rewarded. The given order lends itself to our conceptions (RAT, p. 119). The predicted consequences of actions made on the basis of these conceptions are verified by experience. But the fact that the natural order shows itself to be amenable to our conceptions should not blind us to the fact that the impositions are *originally* the expression of concrete human needs. We call our conceptions rational when they simplify our experience, when they reduce the many to one without crimping the many, when they banish uncertainty by enabling us to correctly anticipate the course of the future. We demand of our theories clarity and elegance (SR, pp. 65-66). All of these elements constitute subjective criteria of rationality, the "marks" which make our theories scientifically intelligible. These are the logical demands which it is the first duty of all our beliefs to satisfy. But as we noted earlier,[15] in cases where two conceptions satisfy our logical demands equally well, that one which best satisfies our esthetic demands and awakens our active impulses "will be accounted the more rational conception." To say that such inner needs should not be taken into account seems preposterous to James. In the scientific field itself "hardly a law has been established, hardly a fact ascertained, which was not first sought after, often with sweat and blood, to satisfy an inner need" (ILWL, p. 55). Thus what is rational is intimately connected from the very outset with human needs and interests even with regard to "theoretic rationality."[16] The very success of science in applying an "ideal system of rational relations" should encourage metaphysics, ethics, and esthetics in the hope that reality is fundamentally congenial to other essential human powers and interests (*Prin,* p. 671; ILWL, p. 55).

Nor is the status of the religious believer an exceptional case, logically speaking. Faith is not a rarity; it is synonymous with "working hypotheses," and it is the stock-in-trade of the scientist. The scientist forms a hypothesis, performs certain actions on the basis of that hypothesis, and "expects the results to disappoint him if his assumption is false" (SR, p. 95). Of course he may be disappointed, but "the longer disappointment is delayed, the stronger grows his faith in the theory." The case of the religious believer is similar, but he is dealing with an hypothesis which may defy ages for its verification. Even a scientific theory like Darwin's "may exhaust the efforts of generations in their corroboration." Religious believers do not pretend that their beliefs are beyond doubt; someday they will perhaps be conclusively confirmed

---

15. See above, p. 155.

16. This point can be better appreciated today in the light of our revised understanding of the history of science and scientific method. Michael Polanyi cites W. I. Beveridge, J. Bronowski, Stephen Toulmin, N. R. Hanson, and Thomas Kuhn as thinkers who have contributed to our understanding of scientific discovery as conditioned by subjectively held passions and values. Polanyi himself is a key figure in this rediscovery of the role of subjectivity within science. See Michael Polanyi, *Science, Faith and Society* (Chicago: University of Chicago Press, 1964), pp. 12-13.

or falsified.[17] Someday the moral key may be shown to fit or not to fit the lock of the universe. How this may come about is perhaps not as clear as we should want it to be. The verification envisioned seems an eschatological affair. When all the evidence is in and human experience is complete, it will become evident whether the world is essentially "vain" or "an even and harmonious unity." Whatever sort of verification is envisioned, it is clear that it will be made possible by our acts, based as they are on risky hypotheses.

This is what James meant by his much misunderstood contention that "there are . . . cases where faith creates its own verification." He certainly did not mean that belief in God could make God exist.[18] (Though he thought perhaps such belief might literally add to God's power and resources.) As he most emphatically states in the Preface to *The Meaning of Truth,* he does not mean to urge "people to say 'God exists,' *even when he doesn't exist,* because forsooth in my philosophy the 'truth' of the saying doesn't really mean that he exists in any shape whatever, but only that to say so feels good" (*MT,* XXXV). Belief in God could not make God exist, but it might make possible the verification of God's existence, just as belief in electrons could not make electrons exist, but it might make possible their discovery and verification. If the theistic hypothesis be true and ultimate reality is personal in nature, then all the sorts of relations possible between persons may be possible here too (WB, pp. 27-28). It is then clear why "we feel, as if the appeal of religion to us were made to our own active good-will, as if evidence might be forever withheld from us unless we met the hypothesis half-way" (WB, p. 28). Faith in God could not make God exist, but it might create the possibility of coming to *know* that God exists. But in the present absence of such knowledge, the act of belief may still be rational — subjectively justified.

---

17. James certainly goes far in accepting a positivistic model for the verification of religious truth claims; it is perhaps just this which makes it necessary for him to provide a subjective justification of religious belief.

18. There are cases where belief in a fact can be one of the factors in bringing the fact about, but this is not one of them.

5

Three Thinkers:
Agreement and Disagreement

S O FAR WE HAVE COMPARED THREE ATTEMPTS TO JUSTIFY
religious belief subjectively. While not ignoring the great
differences among Kant, Kierkegaard, and James, both in
their conclusions and the considerations they appeal to, we
emphasized the structural similarities in their arguments. In
any essay of this type, the question inevitably arises as to
whether the comparisons drawn are forced or artificial.
Questions also arise as to whether the similarities are more
than structural or formal. Does the analysis of subjectivity
lead to any common religious beliefs? Specifically, are the
beliefs which are justified religiously significant? Do the arguments lead to a God who is similar to or different from the
traditional Judaic-Christian conception? To answer these
questions, we must compare the three arguments we have
analyzed in more depth. We shall do this by looking at each of
the aspects of a subjective justification of religious belief in
turn. First, we shall examine the distinction between objectivity and subjectivity in the three thinkers. Next we will
examine their conclusions as to the validity of religion from
the objective or theoretical standpoint, their case for the repudiation of neutrality, and the analysis of the subjective
grounds of belief. Finally, we will take a comparative look at
the content of the religious beliefs justified through the
analysis of subjectivity.

OBJECTIVITY AND SUBJECTIVITY

First, let us examine the basis of the whole approach, which is the distinction between objective and subjective thought, or the theoretical and the practical. We have suggested that all three thinkers employ a distinction between two types of concerns and questions, and that there is an affinity among Kant's distinction of theoretical and practical reason, Kierkegaard's distinction of objective and subjective reflection, and James's distinction between the scientific sphere of theoretic rationality and that realm of practical questions where volitional human needs and preferences are most clearly "a legitimate part of the game."

However, a case could certainly be made that these affinities are superficial. For example, it might be objected that practical *reason* (in its pure form) for Kant is fundamentally reason and that its exercise consists primarily in minimizing the effects of inclination, which at least in part is a matter of desire and emotion. Kierkegaard, on the other hand, sees *passion* as the distinguishing characteristic of subjectivity; to attempt to think subjectively without passion is a contradiction in terms.

Such an objection, however, would do justice to neither thinker. Though Kant does believe that natural inclinations should be governed (though not extirpated) by pure practical reason, he certainly is not ignorant of the emotional component of the good will. Though the notion of reverence is perhaps more sedate than Kierkegaard's passion, and though it arises only when the moral law is thought, it is nonetheless a feeling. And the descriptions given by Kant in *Religion Within the Limits of Reason Alone* show that the exercise of pure practical reason is far from a dispassionate affair. The achievement of a good will is the work of a determined, persistent striving on the part of the individual, who must ceaselessly search out his own motives and deeds. Though technically Kant's ethic requires the individual to take no account of the fact that *he* is the one making the decision, and decide matters as any fully rational being would, to say that Kant's ethic does not require self-concern would be fatuous. As a human being whose nature contains an element of radical evil, the ethical person's mode of existence must be characterized by a *decisive* rejection of evil and a willing of the good. The actual achievement of this condition is more-over a progressive affair which surely partakes of the sort of self-concern and inwardness which Kierkegaard views as the chief characteristics of subjectivity. That Kant and Kierkegaard are talking about a similar quality of existence is made abundantly clear even in Kierkegaard's later Christian works, where one would think subjectivity would take on a more distinctly religious character. It is in these works, however, that Kierkegaard goes furthest in depicting inward-ness in terms of pure motives, ethical earnestness, and a true concern for the right.[1]

If it would be unjust to characterize the Kantian practi-cal reason in its pure exercise as devoid of passion, it would be even more unjust to view Kierkegaard's subjectivity in terms of irrational passion. If passion is not absent from rea-son in Kant, certainly reflection is not absent from passion in Kierkegaard. What he urges on his readers is not mindless emotion, but a disciplined reflection which nonetheless takes its heading from genuine human problems and directs itself with determination and concern to the solution of those problems.

That differences remain it would be foolish to deny. Kant's notion of practical reason concerns the willing of ac-tions as in accordance with principles, and the choice of principles which are to serve as the grounds of actions. Kier-kegaard's notion of subjective thinking conceives of man's willing of actions not so much under the rubric of cognizable principles, but of the willing of actions as stemming from an overall view of life which is conceptualizable in terms of fundamental interlocking categories. Kant's practical reason is more concerned with the question "What shall I do?" Kier-kegaard's subjective reflection focuses more on the question "What shall I be?" But neither thinker would admit the sort of dualism between what a person is and what he does which would fundamentally separate these two questions.

True, Kant does conceive of theoretical and practical rea-son as different employments of the one reason, while Kier-

---

1. See, for example, *TC*, pp. 87, 93. Also many passages in *JY* and *WL*.

kegaard often presents objective and subjective thinking as if
they were fundamentally opposed. However, Kant clearly
recognizes the possibility of a tension between theoretical
and practical reason, unless the limits of theoretical knowledge are clearly recognized. And as we noted,[2] Kierkegaard's
quarrel is not with objective scholarship *per se* at all, but with
the attempt to make objective thought and knowledge man's
primary good. Kierkegaard is defending Kant's belief that "all
interests are ultimately practical" against the counterthesis
of the primacy of the theoretical and objective. Rather than
viewing duty as one more thing to be *known*, Kierkegaard is
arguing that knowledge is one more thing that ought to be
achieved, and not the highest thing. For both Kant and Kierkegaard that highest thing is the achievement of a quality of
existence — a good will or purity of heart — which is only
attained by a distinctive type of passionate conceiving and
willing of ends. Whether this disciplined reflection and reflective striving is so different from objective and theoretical
thought as it seems is a good question, but Kant and Kierkegaard certainly have focused their attention on a fundamental aspect of our human being. The decisive difference
between objective and subjective thinking is the relation of
the thought to the actions and being of the thinker. Even
when Kant urges us to "put out of play" the fact that I am the
one faced with a decision (not let it affect my choice), I can
still never forget, if I wish to act rationally and morally, that
it is *I* who must act in this disinterested fashion. Even if we
accept Kant's view that it is my moral duty to make decisions
as objectively as possible, I must never forget that this is *my*
subjective duty. The objectivity in question is qualified by
subjectivity. Nonetheless, the way in which the two concepts
interrelate may well suggest to us that the disjunction between objective and subjective reflection is overdrawn, a suggestion which we will later explore.

There is a genuine difference between Kant's practical
reason and Kierkegaardian subjective thinking which concerns the relationship of Kierkegaard's religiousness A to re-

---

2. See above, pp. 80-81.

ligiousness B. Kant's *Religion Within the Limits of Reason Alone* is practically a paradigm of a religion of immanence — a state of being in which one's subjectivity is brought to a high point by being related to a moral absolute. For Kant religion is essentially determined by certain concepts which are immanent, contained within mere reason. We have noted that Kierkegaard views this sort of religious attitude as far from antithetical to Christianity. It represents the highest possible natural development of subjectivity, a development without which Christianity cannot even be understood.

Religiousness A cannot be conceived as antithetical to religiousness B, nor can Kant's conception of the "good will" be regarded as antithetical to the subjectivity which characterizes the Christian mode of existence. But neither can religiousness B be regarded as a mere further development of religiousness A. Religiousness B, the paradoxical religion, marks both the highest stage of subjectivity and a break with all immanence. There is a continuity, but the continuity is not a simple "more." Religiousness B represents a distinctive sort of subjectivity because it is a subjectivity qualified by distinctive categories — the categories of the supernatural conceived not merely as an immanent principle but as a reality in time. This is precisely what Kant repudiates again and again in *Religion Within the Limits of Reason Alone;* though we have no grounds to deny the possibility of supernatural revelations, miracles, and works of grace, we can neither understand nor put to practical use any of these things. They are devoid of religious significance except insofar as we may have cause to *hope* they have occurred — a hope which can only legitimately be grounded in a pure moral disposition. For Kierkegaard, however, the pure heart is ultimately achieved through a contact with the God in time, when immanence is deserted and God is known through a particular historical relationship. There is thus a genuine difference between Kant and Kierkegaard: Kant wishes ultimately to restrict *belief* to the realm of theoretically cognizable objects plus those postulates necessary to conceive my moral duty intelligibly. Through Kant recognizes the need to push belief beyond the strictly theoretical realm on the basis of subjective duty, he refuses to affirm with Kierkegaard that religious belief must be pushed beyond the realm of duty to encompass a historical truth. For both thinkers, however, religious belief is not based in any direct sense upon theoretical speculation or scientific evidence, but is seen as springing (legitimately) from that type of reflection which concerns itself primarily with the self and its choices. Religious belief stems primarily from questions as to what I ought to do and who I ought to be, not from what I *know* of the natural order.

The distinction between objective and subjective thought is clearly a part of James's thought as well. In "The Will to Believe" it is the distinction between those questions and concerns which are purely intellectual and can be decided on purely theoretical grounds, and those questions which by their very nature cannot be decided on such grounds and must be dealt with by our "passional nature" (WB, p. 11). This demarcation for James is primarily a matter of distinguishing scientific questions from questions of faith and morals, interpreting science here as the disinterested search for facts.

> Throughout the breadth of physical nature facts are what they are quite independently of us, and seldom is there any such hurry about them that the risks of being duped by believing a theory need be faced. (WB, p. 20)

Such questions here form trivial options; they do not concern our inner being and we can easily postpone judgment in such cases. However, in the practical life, most notably (but not exclusively) in moral and religious questions, issues are raised which can be neither ignored nor settled by our purely intellectual capacities. Where action is required, belief is essential and the passional element comes into its own. James agrees with Kant and Kierkegaard in viewing human reflection as generated by two different sorts of interests and directed to two different sorts of questions.

Though all three thinkers develop this distinction, we must be careful to note that for none of them can the distinction amount to an irreducible dualism. For Kant all interests, including theoretical interests, are ultimately practical. For Kierkegaard objective thought ultimately must be seen as an aspect of human subjectivity. And for James, science itself and the whole theoretical enterprise ultimately stem from our passional nature and are directed towards the satisfaction of concrete human needs. The significance of this runs deep. For James particularly, this fact is seen as *evidence,* however crude, that our inner interests may be in harmony with the innermost nature of things. These relationships between the subjective and the objective suggest that the disjunction between knowledge based on objective thought and evidence, and belief rooted in subjective considerations may not be ultimate in character.

THE THEORETICAL IMPASSE: RELIGIOUS TRUTH AS BELIEVABLE BUT NOT KNOWABLE

Given the distinction between objective and subjective thought, the subjective defense of religious belief first must reckon with the objective evidence pro and con. Basically what must be argued is that theoretical thought reaches an impasse when it deals with religious questions; at least at present it is incapable of deciding as to their truth or falsity. From the perspective of theoretical reason the object of religious faith may perhaps be shown to be a possible object of belief, but cannot be shown to be a necessary object of belief. Kant, Kierkegaard, and James all support some such contention, but they differ on their estimate of the degree of incapacity of theoretical reason, Kierkegaard and James making up the extremes, with Kant in the middle. Comparisons here are somewhat problematic, however, due to the differences in the objects of belief as conceived by the three thinkers.

Kierkegaard comes closest to affirming the total incapacity of objective thought to resolve the crucial religious issue, which was of course for him the question of the incarnation. This event marked for him some sort of absolute limit to objective thought — an historical event which is of such a nature as to make it impossible to decide on a purely objective basis whether it really happened or not. Whatever evidence is adduced will be of such a nature that more than one interpretation is possible. Thus when a man confronts the incarnation

— whether he has faith or does not have faith, whether he chooses to believe or to be offended — his decision is not dependent on objective factors. Each man's choice springs from and reveals "what dwells within him" (*TC*, p. 126). The incapacity of objective thought to resolve the question is total and it is inherent in the nature of the question. Objective thought can recognize only its own limitations and the necessity to yield.

Such a thesis differs markedly from James's belief that there is nothing inherent in religious questions which makes it impossible to resolve them on a purely intellectual basis. James argues only that as a matter of fact these questions have not been resolved; nor do we have at present any way of resolving them on a scientific basis. For James the religious hypothesis not only may be resolvable; ultimately it must be. To be meaningful at all, the religious hypothesis must make some verifiable difference in the course of the world's history, even if that difference cannot be decisively recognized before "the day of judgment" (*ILWL*, p. 62). And James offers the hope that even before that time a science of religion, by study of the facts of personal experience which James believed formed the original material of all religions, could begin to evaluate critically various religious hypotheses, testing them in the light of current scientific knowledge and their own ability to make good their claims (*Var*, pp. 455-457). James, in sharp contrast to Kierkegaard, would have regarded the events recorded in the New Testament, including the incarnation, as simply more data to be critically evaluated.

However possible this might be in theory, James ultimately concludes that the religious hypothesis at present, even when formulated as broadly as possible, cannot be evaluated on purely scientific grounds. In "The Will to Believe" James summarizes the religious hypothesis in two vague propositions: (1) The best things are the more eternal things; (2) We are better off now if we believe (1). Whether some such belief as this be true, we cannot know with certainty. And as we qualify our beliefs further (as James himself does in his espousal of piecemeal supernaturalism), the theoretical warrant for what we believe, negatively or positively, grows less. Nevertheless, James clearly holds that theoretical evidence is not only relevant to the determining of religious truth, but that some such evidence is *necessary* to belief. We have no right to a belief which does not possess enough theoretical backing to make it a live hypothesis.

Kant's view of the conclusions of theoretical reason is perhaps the most complex as well as the most interesting. Kant divides religious belief from knowledge as strictly as Kierkegaard; when theoretical reason attempts to transcend the limits of experience (and we must remember that Kant conceives of God as a being who necessarily transcends those limits), the results can only be sophistry and illusion if taken as knowledge. Nonetheless, the idea of God is *defined* by theoretical reason and it is said to be an idea to which in the course of reflection man is inevitably led. The illusion is a natural one; Kant seems almost to assert with James that "God is the normal object of the mind's belief" (RAT, p. 116). Nevertheless, Kant scrupulously concludes that theoretical knowledge of God is impossible; for true religion such knowledge is neither necessary nor even desirable.

Thus for all three thinkers the final conclusion of theoretical inquiry is that God is a possible object of belief but not a possible object of knowledge. Theoretical reason can recognize its own limitations. From Kant's perspective it must make room for practical faith. From Kierkegaard's perspective objective thought can only say "perhaps"; the reason must yield itself so the paradox may bestow itself. From James's perspective the situation of intellectual suspense which make religious belief a living option is one of the factors which make the "will to believe" possible.

THE REPUDIATION OF NEUTRALITY: UNDERCUTTING SUSPENSION OF JUDGMENT

The case against agnosticism as the proper response to the theoretical impasse requires an interpretation of belief which links it closely with action. Kant views human actions as the embodiment of rational principles and as the conscious seeking of ends. To say that man is rationally obligated to will an end surely implies a belief that that end is attainable, pre-supposing a belief in whatever factors are necessary to attain that end. If a man accepts his rational obligation to seek the highest good he would be less than rational if he failed to believe in the God who makes that end attainable. It is the acceptance of the end as obligatory which makes suspension of judgment irrational, and it is the interpretation of action as fundamentally rational which makes impossible any position which says: "Act morally, but do not form any belief as to whether the end of your action is attainable." Belief is not a purely intellectual affair which can be or ought to be divorced from the exigencies of the human situation.

For Kierkegaard the impossibility of suspension of judgment arises primarily from the connection between religious belief and the quest for a self.

> It is of no avail for such a man to say, "I do not affirm anything about Christ, either yes or no"; for then one has only to ask, "Hast thou then no opinion as to whether thou shalt have an opinion about this or not?"; and if he replies "Well, yes," he has trapped himself, and if he replies "No," then Christianity condemns him all the same, requiring that he shall have an opinion about Christianity. (SD, p. 261)

Man "shall have an opinion about Christianity" because Christian knowledge is wholly wrapped up in the question "What does it mean to be oneself?"—a question with which every man must be concerned (SD, pp. 142-143). Man has a goal which is set before him — the goal of becoming himself — and Christianity, which proclaims itself the only means of achieving that goal, cannot be indifferent to a man so long as he is not indifferent towards that goal. His reaction may not be belief; he may be offended by the goal and the means Christianity proposes, but he cannot remain indifferent.

James seems to appeal to both the Kantian and Kierkegaardian models in this context. If we replace the formal Kantian notion of the highest good with James's pluralistic vision of a world cleansed of evil and populated with enduring goods, one argument James presents is remarkably similar to Kant's. Given that religious belief is a live option, the clincher for James is that a world with a God in it is a world in which James's vision of "salvation" may possibly, though not inevitably, be brought to fruition. Since we are obligated to work towards that end, we cannot heed the skeptic who urges suspension of judgment. He is forbidding us to act as we should if we believed religion to be true.

If we turn from a consideration of "last things" and examine the individual's own situation, James's argument seems to fit the Kierkegaardian model (except of course for the object of belief). The skeptical religious position cuts us off from the possibility of that twice-born state which is at least a *prima facie* answer to the problems of guilt, despair, and meaninglessness. Religious faith is a means of achieving the psychological wholeness characterized by hearty self-acceptance and earnest moral endeavor. While none of these three thinkers succeeds in showing suspension of judgment to be either psychologically impossible or logically self-contradictory, the cumulative force of their conclusions seems to be that such suspended judgment is far from the most rational attitude which a man can take.

THE SUBJECTIVE GROUNDS OF BELIEF

Given that theoretical reason has reached an impasse, and yet some decision is nonetheless rationally called for, why must the decision be the decision to believe in God? Is it not possible that some will find that subjective considerations mitigate *against* theistic belief and rather favor some other religious attitude? After all, men have found religious consolation in skepticism itself, not to mention materialism and mechanism, as Epicurus and Spinoza surely show. The answer to this is of course that such subjective critiques of theism and defenses of other alternatives are quite possible. It is not difficult to imagine an atheistic version of "The Will to Believe" focusing on the pernicious consequences of religion and reminding us of the healthy-minded consolation of a universe free from blame and punishment, eternal gain and eternal loss. What this points to is the fact that the approach we have been considering, while it steadfastly insists on the *rationality* of religious belief, nevertheless does not amount to knowledge.

It is a *subjective* justification of belief. For persons who accept
a certain analysis of man's existential situation and who regard themselves as obligated to achieve certain ends, belief is
justified. Whether that analysis of man can itself be shown to
be correct, and whether the belief that man is under such
obligations can be rationally justified, are distinct questions
to which the answers are by no means obvious.

Nevertheless, we can at least try to become clear as to
what the subjective grounds of the argument may be. Kant
holds that belief in God is subjectively rational, valid for
practical purposes only. In effect, Kant concedes that belief
in God is necessary only to the extent that one accepts the
moral law (in something like the form in which Kant interprets it) as valid, and hence accepts as well the resulting
obligation to achieve the highest good. For Kant the assumption of God's existence is valid only if founded in my subjective apprehension of my moral duty (*KU* 450, p. 118). The
person who rejects the fundamentals of the Kantian analysis
of duty is in no way obligated to believe. To such a person
Kant would be forced to defend not merely religion *per se*, nor
merely the links between moral obligation and theistic belief,
but the fundamental rationality of moral obligation as Kant
construes it. If it turns out that such a view of morality ultimately cannot be proved, but presupposes that a man has
adopted a moral point of view, then religious belief, if justifiable at all, will be only subjectively justifiable — justifiable
only to a person who accepts this point of view.

For Kierkegaard the analogous problem would be the justification of his claim that the Christian mode of existence
represents the highest degree of development of subjectivity
— the highest stage on life's road. For a person who sees the
shortcomings of the esthetic and ethical modes of existence
when taken alone, who recognizes the possibility of an eternal
happiness and sees that such an eternal happiness cannot be
achieved via immanent religious categories, Christian faith
— which involves the giving up of theoretical reason in a leap
— can be shown to be rational. (Reason *yields itself* and the
individual attains the state of *faith*.) It is a different question
as to whether the Christian view that faith is the highest

mode of existence can itself be rationally defended. As a matter of fact, Kierkegaard himself does not seem to believe that such a justification is possible. At times he even seems to offer a reverse apologetic in which the mark of the truth consists in the fact that it disappoints rational human expectations. Hence he claims that offense and faith are *equally* possible. The closest thing to a justification would be Kierkegaard's indirect communication — an attempt to help the reader along the road towards self-understanding, but an attempt which presupposes that the reader must travel the road himself. Kierkegaard can only hope that the earnest reader who achieves existential depth will come to *see* the profundity of the Christian analysis of man and the failings of alternative conceptions. But the "coming to see" which is referred to here is a subjective process and apparently cannot be justified in any objective sense.

James, with his quick eye and deep appreciation for the role temperament plays in philosophical discussions, clearly recognizes the role which the passions play in these matters.

> Pretend what we may, the whole man within us is at work when we form our philosophical opinions. Intellect, will, taste, and passion cooperate just as they do in practical affairs; and lucky it is if the passion be not something as petty as a love of personal conquest over the philosopher across the way. (SR, p. 92)

We have interpreted James's defense of religion as something of a synthesis of the models developed by Kant and Kierkegaard. James sketches the relationships between religion and morality, and he also connects religion with the quest for the unified self. Quite clearly then, our beliefs in those areas will largely determine our religious beliefs, and James regards those two areas as especially related to man's passional preferences.

Science may tell us what exists, but to know the *worths* of what exists James says we must go to what Pascal terms the heart (WB, p. 22). The interpretation of the universe as a moral universe, grounded in a supremely moral being, is itself a moral belief, the expression of a passional preference. It cannot be proved as such, at least in the foreseeable future.

But James believed quite definitely that moral obligations are not constituted merely by *our* passions and preferences; moral obligations are not the sorts of things which we can "play fast and loose with" (SR, p. 103). James holds that for those who find this view appealing, who are willing to exercise their faith in it (a perfectly legitimate faith), theistic belief is rational.

With regard to the achievement of the ideal self, James is equally aware of subjective proclivities. In the *Varieties* he not only distinguishes religious personalities with distinctive religious needs from those who do not seem to possess those needs; he also classifies the religious sensibility itself into the once-born and twice-born types and describes many varieties of each in loving detail. Thus there is no one "ideal self."

> I do not see how it is possible that creatures in such different positions and with such different powers as human individuals are, should have exactly the same functions and duties. No two of us have identical difficulties, nor should we be expected to work out identical solutions. (*Var*, p. 487)

Nevertheless an overwhelming number of persons do seem to have distinctive religious needs to some degree. This is clearly seen if we reduce religion to its simplest terms: the belief that there is something wrong about us as we naturally stand and that we can be saved from this wrongness by getting into a right relationship with the higher powers (*Var*, p. 39). However vague our notion of those higher powers may be, James argues that the fact that religion can transform personalities in beneficial ways is quite undeniable. Whether the wider self from which these transformations come really be a supernatural being or merely an aspect of the human psyche cannot perhaps be established at present. James himself finds it plausible to believe that a God does exist and that in prayer real business is accomplished; in short, "God is real since he produces real effects." To all those individuals who lack a robust optimism, who feel the sense of something wrong, and who also feel the need of a helper who is continuous with my better self to overcome that wrong condition, religious faith will be a rational step, though the character of the faith may differ in proportion as the individual's sense of need approaches the depths of the divided self and the sick soul. The thrust of James's analysis is then subjective in a sense similar to that of Kant and Kierkegaard. Given that the individual has certain moral beliefs and understands his own human condition in terms of certain kinds of ideals and needs, religious faith can be shown to be rational.

One should not misunderstand this contention that religious faith as viewed by these three thinkers rests on considerations which cannot ultimately be rationally justified in some objective sense. To say the Kantian analysis of moral duty and the Kierkegaardian analysis of the human condition are not theoretically justifiable is not to say they fail to meet conditions which other superior views on these matter do meet. It seems rather that they represent distinct controversial opinions in matters where it is not presently clear how one could arrive at any sort of objective consensus. It is quite possible, of course, that in intellectual areas where consensus cannot be achieved, that some parties in the dispute are nonetheless right, and even that they have good reasons for their beliefs. The nature of man and the status and character of moral obligations are two areas in which subjective opinions, feelings, and attitudes come into full play. This does not mean, however, that these questions are not genuine questions, nor that thought has no role to play in answering them.

> However particular questions connected with our individual destinies may be answered, it is only by acknowledging them as genuine questions, and living in the sphere of thought which they open up, that we become profound. (*Var*, p. 500)

THE ADEQUATE RELIGIOUS OBJECT

We have examined points of similarity and disagreement in the arguments given by Kant, Kierkegaard, and James to justify religious belief. In conclusion, let us briefly examine the content of their religious beliefs. Does the analysis of subjectivity lead to beliefs which are religiously adequate? Are these arguments relevant to thinkers who wish to hold to the traditional Judaic-Christian concept of God? (Of course those two questions are not identical.)

We can best answer these questions by looking at what we shall term the adequate religious object. The adequate religious object for each thinker will be the most adequate conception of the supreme object of belief of the most adequate religious world-view. For Kant the adequate religious object is the supreme moral person. Kant's adequate religious object is a version of the God of traditional theism; he is conceived as creator of the natural order, but this conception must be seen as dictated by moral purposes. Our practical reason demands that the natural order be subject to a moral purpose. The various aspects of divinity are all essentially related to moral duty: God is conceived as moral ruler and judge, the founder of that moral commonwealth known as the people of God, and the one of whom, if we do all that is in our power to become moral persons, we may *hope* will lend us his assistance in our moral endeavors and pardon our previous failings. (Though we can have no *knowledge* of such things.)

Although belief in God is for Kant dictated by moral concerns, it is important to realize that the concept of God is initially defined by theoretical reason. Kant says that it is of the utmost importance to realize that the traditional attributes of God are transcendental predicates which are derived from the speculative employment of reason (*KRV* A640-642, B668-670). The belief in God is not merely a fiction designed to give added stimulus to our moral efforts, but a genuine theoretical belief, which, while never amounting to knowledge, is a belief in the God who provides the ultimate reason why things are as they are.

The adequate religious object for Kierkegaard is the God in time, the traditional God of theism become a historical person. Thus for Kierkegaard our knowledge of the adequate religious object is historically conditioned in a way which it is not for Kant. Though historically conditioned, the adequate religious object represents the limit of all human cognition; it is the supreme paradox, bringing with it the possibility of offense. For the Christian, the one who has been born, this paradox is not an offense; it is rather a Savior, and my task as a human being is to achieve contemporaneousness with that event. The God in time becomes "the Pattern" for my life (*JY*, pp. 161-217). The belief is essentially bound up with one's manner of existence.

Though bound up with a person's existence in an essential way, it is also important to see that Kierkegaard's belief in the incarnation is not an ethical fiction whose objective truth is of no concern to the believer, as some have charged.[3] While faith in the God-man is not grounded in historical evidence, it is a genuine historical belief because the event is believed to be genuinely historical. "The absolute fact is an historical fact, and as such it is the object of faith" (*PF*, p. 125). There is thus an ineradicable factual element in Christian faith for Kierkegaard.

James's conception of the adequate religious object is less definite. James usually characterizes his religious belief as "theism," by which he means to indicate belief in a personal deity, "less than the Absolute of Idealism," and even less than the God of scholastic theology. In a letter to Thomas Davidson, James explains his belief in this way:

> He (God) need not be an all-including "subjective unity of the universe." . . . All I mean is that there must be *some* subjective unity in the universe which has purposes commensurable with my own and which is at the same time large enough to be, among all the powers that may be there, the strongest. . . . In saying "God exists" all I imply is that my purposes are cared for by a mind so powerful as on the whole to control the drift of the universe.[4]

Thus James believes in a God somewhat like the God of traditional theism, only "finite, either in power or in knowledge, or in both at once" (*PU*, p. 311). James's conception of God is intimately linked with the concept of meliorism developed in *Pragmatism,* which is the belief that the salvation

3. See Wesley K. H. Teo, "Self-Responsibility in Existentialism and Buddhism," *International Journal for Philosophy of Religion,* 4 (1973), 80, for an example of a thinker who regards Kierkegaard's belief as a non-theoretical "fiction." For a response to Teo see C. Stephen Evans, "Kierkegaard on Subjective Truth: Is God an Ethical Fiction?" *International Journal for Philosophy of Religion,* 7, 1 (1976), 288-299.

4. Quoted in Ralph Barton Perry, *The Thought and Character of William James* (Boston: Little, Brown and Co., 1935), I, 737.

of the world is neither an impossibility or bare possibility, nor a certainty, but a real possibility. This means that no conditions are extant which would make this impossible, and *some* of the conditions which would make it possible are realities (*Prag,* pp. 283-284). Both atheistic and absolutistic metaphysics seem lacking to James in that they do not define reality in such a way as to stimulate human moral efforts.

In a recent essay, Robert Vanden Burgt emphasizes this connection between human freedom and creativity and James's conception of God, noting that James even goes so far as to assert that God is dependent, in part, upon acts of human consciousness for his very being.[5] If this is so, then Burgt feels it makes sense for James to include religious beliefs in the class of beliefs which may help "create the fact." To say this is to say too much. James says that the existence of the divine order is dependent on our good will only in part (WB, p. 61). God's being is seen as drawing strength and support from our actions, but there clearly is a sense in which James believes the spiritual order to be "there" prior to belief. Nonetheless, Burgt's point is sound insofar as it emphasizes the close and reciprocal relations which hold between God and the natural order. God is first among equals, a free being who works for good with the help of other free beings.

In *A Pluralistic Universe* and in the Ingersoll Lecture on *Human Immortality* James displays an affinity for Fechner's pan-psychism. Though James never explicitly adopted panpsychism, it does seem that he began to conceive of the human consciousness as in some way rooted in a broader consciousness. If this broader consciousness (mother sea) is identified with God, then Vanden Burgt's emphasis on the dependence of God on our efforts would make even better sense. Such a conception of God would be more immanent than theism in any traditional sense.

We must remember, however, that James never explicitly embraced Fechner's view, and that he certainly never identified the "mother consciousness" with God. Even if James

---

5. "William James on Man's Creativity in the Religious Universe," *Philosophy Today,* 15 (Winter, 1971), 292-301.

accepted a "transmission theory" of consciousness, he does not interpret this theory in such a way as to compromise the individuality of particular minds.[6] Nothing could be clearer than James's desire to see God not as "the whole" but as one particular being among others, a being with his own self-consciousness and value-orientation. In the Postscript to the *Varieties* James makes it clear that he is willing to entertain the possibility of a number of super-human conscious beings (*Var*, pp. 525-526). If that were in fact true, James's definition of God as the most powerful of these beings would still be adequate.

In summary, James conceived of the adequate religious object as a being superior to man in knowledge and power, concerned to overcome evil and replace it with good. Attempts to pin down the nature of God James regarded as doubtful. Nevertheless, James's God appears as a somewhat finite version of traditional theism — a powerful being who is in some respects limited and dependent on human cooperation to accomplish his purposes.

These differences in the adequate religious object are marked, as are the differences in their arguments. Nevertheless, these various conceptions are far from totally dissimilar. All may be regarded as variants of traditional Western theism. Though these arguments, rooted as they are in personal concerns, are far from leading to full agreement as to the nature of the adequate religious object, they do seem to lead to a conception of God which is personal in character. And that is precisely what is to be expected. Religious beliefs which are grounded in the deepest moral and psychological concerns of persons naturally lead to belief in a God who himself cares about those concerns: a Person who cares about personhood. While such a God cannot be automatically identified with the God of Abraham, Issac, and Jacob, he is clearly the sort of God to whom these patriarchs prayed. Such a God cannot but be of concern to contemporary individuals struggling to achieve meaning and purpose in a universe which seems to many to offer none.

---

6. See the preface to the second edition, *HI*, pp. v-ix.

6

Conclusions: General Features of a Viable Defense of Religious Belief

INTRODUCTION

WE HAVE COMPARED THREE ATTEMPTS TO JUSTIFY RELIgious belief. Clearly these three attempts differ markedly, not only in the considerations they appeal to, but also in the conclusions they reach. However, we have interpreted these attempted justifications as structurally similar. All presuppose a distinction between theoretical and subjective thought and attempt a subjective justification of religious belief which contains the following elements: (1) an attempt to show that God is a *possible* object of rational belief, though theoretical reason is inadequate to resolve the issue of religious truth; (2) suspension of judgment with regard to religious beliefs is undesirable or impossible; (3) certain subjective factors (factors essentially related to the subject as a willing-feeling being) make it existentially desirable and rationally justifiable to opt for religious belief. Hence, although we may not properly be said to know that God exists, we may legitimately be said to possess a rationally justified belief.

It is time to draw some conclusions as to the general strengths and weaknesses of such arguments, and the general nature of a viable version. The following are tentatively offered. I shall first summarize the lessons to be learned and then try to defend these conclusions, in part by drawing on our earlier historical analyses.

1. Subjective justifications of religious belief are partially dependent on theoretical considerations; that is, subjective arguments can supplement but never totally supplant theoretical argument and evidence.
2. If a defense of religious belief can be constructed on the

basis of an analysis of human subjectivity, "subjectivity" must not be taken in an idiosyncratic way, but must be regarded in a universal or generic sense; that is, the categories of "existence" and "the individual" must be universal categories.

3. Even so, the effectiveness of the arguments will still be person-relative; the acceptance of the argument will depend upon the individual's acceptance of ethical and psychological beliefs which are not beyond question, and which present peculiar epistemological problems.

4. Partly as a consequence of (1) and (3), such defenses of religion offer no promise of finally resolving the basic disputes in the philosophy of religion.

5. With these qualifications, the sorts of considerations advanced by the subjective defense of religious belief are relevant to deciding questions of religious truth, and in general, it is legitimate for individuals to take moral and existential concerns, usually regarded as subjective, into account when dealing with metaphysical beliefs of religious import.

THE DEPENDENCE OF THE PROJECT ON OBJECTIVE CONSIDERATIONS

The first lesson which we shall offer concerns the relationship of subjective concerns to theoretical concerns. Given the distinction between subjective justifications of belief and objective evidence, we hold that subjective considerations can supplement but never totally replace theoretical evidence and argument. If this thesis is correct it will follow that any appeal to subjective considerations which denies the importance of such traditional epistemological concerns as theistic proofs, historical evidence for claims of revelation, and appeals to religious experience will be illegitimate.

Taken in a weak sense, this contention seems obviously true. One of the key elements of the subjective approach has been shown to be an analysis of theoretical reason to show that its conclusions must necessarily be inconclusive *vis a vis* religious questions. Theoretical reason can at best show that God's existence is *believable*. Obviously this contention requires careful consideration of the evidence pro and con,[1] and

---

1. One weakness in the defenses of religion given by these three thinkers is that they do not pay sufficient attention or provide adequate answers to theoretical *objections* to belief in God such as the problem of evil.

each of the three thinkers considered provides this analysis. In the *Critique of Pure Reason* Kant gives a detailed criticism of the traditional natural theology. In the *Philosophical Fragments,* Kierkegaard gives his critique of theistic arguments, and in the *Concluding Unscientific Postscript* he devotes chapter one of Book I to an attempt to demonstrate the impossibility of establishing Christianity on the basis of objective historical evidence. In *The Varieties of Religious Experience* James devotes chapter eighteen to the weaknesses of philosophical arguments and chapters sixteen and seventeen to mysticism and appeals to religious experience with a view towards showing that such appeals, while tending to cast doubt on dogmatic naturalistic views, ultimately possess no authority to resolve the fundamental religious truth-questions. Thus it is clear that subjective arguments require consideration of the objective evidence pro and con at least to the extent of showing the inconclusiveness of the objective approach.

However, we shall argue that any truly viable defense of religious belief depends on theoretical argument and evidence in a still more significant sense. Any viable subjective argument will require theoretical evidence or argument to show that religious belief is rationally credible or plausible. James recognizes this clearly and we have argued that it is an implicit part of Kant's procedure. Only Kierkegaard seems to deny this and we shall question whether his denial of the necessity of objective evidence is itself plausible or consistent with other views which he holds.

In our interpretation of James we argued that James's notion of a live option presupposes that the hypotheses under consideration possess enough evidential backing to make them intellectually plausible. The "right to believe" presupposes that a hypothesis is live enough to tempt our will. Unfortunately, this is a rather vague notion. Part of the vagueness stems from difficulties in the concept of evidence. It is a notorious fact that religious believers and critics usually fail to agree as to what would constitute evidence for religious beliefs. But even assuming agreement as to what constitutes evidence, the notion is far from clear. How much evidence is required to give a hypothesis the status of "plausibility"?

One way of sharpening the concept is suggested by Robert Ackermann. In a discussion of rational belief Ackermann points out that the attractiveness of a possible belief is often not a function of the evidence *per se* but of the likelihood of a possible answer relative to the alternatives. This is due to the fact that a problem often presents itself with a "fixed set of possible solutions from which we are to choose an answer."[2] The "forced-option" condition which James has added clearly entails that genuine religious options will be options of this sort, where the alternatives are finite and where the thinker may be "forced to take a view about things under pressure of relieving a bad situation before some sort of deadline."[3] If this account is defensible it will mean that defenders of religious beliefs (if they can show that the alternatives are finite and that some decision is required) are freed from the necessity of showing religious beliefs to be plausible relative to some absolute scale. To show that a religious belief is rational from a theoretical basis, one will have to show only that it seems more likely to be true than any of its competitors.

However, even this requirement seems too stringent a condition for intellectual plausibility as it would entail that for every belief-problem there is only one plausible answer. But is seems clear that for many problems there may be more than one plausible solution. Thus, if we assign evidential values to beliefs on a scale of 0 to 1, in a situation where a decision must be made and the two known solutions possess the same evidential value, say 0.4, it makes sense to speak of both alternatives as plausible. And in a situation characterized by great uncertainty, when much of the relevant evidence is unattainable and where the assigning of evidential value itself seems uncertain, it would by no means be considered strange or unusual for a person with a strong hunch to believe a hypothesis with an evidential value somewhat lower than another alternative. While one might not regard such a belief as a model of a rationally chosen belief, it is not

---

2. *Belief and Knowledge,* Anchor Books (Garden City: Doubleday & Co., 1972), pp. 47-48.

3. *Ibid.,* p. 49.

clear that such a belief would be *irrational*. One might at least regard such a belief as answering James's condition that it be "live enough to tempt our will." It could be regarded as a potentially rational belief, a belief which may be rationally justifiable if other relevant factors (such as the exigencies of action and moral obligation) require it. Clearly, however, any such subjective justification of belief depends to some extent on objective argumentation and evidence, and the rationality of the belief will be to a great extent determined by objective considerations. The greater the objective evidence, the more plausible will be the subjective argument.

With regard to Kant it is more difficult to discern the positive role of theoretical reason. There is of course the negative function of protecting the postulated beliefs of practical reason from attack, a service which Kant compared to the policeman who has what he calls the negative role of protecting the populace. Kant constantly affirms the impossibility of theoretical religious knowledge. The path to wisdom certainly must pass through science, but "we can be sure that it leads to that goal only after the completion of science" (*KPV* 141, p. 147). At the risk of making too much of a metaphor, it might be said nevertheless that the path to science is the same path that leads to wisdom after the completion of science, and that it is important that science itself seems to point in a certain direction, even if science itself cannot travel to the destination. In view of Kant's repeated contention that speculative reason not only necessarily forms an idea of a supreme being, but presents arguments in support of that idea which, whether strictly valid or not, are nonetheless natural and convincing not only to common sense, but to speculative reason itself (*KRV* A604, B632), it is hard not to see the role of theoretical reason as providing the foundations of a practical defense of religious belief by establishing the theoretical plausibility of belief in God. The overall force of Kant's defense of religious belief derives in large part from the coherence between the conclusions of theoretical and practical reason. Thus for Kant as well as James, despite the primacy of the practical and the insufficiency of theoretical reason taken alone, there is a sense in which practical reason is also insufficient taken alone.

However, when we consider Kierkegaard, we meet a sharp challenge to our thesis. No fair-minded reader can fail to see that much of Kierkegaard's writing, in both the pseudonymous and the Christian works, is directed towards depreciating the relevance of objective evidence for religious belief. Kierkegaard seems to regard a concern for the validity of theistic proofs and historical evidence and other objective questions, far from being important to the seeker after religious truth, as a positive hindrance. They are distractions which keep me from asking the truly important questions which concern me and my relationship to the truth: "Is it certain that I have faith? Do I understand what it means to exist as an individual human being?" Though Kierkegaard clearly holds that the incarnation is a genuine historical event, the God in time, he nonetheless wishes to say that questions of historical inquiry have no bearing on the decision to believe in that historical event. Whether the evidence for Christ's existence be great or small is unimportant, as evidenced by the famous statement in the *Fragments* concerning the value of the historical record left by the people of the time:

> If the contemporary generation had left nothing behind them but these words: "We have believed that in such and such a year the God appeared among us in the humble figure of a servant, that he lived and taught in our community, and finally died," it would be more than enough. . . . This little advertisement would be sufficient to afford an occasion for a successor, and the most voluminous account in all eternity can do nothing more. (*PF*, pp. 130-131)

Kierkegaard seems to have two objections to any attempt to connect religious faith with historical inquiry. The first objection stems from the incommensurability between the conclusions of historical inquiry, which are always approximations, and the passionate certainty of faith, which requires a total subjective commitment. For Kierkegaard all knowledge of fact, even knowledge of one's historical externality, is at best an approximation; all historical conclusions therefore require an act of will, or an element of faith in an ordinary sense. But religious faith possesses a decisiveness and totality which is incommensurable with the tentativeness of the historical inquiry, and no amount of historical evidence would be enough to produce faith[4] in this special sense (*PF*, p. 106).

This first objection of Kierkegaard's to linking religious belief to objective evidence can be answered forthrightly by simply pointing out that to show that historical evidence is not *sufficient* to produce religious faith by no means entails that such objective evidence is irrelevant. If the belief in the God in time is to be a genuine historical belief (a belief in the factuality of the occurrence), and Kierkegaard insists that it must be genuinely historical (*PF*, p. 125), then it is clear that we must learn about the event via the ordinary historical channels or written records, artifacts, and the like. Thus the passage in the *Fragments,* though it may minimize the role of such historical evidence, nonetheless admits the necessity of *some* such evidence. Kierkegaard does not follow Kant's view found in *Religion Within the Limits* in which the Son of God is viewed as a rational ideal whose validity is independent of historical factual existence. For Kierkegaard, though the believer does not believe in virtue of historical testimony *alone,* this does not mean that historical testimony is not *necessary* if he is going to believe (*PF*, p. 106). And having asserted that religious faith is historical faith (belief in the factuality of an event) and admitted that historical evidence is a necessary (but not sufficient) condition for religious faith, it is difficult to see why the quality and amount of that historical evidence is irrelevant or unimportant.[5] While it is clear that the transition from historical belief to Christian faith is not a direct or immediate transition, if for no other reason but the obvious one that faith requires an interpretation of the event not evident on the face of things, still the religious meaning cannot

---

4. For an examination of Kierkegaard's use of "faith" in these two senses see Richard Campbell, "Lessing's Problem and Kierkegaard's Answer," *Essays on Kierkegaard,* ed. Jerry H. Gill, p. 84.

5. See *ibid.,* pp. 74-89, for a convincing argument that Kierkegaard's analysis of the religious situation actually entails that ordinary historical argument is relevant to religious faith, although Campbell emphasizes that Kierkegaard did not realize this himself.

be logically unrelated to the historical event of which it is the interpretation. Even if the distinctive character of faith — its decisiveness, totality, commitment — stems not from objective evidence but from subjective concern, it still would not follow that an honest thinker (and surely honesty is a characteristic of the highest forms of subjectivity) would be indifferent to ordinary historical evidence which has a bearing on the factuality of his belief. If this contention is correct, then Kierkegaard's contention that an objective concern with Christianity is preverse is either groundless, or else stems from an assumption (surely mistaken) that the historical evidence for Christianity was so overwhelmingly strong that the continuing inquiry about objective questions was an obfuscation, an attempt to evade asking the subjective questions and find a security which the merely historical could never in principle supply.

The second source of Kierkegaard's contention that objective evidence is irrelevant to questions of religious belief seems to center in the nature of the adequate religious object itself, the incarnation conceived as a paradox. "One cannot find historical certainty for that which is absurd because it involves the contradiction that something which can become historical only in direct opposition to all human reason, has become historical" (*Post,* p. 189). Thus, in the case of Christianity there is a further difficulty which separates historical evidence from belief. Here we have not only the uncertainty which attaches to all historical belief, but the further uncertainty that the object of the belief is a paradox. It is this sort of belief which is the cognitive component of faith in the pre-eminent sense.

Despite these strong words, it can be argued, I think, that even faith in the incarnation is partially dependent on objective historical evidence. First, we must accept our earlier contention that Kierkegaard is not an irrationalist and that a paradox is not a logical contradiction.[6] Rather we must interpret the paradox as the limit of historical understanding, or more precisely, that limiting case in which the estimation of

---

6. See above, pp. 89, 117-120.

the probability (or rather improbability) of an event completely balances the actual testimony for the event.[7] Second,
we must once again emphasize the thoroughly polemical
character of human reason. It is *humanly* speaking that the
incarnation is a fantastic aberration, and an insane combination. The incarnation goes against all our *human* expectations,
and yet it is the historical fact which purports to be of eternal
significance to the individual who confronts it. The character
of the event is such that it shocks the individual, grabs his
attention, and provides the possibility of offense. He is forced
not merely to think about the question of whether the event
occurred, but to react to the event.

If we view the paradox of the incarnation in this light, it
seems that there is still a connection between ordinary historical faith and faith in this pre-eminent Christian sense. So
long as religious faith still involves genuine factual belief,
then some sort of historical evidence will still be a necessary
condition for such faith, though as a sufficient condition for
such faith, objective historical evidence will be even more
inadequate. The paradox is still introduced to me by ordinary
historical means; if there were no evidence, the question of
belief in the incarnation would not even arise. The decision
which faces the subjective thinker is constituted precisely by
the fact that *there is evidence* for an event which seems inherently improbable, but which purports to be decisive for him
with respect to his eternal happiness. Now as a matter of fact
Kierkegaard apparently thought the evidence for the incarnation was quite good as historical evidence goes (*Jour,* p. 109).
If there is good evidence for the event itself, and the impossibility or improbability of the event is relative to human per-
ceptions of what is likely and impossible, then it makes sense
to see the difficulty of believing as a subjective difficulty. The
difficulty consists in "willing subjectively to aspire to
knowledge about the historical in the interest of one's own

---

7. See above, pp. 87-88. Also see Vernard Eller, "Fact, Faith, and
Foolishness: Kierkegaard and the New Quest," *Journal of Religion,* 48, 1
(1965), 54-68, for a development of this reading of Kierkegaard. Eller distinguishes between an "absurdity" and Kierkegaard's analysis of "the absurd"
and shows in what sense historical evidence is relevant to the latter.

blessedness" (*Post,* p. 512), and in the fact that the historical knowledge in question seems inherently improbable to the finite understanding. The event is not necessarily offensive; it brings with it merely the *"possibility* of offense." Faith and offense are the two possible reactions; each is determined not by the event or the evidence *per se,* but by the nature of the self considering the event. But this does not mean that evidence is unnecessary. What I should wish to argue here is that only if there is reliable evidence for the incarnation does Kierkegaard's description of the situation make sense. The paradoxical character of the incarnation lies in its having really happened; the difficulty is not merely in understanding the concept of the God in time, but in believing that the God-in-time event actually occurred. And the factual element of this belief is only presented to the understanding via historical means. The stronger the evidence, the more strongly this event is presented. Without the evidence there is no presentation, hence no contradiction or absurdity. And there seems to be no good reason for denying that the stronger the evidence the more strongly will the contradiction between one's worldly expectations and the purported fact be felt.

Kierkegaard feels that no amount of evidence could suffice to produce belief in this event. But this does not entail that some amount of evidence might be *necessary* to produce belief. *Given* that there is evidence for this belief, a situation he describes in which belief and offense are equal possibilities and a man's choice is determined by his subjective character is perhaps comprehensible. But if the evidence is not there, the question of belief will not even arise. And though Kierkegaard may have good reason for arguing that objective evidence could never lead of necessity to religious faith, I fail to see why a consideration of that evidence should be irrelevant to religious faith. Thus in all three of the cases considered, the subjective considerations advanced on behalf of religious beliefs presuppose both the importance of objective argumentation and evidence and the evidential value of religious beliefs.

SUBJECTIVE CATEGORIES AS
UNIVERSAL CATEGORIES

Our second lesson, which is perhaps less controversial, is that the self with its needs, values, and obligations must be taken in a universal and not an idiosyncratic sense if it is to serve as a basis for rational belief. Paradoxical as it may sound, the concept of the individual is a universal concept in the sense that the categories which describe the structure of existence are universal categories. If obligations are to give rise to rational beliefs, those obligations must be taken as objectively valid; if needs are to give rise to rational beliefs, then they must be genuine human needs, needs which bring with them some sort of right of satisfaction. This seems doubly paradoxical because nothing seems more subjective in the sense of "unique" and "individual" than needs and obligations. Kant's notion of the highest good as a rational ideal differs widely from James's concept of a world of pluralistic goods from which we are to select and strive along basically utilitarian principles. Kierkegaard's picture of the self which I am to become differs widely from many other psychological views. Nevertheless, we must regard those ends which we believe we are *obliged* to seek as ends which are universal.

That Kant's conception of practical reason is not subjective in an idiosyncratic sense is of course as clear as can be. Kant made a clear distinction between needs which are "based on an objective determining ground of the will" and needs based on inclinations which are the ground of mere wishes. The second kind of need could never serve as a ground for belief that the conditions of satisfying the need exist; only when the need is the sort of need which binds every rational being is such belief justified (*KPV* 143, p. 149 footnote).

That Kierkegaard's descriptions of subjectivity are also attempts to describe the universal structures of the self, albeit in concrete fashion, may not be as obvious, but it is nonetheless so. His attack on Hegel and speculative understanding on behalf of the individual is by no means a romantic glorification of the individual. The Kierkegaardian notion of the individual is certainly not equivalent to Dostoevsky's Underground Man, who perversely wills his own destruction to preserve his uniqueness. Kierkegaard does demand that the individual come out from the crowd and become himself, but the self he is to become is not created *ex nihilo;* it is constituted by the Creator and describable in categories which are universal. Surely Kierkegaard makes this perfectly clear in his analysis of the self in the first section of *The Sickness Unto Death* (pp. 146-148). For example, when he says that to have *willed* in a decisive way is the absolute condition for having existed as a human being (*Post,* p. 270), the concept of a human being is functioning as an objective, normative concept.

It would be a misunderstanding to object to this on the basis of the three stages on life's way. Certainly Kierkegaard recognized that different ways of life which embody different sorts of selves are possible. But these possibilities themselves are rooted in the structure of the self as such. Whether he was right or wrong, Kierkegaard undoubtedly regarded these different spheres as universal possibilities. And only the most superficial and selective reading of Kierkegaard could possibly lead to the conclusion that he thought these different spheres were equally adequate to achieve self-actualization. Even in a work like *Either-Or,* where no direct conclusion is given, he tells us that a conclusion is pointed at existentially. "It is left for the reader to put two and two together" (*Post,* p. 264). That implies that two and two must be there to be put together.

It is only if the category of the individual is an objective, normative category that Kierkegaard's notion of original sin makes sense. In *The Concept of Dread* he tells us "the fact is that at every moment the individual is himself and the race. . . . Perfection in oneself means therefore the perfect participation in the whole" (*CD,* p. 26). We have already noted Kierkegaard's claim that to will to live as a human being relying upon a *difference* is the weakness of cowardice.[8] The task of becoming an individual is structurally the same for

---

8. See above, p. 99.

everyone. Nor should we be misled by Kierkegaard's constant identification of the universal with the ethical into believing that universality is absent from the religious. It is just this element of the "universal human" which ties the ethical and the religious together and plays such a dominant role in his specifically Christian works (*TC*, p. 235). Every man has an equal capability and equal need for a God-relationship.

This is not to say that Kierkegaard's norm of personality involves some sort of conformity. Each man must become himself, and it is *he* who must achieve the norm. One of the universal elements of the norm is an inner-directedness whereby the individual does not pattern himself after the crowd. And there is much room and latitude within the norm for individual differences, which are not as such a fault (*Post*, p. 312). But to make a difference a norm would indeed be a fault (*Post*, p. 312). If our contention is correct, Kierkegaard is clearly not a subjectivist in an irrational sense. The person who chooses to believe in Christ will be a person who recognizes the objective validity of an ideal and believes in the reality of the condition necessary to attain that idea. Formally the argument is exactly parallel to Kant's, though the object of belief differs.

It is with James that the thesis that the needs and obligations which ground religious beliefs are universal and objectively valid threatens to break down. It must be admitted that James not only admits but seems to emphasize the idiosyncratic nature of the human personality, and this emphasis on individual differences carries over into his defense of religious beliefs. However, we shall argue that despite this latitudinarianism on James's part, he still wishes to hold that a certain range of needs and obligations are genuinely *human* needs and form a fundamental aspect of human personality, although their degree of importance may differ somewhat from person to person, as may the means of satisfying those needs and obligations. If this is so, James is still employing normative concepts and relating religious belief to those objectively valid norms, not to mere "subjective" wishes and desires. The distinction between wishes and whims and objectively valid obligations is difficult to draw in James's philosophy, precisely because he views the validity of norms as arising from the subjective desires of creatures. Nevertheless, it is a distinction which must be drawn.

It is precisely the tendency in James to ground religious belief in desires, wishes, and passions (taken as subjective in the idiosyncratic sense) that makes James's defense of religious belief appear weak. It is undoubtedly this tendency which made critics view his defense of the "right to believe" as a defense of wishful thinking, a justification of self-deception. James invites this by a strong defense of religious tolerance, and by making his defense seem to rest on differences of temperament.

> Ought it, indeed, to be assumed that the lives of all men should show identical religious elements? In other words, is the existence of so many religious types and sects and creeds regrettable?
> To these questions I answer "No" emphatically. And my reason is that I do not see how it is possible that creatures in such different positions and with such different powers as human individuals are, should have exactly the same functions and the same duties. No two of us have identical difficulties, nor should we be expected to work out identical solutions. (*Var*, p. 487)

Such a statement certainly lends support to interpreting James as a thinker who urges us to conform our beliefs to our psychological needs: "Believe what you need to believe to get yourself through." And such a view seems to smack of intellectual dishonesty and self-deception. However, such a reading of James simply does not do justice to his overall position. Notice he does not say that these human functions and needs are totally disparate, but only that they are not exactly the same. That the needs and functions which give rise to religious belief have a basic similarity and that the religious beliefs which they give rise to have a common core is the main point of the *Varieties*. Religious tolerance and pluralism are a necessary consequence of the uncertainty and low degree of probability of the various religious systems when they are taken in their full particularity. Our systems are partial systems and it is James's belief that the full truth, the total human consciousness of the divine, can only be revealed (at present) through a plethora of different views. This is necessary because no one of us possesses human nature in its fullness; we are partial creatures and it takes the whole of us to spell out "human nature's total message" (*Var*, p. 487). Thus I take James to be saying, not that the truth for me is not the same as the truth for you, but rather that the total truth may only emerge by adding my mixture of truth and error to your mixture. The under-pinning of James's view is that human nature *does* have a message to convey, that in the field of religion, as in other fields, we believe that "the reality is congenial to powers which you possess" (SR, p. 86).

The difficulty stems from James's view of human nature with its needs and obligations and its connections with our passional life. James believed that obligations were consti-tuted by the demands and desires of conscious creatures.

> Take any demand, however slight, which any creature, however weak, may make. Ought it not, for its own sole sake, to be satisfied? If not, prove why not. The only possible kind of proof you could adduce would be the exhibition of another creature who should make a demand that ran the other way. (MPML, p. 195)

Thus for James legitimate obligations and needs are grounded in unique, individual centers of consciousness in all their particularity. The distinction we have been making between idiosyncratic desires and legitimate human needs and obligations is not an *essential* difference or difference in kind. Nevertheless, James does not say that we should actu-ally try to satisfy every human demand. In the actual world many demands do conflict; to satisfy some ideals would in-volve the destruction of many others. We thus recognize as obligatory those actions which after critical testing are seen to make for the "best whole" and least amount of dissatisfac-tion.[9] Clearly the satisfaction of needs which are universally or nearly universally felt, and which are in themselves life-

---

9. This is similar to Dewey's distinction between immediate goods and goods approved on reflection. See John Dewey, *Experience and Nature* (2nd ed.; Chicago: The Open Court Publishing Co., 1926 [1929]), pp. 396-417.

enhancing, will be among those which are rationally judged to be worthy of fulfillment. And James has contended that the distinctive moral and psychological needs which require religious belief for their fulfillment are of that category.

No subjective defense of religious belief which purports to be of logical significance can rest its case on idiosyncratic features of human nature. The analysis of subjectivity must be an analysis which purports to be general in nature and objectively valid. To a greater or lesser extent this procedure is exemplified in Kant, Kierkegaard, and James.

SUBJECTIVE ARGUMENTS AS PERSON RELATIVE

Despite the fact that subjective justifications of religious belief rest their case on analyses of the human condition which purport to be objectively valid, judgments as to the strength of these defenses will be directly related to values — and beliefs about values — subjectively held by the person making the judgment. This is a simple consequence of the fact that the analyses of the human condition which are offered, while purporting to be universally valid, are not universally accepted as valid.

Even Kant recognized this by affirming that the justification of belief in God which he offered was subjectively valid, valid for moral persons only (*KU* 451, p. 119, note). In effect, Kant says that *if* a person recognizes certain obligations, then he ought to believe in God. Of course Kant believed that those obligations were themselves rational obligations which could not be denied without rational inconsistency. But many philosophers have disagreed with Kant both about the kinds of actions and ends I am morally obligated to seek, and about Kant's thesis that moral obligations are grounded in the nature of reason itself and hence are trans-culturally and trans-temporally valid. We cannot here resolve such a dispute nor even indicate how such disputes could be resolved without plunging headway into a discussion of the whole of moral philosophy. But the implications of the disagreement would surely extend to Kant's defense of religion.

Kierkegaard's analysis of the human condition and his

construction of an ideal of personality have been even less well-received than Kant's moral philosophy. (Though perhaps Kierkegaard's views have been studied less carefully and no doubt misunderstood in part.) Yet, clearly the leap of faith will be a rational leap (rather than a leap into the dark) only to the person who accepts Kierkegaard's conception of the human ideal and his contention that this ideal is most fully realizable through Christian faith. Thus many thinkers will find Kierkegaard's defense unconvincing for two possible reasons: (1) They may find his picture of the human ideal to be faulty, or (2) they may reject his contention that the ideal can only be realized in the context of Christian faith. James's attempt to connect religious belief to moral earnestness and psychological integration will be open to similar objections.

Thus what these three thinkers have really shown is that certain forms of religious belief are rational, *given* the individual's acceptance of ethical and/or psychological beliefs which are not universally accepted. Of course the fact that Kant's or Kierkegaard's views on these matters are not widely accepted does not entail that they are not correct. Nor does it entail that thinkers who hold these views have no good reasons for holding them. It is quite possible for a thinker to have a good reason for a view which is nonetheless not widely shared. Hence we are not saying that religious beliefs which are justified subjectively are necessarily irrational; we are simply pointing out that judgments as to their rationality will be relative to certain beliefs about values which appear controversial. They will thus be person-relative, not only in the general sense in which George Mavrodes points out is applicable to proofs and claims to know in general,[10] but in the still stronger sense that their convincingness is relative to opinions concerning matters about which there is at present much controversy and little consensus, even as to how to resolve the controversies. At least in part, James and Kierkegaard seem to recognize this problem and deal with it, Kierkegaard through his methodology of indirect communication and

---

10. See George Mavrodes, *Belief in God* (New York: Random House, 1970), pp. 31-41.

James through his appeal for tolerance and religious pluralism.

THE INCONCLUSIVE CHARACTER OF SUBJECTIVE ARGUMENTS

Mostly as a consequence of (3) (disagreements over values and beliefs about values), but also a partial consequence of (1) (the dependence of subjective arguments on objective or theoretical evidence combined with the fact that there are disagreements as to the value of objective evidence concerning religious questions), it is plain that subjective defenses of religion offer no promise of finally resolving basic disputes in the philosophy of religion.

No doubt this contention seems obvious from what has been said, and we shall offer no further argument to support it. However, we should point out that from our study it is clear that even if it were argued that subjective considerations did justify some form of religious belief, the question as to the exact form of that belief would still remain. The different conceptions of the adequate religious object held by Kant, Kierkegaard, and James illustrate this fact well. No doubt these disagreements tend to cast doubt on the value of such arguments in general. We should remember, however, that those differences hide some fundamental similarities.

SUBJECTIVE ARGUMENTS AS POSSIBLY AND LEGITIMATELY DECISIVE FOR THE INDIVIDUAL

Despite thesis (4) with the qualifications we have noted, we shall argue that the sorts of defenses of religion examined in this paper are epistemologically significant. The considerations advanced by Kant, Kierkegaard, and James are relevant to deciding questions of religious truth, and in some cases may be for individuals the decisive determinants of rational religious beliefs. In general we shall argue that it is legitimate to take into account value-questions when dealing with metaphysical beliefs. This contention cuts against the grain of much of modern philosophy.

Take for example Richard Taylor's account of the bearing

of moral responsibility on the question of freedom and determinism. In his small book *Metaphysics,* an excellent and
provocative introduction to a number of key metaphysical
problems, he attempts sharply to separate metaphysical problems from ethical problems. After a discussion of whether
determinism is in fact compatible with moral responsibility,
Taylor dismisses the inquiry as irrelevant to questions of
metaphysical truth.

> We are happily spared going into all this, however, for the ques-
> tion whether determinism is true of human nature is not a
> question of ethics at all but of metaphysics. There is accord-
> ingly no hope of answering it within the context of ethics.[11]

Taylor does admit that ethical beliefs may have
metaphysical implications and *vice versa.* Hence we can *assume* that some metaphysical view is true and see what the
implications may be for ethics, or assume some ethical theory
and see what the implications may be for metaphysics. Taylor
claims that this does not make us any wiser, as far as any
fundamental question is concerned. "We shall still not know
what theories are true; we shall only know which are consistent with each other."[12] Taylor's view here is extremely significant because the logical structure of the subjective defense of religious belief is very similar to defenses or attacks
on freedom which are rooted in moral responsibility. It is
common for thinkers to urge "We must believe we are morally
responsible, and determinism (or freedom) is inconsistent
with moral responsibility; hence we must be libertarians (or
determinists)." The parallel with Kant's argument for belief
in God is obvious, and not surprising, since Kant used a similar argument to justify freedom.

If ethical considerations are of no help, how does Taylor
feel the question of the truth of determinism can be
answered?

> It can, like all good questions of philosophy, be answered only
> on the basis of certain data; that is, by seeing whether or not it

---

11. (Englewood Cliffs, N. J.: Prentice-Hall, 1963), p. 36.
12. *Ibid.*

squares with certain things which every man knows, or believes himself to know, or things of which every man is at least more sure than the answer to the question at issue.[13]

Taylor's view here as to the nature of metaphysical thinking seems generally sound. Certainly, as Aristotle and others have noted, we cannot prove everything, and once this is recognized, the idea of beginning with common-sense beliefs seems eminently sensible. Taylor does not claim that such common-sense beliefs are self-evident or necessarily true; as a matter of fact, some are undoubtedly false and the course of reflection will require that some be given up, as metaphysical problems seem to be engendered by conflicting common-sense beliefs.[14] Nevertheless it seems sensible to begin with what we know most certainly, or at least believe we know most certainly. Surely our metaphysical beliefs ought to account for and not conflict with what we know.

With this view of metaphysics, why should Taylor exclude ethical considerations in examining metaphysical problems? He tells us our metaphysical beliefs must be consistent with the data, which consist of things every man or almost every man knows or thinks he knows. Why should ethical or moral data be excluded from consideration? Taylor has admitted that ethical beliefs have metaphysical implications. Could not a person claim that among the things he *knows* are such things as "certain kinds of actions (feeding a hungry child, assisting an elderly person, etc.) are obligatory," and "other kinds of actions (running over a child in a motor car) are wrong and should be avoided"? Many persons have claimed to know such things and even claimed to know them with great certainty. If they are right, then it would seem that these sorts of beliefs should be included (at least initially) among the data of which metaphysical beliefs must take some account.

One possible response to this would be to affirm that ethical beliefs do not amount to knowledge — all knowledge is knowledge of facts. Without getting into the whole area of

---

13. *Ibid.,* p. 37.
14. *Ibid.,* pp. 2-3.

emotivist ethics, let us say only that this response leads either to an uninteresting semantic quarrel (if someone wishes to use "knowledge" in some special restrictive sense he may, but no substantive philosophical issue is thereby resolved), or else it rests on prior assumptions. One cannot justify the denial that moral truths can be *known* on the basis of common sense; such a restriction must be defended as a philosophical theory, and it would not be surprising if such a theory involved prior metaphysical commitments.

A second and more plausible argument against including moral concerns among the metaphysical data would be the one which Taylor himself seems to appeal to. Taylor calls the realm of ethics a "nebulous realm," and points out how doubtful it seems to many whether they are morally responsible.[15] That is, he points out what we have earlier stressed, that value-questions are matters about which there is much disagreement. Metaphysical data, on the other hand, must consist of "things which every man knows, or believes himself to know, or things of which every man is at least more sure than the answer to the question at issue."[16]

This requirement that metaphysical beliefs be responsible only to things which "all men know" seems very questionable to me. For one thing, it seems questionable as to whether there are any propositions which all men know or think they know. If there are any, it seems likely to me that George Mavrodes is right in contending that they will be extremely simple propositions like "There is a world," from which it is unlikely that any interesting conclusions will follow.[17] It also seems likely to me that very simple ethical truths, such as "Some actions are right and others are wrong," are as good candidates for truths which all men know as any other type of proposition.

But the main thing that is wrong with Taylor's rather stringent requirement is that it ignores the fact that each person is not "all men"; each person is an individual and

---

15. *Ibid.*, p. 37.

16. *Ibid.*

17. Mavrodes, pp. 45-46.

individuals know many things not known by all men (or perhaps even by many men). Mavrodes makes this point against those who claim that natural theology must be based on propositions which are obviously true and accepted by nearly every sane man.

> So far as I can tell, the vast majority of the things that each of us knows are neither necessary truths nor truths "accepted by nearly every sane man." Why, then, should not each of us make use of his own knowledge, and extend it by argument if he can, even it if happens not to be universally shared? It would seem foolish for anyone else to construe another's ignorance as a limit upon his own intellectual life.[18]

Why then should not a person form his metaphysical beliefs in response to all that he knows? The stringent requirement that we consider only "what nearly all men know" is perhaps thought advisable because individuals believe they know many things which are false. Where people disagree we may be relatively sure that some if not all of the views held are mistaken. However, this is stultifying as a requirement of knowledge. Surely the mere fact that there is disagreement over an issue does not mean that no one has any knowledge about the matter in question. It is simply a fact that every piece of knowledge is not universally shared (if indeed any piece is). Therefore, the fact that there are moral disagreements does not entail that no one has any moral knowledge. As a matter of fact, William Frankena holds that many so-called moral disagreements may be disguised factual disagreements, and it is not clear as to how much actual moral disagreement can be found in human judgments.[19] If someone does have any moral knowledge, and if what he knows entails or requires metaphysical beliefs, then such beliefs would certainly merit the title "rational." Even if he does not claim to possess moral *knowledge,* but merely claims that moral propositions are among those he believes very strongly for good reason, it seems logical to require of him that he hold what-

---

18. *Ibid.,* pp. 46-47.

19. *Ethics* (Englewood Cliffs, New Jersey: Prentice-Hall, 1963), pp. 92-94.

ever other beliefs which those moral beliefs require, and regard those other beliefs as rational.

When we consider the situation of the individual, who is limited by time and circumstances, and who must act and make decisions, the relevance of value-beliefs to metaphysical inquiry is plain. So long as he continues to act and make moral decisions (which is practically equivalent to existing as a human being), he is in effect holding certain value-beliefs. So long as he believes that actions should be rational, that they should be the outgrowth of reflection and one's beliefs about what is the case and what is not, he will be forced to recognize the relevance of his moral beliefs to his metaphysical beliefs. Thus, though the subjective approach to religious belief will not and cannot produce any objective consensus in the field of philosophy of religion, the sorts of considerations advanced by Kant, Kierkegaard and James are relevant to deciding these questions. Discussions of religious truth ought to take them into account, and these sorts of concerns may be for particular individuals decisive determinants of religious beliefs which merit the appellation "rational."

7

Conclusions: Subjective Concerns as Metaphysical Data and Subjective Concern as the Ground of Personal Faith

THE THEORETICAL VALUE OF THE ANALYSIS OF SUBJECTIVITY

SUBJECTIVE JUSTIFICATIONS OF RELIGIOUS BELIEFS DO constitute a distinctive type of religious apologetic. The approach we have been examining differs not only from rationalistic attempts to establish the truth of theism through rigorous logical argument; it is also distinct from more empirical, probabilistic justifications of theism exemplified most notably in the work of F. R. Tennant. The subjective approach possesses at least a *prima facie* attractiveness due to the difficulties faced by these other approaches. The difficulty which the probabilist approach faces is giving some kind of clear meaning to "probability" in this context. The subjective approach attempts to avoid this problem by requiring of theoretical reason only that it demonstrate the plausibility or believability of theism, which seems to be a somewhat weaker notion. It then goes on to argue that belief in God is justified, even in the absence of probable knowledge, because such belief is a presupposition or precondition of the acceptance and attainment of certain values which are put forward as objectively valid ideals for which a man is rationally obligated to strive. If a person does accept the rationality of action on behalf of these ideals, belief which accompanies that acceptance could be said to be subjectively rational — rational, given that person's acceptance of those ideals and his interpretation of those ideals as requiring belief in God. Proponents of this approach give up the claim to know: knowledge is grounded on objective, theoretical concerns. Religious belief is rooted in subjective, practical human needs and values. We must, however, look more closely at this disjunction between subjective rational belief and objective rational knowledge. At several points in our consideration of the subjective approach, questions were raised about the validity of this disjunction between the objective and the subjective, between the theoretical and the practical.[1] On the one hand, a careful consideration of the objective and the theoretical led us in the direction of seeing objectivity as a dimension of subjectivity; theoretical knowing is a practical activity of man, and the knowledge which is gained by that objectivity is a *value*. Even scientific knowledge is the upshot of the activities of persons. As Polanyi notes, "Scientific passions are no mere psychological by-product, but have a logical function which contributes an indispensable element to science."[2] On the other hand, as I argued in chapter six, any coherent subjective defense of religious belief cannot ground belief in relative values; the ideals which are put forward must be put forward as objectively rational ideals. If these contentions are sound, then the hard and fast distinction between "subjective belief" and "objective knowledge" cannot stand. Knowledge is subjective in the sense of being the upshot of human decisions and acts which are the expression of fundamental human values, and values are objective in the sense that if they are in fact true values, their validity is independent of the wishes and desires of particular individuals. That certain ideals of personality — those revolving around love, for instance — are inherently desirable is a truth about the world which is discovered, not invented.[3]

This suggests to us the possibility of reformulating subjective justifications of religious belief in the form of theoretical arguments for religious truth. Let us take a rather crude example to illustrate the difference between a subjective justification of belief and a theoretical argument from subjectivity for the truth of a belief. (1) John desires to become a good

1. See above, pp. 56, 80-82, 153-157, 161-162, 164-165.

2. Michael Polanyi, *Personal Knowledge* (New York: Harper and Row, 1964), p. 134.

3. For a convincing argument for this point, see Peter Bertocci, *The Person God Is* (New York: Humanities Press, 1970), pp. 26-34, 119-139.

person (it is unimportant how "good" is defined here) and he believes he ought to become a good person. John further believes that he can only become a good person with the help of God and that God offers such help to religious believers. John concludes that he ought to believe in God. (2) John's more reflective brother Paul also believes he ought to become a good person, and he also believes that he can only become good through divine assistance. In reflecting on the matter, Paul decides it would be very queer if reality were such that he found himself rationally obligated to achieve something for which the essential conditions were lacking. Paul concludes that God (probably) exists.

Notice that the conclusion to argument (1) is "John ought to believe God exists," while the conclusion to argument (2) is "(Probably) God exists." Argument (1) is a subjective argument which purports to justify an individual's decision to believe. Argument (2) takes as its starting point essentially the same considerations. But argument (2) is a theoretical argument which takes these subjective considerations as data to be made intelligible. "The existence of *this* sort of being would be unintelligible unless the world of which that being is a part was of a certain character." This is the general pattern for argument (2). Kant, Kierkegaard, and James all present to us an ideal of human personality for which men ought to strive and then suggest that this ideal can only be achieved in the context of religious belief. If their contentions are sound, then this is itself a remarkable piece of evidence for the truth of religion.

Why then did these thinkers present us with subjective arguments? Why then did they expressly deny that religious truth-claims could be *known* (even minimally), and content themselves with a subjective justification of belief? One plausible answer is that they were operating with a restrictive view of knowledge; they wished to identify knowledge with scientific knowledge. Only that which can be verified through certain public, empirical procedures qualifies as knowledge. At the level of metaphysics, cognitive judgment does not seem to them to satisfy this requirement and hence can only be subjective belief. It has been charged that such

conceptions of knowledge, together with related conceptions
of experience, presupposing mathematical and physical
knowledge as paradigms, may function as a priori filters,
screening out the religious dimension of experience (along
with other dimensions) and making religious knowledge impossible in advance.[4] With respect to these three thinkers
this charge has merit. The resort to subjective arguments is
at least partially the consequence of their acceptance of a
positivistic view of knowledge, an acceptance which could be
challenged.

We do not wish to engage in unproductive semantic quar-
rels and there may well be justification for using the honorific
title "knowledge" in the restrictive way Kant and others do.
Whether this be so or not, one must not let titles blind us to
the actual similarities and differences which exist between
different sorts of rationally grounded beliefs. Perhaps the
term "knowledge" should be put in quotes when we speak of
moral knowledge and personal knowledge; perhaps not. The
notion of metaphysical knowledge may seem to some to be a
contradiction in terms. But we must not allow terminology to
dictate to us over-neat and reductive classifications.
Metaphysical systems may not be known in the sense in
which scientific theories are known, but neither are they
"merely believed" in a subjective or arbitrary sense.

What are the criteria which must be employed in the
rational evaluation of metaphysical perspectives? Over the
last thirty-five years a view of metaphysics has been developed by a variety of philosophers operating from very different traditions which attempts to mediate between dogmatic and skeptical accounts of the metaphysical undertaking.[5]

---

4. See John Smith, "Religious Insight and the Cognitive Problem," *Religious Studies,* 7 (May, 1971), 99-102.

5. See Frank Dilley, *Metaphysics and Religious Language* (New York: Columbia University Press, 1964). Arthur Holmes in *Christian Philosophy in the
Twentieth Century* (Nutley, N. J.: Craig Press, 1969), pp. 181-215, reviews the
contributions made by such philosophers as Stephen Pepper, Everett Hall,
and Dorothy Emmet to the development of this view of metaphysics. John
Hick's discussion of theistic faith as a "total interpretation" seems to embody
essentially the same conception of a metaphysical world-view. See Hick,
Faith and Knowledge, pp. 109-134.

Metaphysics is seen neither as a rational super-science founded in a priori principles, nor as simply emotive nonsense or psychoanalytic projections. It is rather the attempt to articulate an interpretive, categoreal scheme in terms of which the whole of experience can be understood. Metaphysical systems are perspectival in that the categories are the exemplification of a basic analogy or root metaphor drawn from some limited aspect of experience, and they are synoptic in that they attempt to develop this perspective in a way which makes possible the grasping of things as a whole. On this view, though there may be a variety of relatively adequate metaphysical systems, the choice of a metaphysic is not arbitrary, and some degree of rational evaluation is possible, appealing to the twin tests of empirical adequacy and rational coherence.[6] Though metaphysical schemes are not verifiable in any direct or naive manner, their success in not only covering but illuminating diverse ranges of human experience is clearly relevant to judging their truth or falsity. Even more significant may be the demand that metaphysical systems be more than logically consistent; to possess merit, they must provide an experiential, growing coherence to the diverse ranges of experience itself.

If reason is not dogmatically identified with the procedures of formal logic and empirical science, then even if metaphysics does not amount to knowledge, it might nonetheless be a rational activity. Peter Bertocci suggests that reason is "the complex cognitive activity in the life of a person that, sensitive to the qualitative differences and similarities in the content of experience, follows connections or links — such as time, space, causality, purpose, unity, valuational differences, which experiences themselves suggest."[7] Bertocci suggests that logic itself is a phase or aspect of the "wider rela-

---

6. John King-Farlow and William N. Christensen, in "Faith — and Faith in Hypotheses," *Religious Studies*, 7 (June, 1971), 122-124, propose a list of rational criteria for the evaluation of metaphysical beliefs which are religious in character, emphasizing the need for metaphysical systems to make contact with experience at their "edges," and the necessity for openness to criticism and dialogue with contrasting views.

7. Bertocci, p. 211.

tional life of reason." If reason is the attempt to understand experience in terms of coherent categories and themes found within experience, metaphysics may be seen as the attempt to extend that search for experiential coherence to the whole of human experience. John MacMurray suggests a similar view of reason and experience when he says that the job of speculative philosophy ought to be to *think* the unity of experience.

> The common objection that experience cannot be a totality and so cannot be thought as a unity is beside the point, and Kant himself would surely have treated it with contempt. For no philosopher has ever insisted with greater force that the world we know cannot be a totality; yet none has ever made a more strenuous effort to achieve systematic adequacy in philosophy by thinking the unity of experience. The unity of experience as a whole is not a unity of knowledge, but a unity of personal activities of which knowledge is only one. It consists in the fact that the same person may be at once scientist, artist, moral agent, and sinner.[8]

In all of these activities man is not an isolated subject but a participant in an objective, interpersonal order. To understand the unity of experience in this sense is to view the whole of experience from a certain perspective; it is to form metaphysical beliefs about one's self and the reality of which the self is a part. These beliefs about the world which man experiences as a knower, willing agent, esthetic senser, and the like, may not themselves be knowledge, but they are surely conceptual in nature and susceptible of rational evaluation.

If this view of metaphysics possesses merit, then the possibility opens up of recasting the subjective arguments of Kant, Kierkegaard, and James into theoretical arguments from the nature of subjectivity. If metaphysics as a discipline is not judged in terms of the cognitive procedures developed for empirical science, then the ranges of subjective experience explored by these thinkers can be seen as data to which any adequate metaphysical scheme must pay some attention.

---

8. *The Self as Agent* (London: Faber and Faber, 1957), p. 66.

We are not proposing that an analysis of subjectivity could provide the basis for a linear argument sufficient to rationally justify theism, but rather that the consideration of these aspects of the human condition *in conjunction with* cosmological and teleological considerations would lend itself favorably to a theistic metaphysic. We have already seen that the subjective approach is inevitably partially dependent on objective argument. It is logical to conclude that the interpretive and illuminative power of a theistic perspective rests not only on the ability of theism to account adequately for these objective ranges of human experience, or merely on its power to illuminate human subjectivity itself, but on its ability to account coherently for the togetherness of the objective and the subjective. Man is the objective knower, positing a first, unconditional cause of the cosmos; man is also the subjective thinker, positing a ground and measure of his being through which he alone attains ultimate personal realization. And man is the reflective thinker, viewing his objective knowing as a dimension of human subjectivity, and viewing the nature of his subjectivity in as objective a manner as possible. The theist ultimately concludes that the God-hypothesis makes intelligible not only the objective order, but his own subjective being, and the fact that his subjective being is grounded in and helps to make up that objective order. On this view of metaphysics we could hold, for example, that the power of Kant's defense of theistic belief lies in the harmonious coherence which the three *Critiques* render to viewing the phenomenal world as grounded in an intelligible world.[9] John MacMurray, though ultimately critical of the Kantian philosophy, holds that there is a sense in which the Kantian philosophy is more adequate than any other modern philosophy, in that it does more justice to the diverse aspects of human experience (man as knower and willing agent) and attempts to grasp these diverse aspects of experience as a unity.[10]

---

9. See above, pp. 52-53, 71-73.

10. See MacMurray, pp. 60-61.

THE SUBJECTIVE VALUE OF THE
ANALYSIS OF SUBJECTIVITY

Whether this type of argument be ultimately cogent or not, surely the attempt could be made to employ the analysis of subjectivity in such a theoretical argument. However, if we left the matter at that, we would fail to recognize one important source of the appeal of the subjective justifications of belief which we have analyzed. For the fact is that there is a gap between the sort of dispassionate metaphysical analysis we have just brought forward and vital religious faith. Metaphysical arguments are at best tentative or plausible; without a doubt, they guide human thought through areas where the footholds are all too insecure. Religious faith, however, summons a man to a commitment which is in some way absolute or total; it demands that he regard the notion of God not as a provisional hypothesis but as the basis of a world-view and a way of life. There seems to be an incommensurability between the degree and nature of the objective evidence and the degree and nature of the religious commitment. There is in James's words, an element of "over-belief," or in Kierkegaard's terms, there is necessarily an element of "leaping." The transition from the objective evidence to faith is not a direct or immediate transition.

Whatever else is said about this incommensurability, it is precisely what is to be expected from the point of view of religion itself, at least on some analyses of religion. Most religious believers do not regard faith as necessarily the outgrowth of scientific knowledge, or even metaphysical acuity. There is no direct correlation between intelligence and religious faith, or even logical discernment and religious faith. Faith is held to be something as easily attainable by the simple as the wise. The breeding ground of faith is subjective thought. Am I the person I ought to be? Have I failed to measure up to a certain standard? Where can I find true fulfillment and meaning as a person?

If subjective thinking is the main source of religious belief and thus accounts for the degree of commitment which we termed "overbelief," does this have any epistemological significance? Let us distinguish, at least initially, the value subjectivity may have in *producing* religious belief from its cognitive or epistemological value. Personal commitment — faith — may stem from all sorts of psychological roots. Religiously it may be true that the roots of faith ought to be subjective concerns. We have just suggested that subjectivity may also possess cognitive or epistemological value as data which an adequate metaphysic must take account of. Closely related as these two may be, it would surely be a blunder to confuse the two, and perhaps take the psychological certainty which attaches to religious belief as providing epistemological security.

But it is perhaps just here that subjective arguments, which do not attempt to demonstrate the truth of religion theoretically, but rather attempt to justify a personal decision to believe, come into their own. The potential religious believer analyzes the actual situation which confronts him: (1) He possesses some theoretical warrant for his belief, insofar as a theistic metaphysic can be justified by the sort of theoretical argument previously outlined. (2) He sees clearly the nature of religious belief and the religious way of life; though religion certainty does not preclude honest doubt, it does preclude the taking of the central core of religious belief as tentative or hypothetical. He is called to make a commitment of himself, and neutrality is impossible. (3) He accepts an obligation to become a certain type of person and perform certain types of actions. (4) He believes that this personal fulfillment and moral way of life are achievable only through religious belief.

If such a person decides to become a believer, what are we to say? The real issue here concerns the rationality of *confidently* and *decisively* holding a belief for which the evidence is not completely decisive. To resolve it we must first ask a question about the nature of belief itself. How are beliefs held? Is belief a matter of degree such that we can be said to believe something more strongly or less strongly? If so, how ought the manner in which the belief is held be related to the evidence for the belief?

H. H. Price gives a masterful treatment of this problem

in his Gifford Lectures on *Belief.*[11] Price regards Locke and
Newman as the classic representatives of the opposing views.
In Book IV of the *Essay Concerning Human Understanding*
Locke holds that belief is a matter of degree and that it is the
characteristic of a rational person to apportion his belief to
the evidence, thus giving rise to an "ethics of belief" of the
sort represented by W. K. Clifford. Newman, on the other
hand, in his *Grammar of Assent,* maintains that Locke confused belief with inference, and that belief is an all or nothing,
unconditional affair. Price concludes that clearly there is
something different about the manner in which we hold our
beliefs, and thus Locke's view is more nearly correct. Since it
is possible to hold belief in a tentative and conditional way,
we ought to hold beliefs in that manner in cases where the
evidence is not conclusive.[12]

Price's conclusion here is generally sound. Surely we do
hold beliefs with greater or lesser confidence. However, we
should not be too hasty in jumping to the conclusion that the
manner in which a belief should be held ought to bear a direct
or immediate correlation with the evidence. As Price himself
admits,[13] Newman's view is not completely wrong. Belief
does involve an element of decisiveness (or preference as
Price terms it). We cannot believe P without disbelieving
"not P"; belief has some of the characteristics of a choice.
In discussing the "degree of a belief," Price prefers to speak
of the degree of confidence we have in a belief. But there
are issues about which the important question is, "Do you
believe at all?"

Certainly the manner in which we hold our beliefs is
important. Beliefs may be held in all sorts of ways — tentatively, timidly, fearfully, cautiously, boldly, joyfully, lov-
ingly, and so on. And clearly the evidence which supports a
belief has or ought to have an impact on the manner in which
a belief is held. But it is not clear that the evidence will be the
only factor which ought to influence the manner of believing,

---

11. *Belief* (New York: Humanities Press, 1969), pp. 130-156.

12. *Ibid.,* p. 155.

13. *Ibid.,* p. 207.

nor that the relationship will be as direct as W. K. Clifford thinks.

The three thinkers we have analyzed tend towards a dispositional analysis of belief, rather than viewing belief merely as a mental occurrence. That is, they view beliefs as rules of action and actions as the embodiments of beliefs. This account of belief is over-simple; to have any plausibility the concept of an action must be greatly broadened. Nevertheless, Price notes the plausibility of the analysis of belief as a multiform disposition. From the dispositional interpretation, to say that "A believes that P" is to make a very complex dispositional statement about A, a disposition which manifests itself not only in A's actions, conceived narrowly, but also in his inactions, emotional states such as hope and fear, feelings of doubt, surprise, and confidence, and in the practical and theoretical inferences A makes.[14] This dispositional account of belief is not behavioristic. Price does not deny that special mental events occur, which many people refer to as "beliefs," though Price prefers to call these mental acts "assents." These mental acts obviously play an important role in the acquisition of those dispositions we term beliefs, and they may be one of the most important ways in which those dispositions manifest themselves. Nevertheless, it is implausible to equate beliefs with those mental acts. At any moment, individuals believe many things which they are not consciously thinking about. These beliefs obviously consist, not of mental acts, but of dispositions to perform certain acts, including perhaps mental acts, if the circumstances are appropriate. If I am asked if I believe that I am living in Illinois, I will answer affirmatively, even though I may not have been thinking at all about my place of residence at the time. Nor do I lose my beliefs when I go to sleep or in other such situations. Furthermore, it is clear that my beliefs, viewed as such dispositions, do not manifest themselves solely in mental acts, but in my actions in general.

If belief is a disposition of this sort, then it is not quite so clear as to what it means to hold a belief confidently or tenta-

---

14. *Ibid.,* pp. 294-295.

tively, as it would be if belief were merely a mental oc-currence. If a man holds a belief in some proposition P with a low degree of confidence, does that mean he ought to act on the basis of such a belief only part of the time? Or would such vacillation merely be evidence of the person's indecisive character? If he always behaves as a man would who believes that P, does this mean that he holds the belief confidently? Might not such a person still entertain grave doubts?

On such a dispositional analysis of belief it is clear that some sense can be given to the all or nothing account of belief. This is because actions partake of this all or nothing charac-ter. If a person believes that P, he will perform certain dis-tinctive actions; if he does not believe that P, he will not perform those actions. And it is surely false to argue that the *way* in which he performs those actions merely ought to re-flect the degree of confidence he has in the belief. Certain sorts of acts, if they are to be performed at all, must be per-formed in a decisive, resolute manner. James's illustration of the mountain climber jumping a crevasse is an excellent example. *If the quality of a belief is measured by the quality of the actions it gives rise to, then it seems possible for a rational man to hold a belief in a bold, resolute manner, even though conclusive evidence for the belief is somewhat lacking.* Such beliefs are essential conditions for accomplishing many of the most sig-nificant and challenging human tasks. Among those tasks some thinkers would list such goals as achieving the highest good or arriving at psychological wholeness or maturity. And a religious belief which is directly required for such a task might participate in this decisive, bold character.

That a belief is held boldly and resolutely in this sense does not mean that the thinker is unaware of difficulties, or has lost his critical wits. The truth contained in the ethics of belief position is that a thinker ought to be honestly aware of the evidential status of his belief and be sensitive to that evidence. But if belief is a multiform disposition it is com-prehensible how *conviction* and doubt can co-exist within a personality.[15] (That doubt and conviction do co-exist within

---

15. See King-Farlow and Christensen, "Faith — and Faith in Hypoth-

the life of many religious believers is indisputable.) Rational questioning and doubt may manifest themselves in a readiness to entertain new evidence and look at the old evidence again, or perhaps in a tolerance for opposing views. Conviction may manifest itself in acts of piety and charity — singing hymns with feeling, praying with pathos and confidence, loving in a sacrificial manner. Both doubt and conviction may be manifested in feelings which alternate, intermingle, perhaps even fuse, and which co-exist through all these actions. The man who worships with conviction in church can also be a critical philosopher who questions his faith and is continually rethinking the evidence on which that faith rests.

It is therefore possible rationally to maintain a positive faith and commitment to a view for which the evidence is tentative and incomplete. Kant, Kierkegaard, and James have attempted to describe for us the sort of situation in which such a commitment may be regarded as the result of rational reflection. That such commitments in a certain sense outrun the evidence is not denied. Such decisions may involve risks, but if the situation has been correctly described, whatever decision which is taken will involve risk — and not only the epistemological risk of being wrong. The thinker who fails to act on his religious impulses risks the destruction of his personality; in more traditional terms, he may lose his own soul. The significance of the subjective defense of religious belief lies in its argument that such risks are not unique to religious beliefs, and that in the case of the religious believer the necessity for such risky belief stems from the exigencies of the human situation.

However, to merit the appellation "rational," religious belief, though it may outrun the evidence, must remain in constant communication with that evidence. A concern for truth which is reflected in an openness to all of the experiential data may not be a sufficient condition for faith, or even a necessary condition. But it is surely a necessary condition of *rational* faith.

---

eses," pp. 113-124, for support of the thesis that reflective doubt and affective commitment are not only compatible but jointly necessary elements of mature religious belief.

It therefore seems that a philosopher of religion who wishes to construct a religious apologetic is left with a twofold task. On the one hand, he must characterize the various dimensions of human experience, including the data of human subjectivity, in such a way as to show their evidential value for theism; on the other hand, he must analyze the nature of the subjective situation which faces the religious believer in such a way as to show the rationality of a decisive commitment which rests on grounds which are neither deductively or inductively certain. Unsettling as it may be to rationalistic pretensions, human decisions are subject to uncertainty, as even Descartes was forced to recognize.[16] It may even be that authentic religious character requires for its nurture a situation characterized by risk. We thus conclude with Peter Bertocci that "personal convincedness may therefore in a reasonable life be interfused with philosophical probability."[17]

16. Descartes, *Meditations,* in *The Philosophical Works of Descartes,* trans. by Elizabeth S. Haldane and G. R. T. Ross (Cambridge: Cambridge University Press, 1969), I, 199.

17. Bertocci, p. 171.

Selected Bibliography

Ackerman, Robert. *Belief and Knowledge*. Anchor Books. Garden City, N. Y.: Doubleday & Co., 1972.

Acton, H. B. *Kant's Moral Philosophy*. London: Macmillan, 1970.

Barth, Karl. *Protestant Thought from Rousseau to Ritschl*. Translated by Brian Cozens. New York: Harper and Row, 1959.

Beck, Lewis White. *A Commentary on Kant's Critique of Practical Reason*. Chicago: University of Chicago Press, 1960.

Bertocci, Peter. *The Person God Is*. New York: Humanities Press, 1970.

Bixler, Julius Seelye. *Religion in the Philosophy of William James*. Boston: Marshall Jones Co., 1926.

Borst, C. V., ed. *The Mind-Brain Identity Theory*. London: Macmillan, 1970.

Collins, James. *God in Modern Philosophy*. Gateway Edition. Chicago: Henry Regnery Co., 1967.

Descartes, Rene. *The Philosophical Works of Descartes*. Translated by Elizabeth Haldane and G. R. T. Ross. 2 vols. Cambridge: Cambridge University Press, 1969.

Dewey, John. *Experience and Nature*. 2nd ed. Chicago: The Open Court Publishing Co., 1926 (1929).

Diem, Hermann, *Kierkegaard: An Introduction*. Translated by David Green. Richmond, Va.: John Knox Press, 1966.

Dilley, Frank. *Metaphysics and Religious Language*. New York: Columbia University Press, 1964.

Ducasse, C. J. *A Philosophical Scrutiny of Religion*. New York: Ronald Press Co., 1953.

Eisendrath, Craig R. *The Unifying Moment — The Psychological Philosophy of William James and Alfred North Witehead*. Cambridge: Harvard University Press, 1971.

England, Frederick Ernest. *Kant's Conception of God*. London: George Allen and Unwin, 1929.

215

Ewing, A. C. *A Short Commentary on Kant's Critique of Pure Reason.* Chicago: University of Chicago Press, 1938.

Frankena, William, *Ethics.* Englewood Cliffs, N. J.: Prentice-Hall, 1963.

Gill, Jerry H., ed. *Essays on Kierkegaard.* Minneapolis: Burgess Publishing Co., 1969.

Hampshire, Stuart. *Thought and Action.* New York: Viking Press, 1959.

Hepburn, Ronald W. *Christianity and Paradox.* New York: Pegasus, 1968.

Hick, John. *Faith and Knowledge.* Ithaca: Cornell University Press, 1957.

Holmes, Arthur. *Christian Philosophy in the Twentieth Century.* Nutley, N.J.: Craig Press, 1969.

Hook, Sidney. *The Quest for Being.* New York: St. Martin's Press, 1961.

James, William. *Human Immortality.* 2nd ed. Boston: Houghton Mifflin Co., 1898.

————. *The Meaning of Truth.* New York: Greenwood Press, 1909.

————. *A Pluralistic Universe.* New York: Longmans, Green, and Co., 1909.

————. *Pragmatism: A New Name for Some Old Ways of Thinking.* New York: Longmans, Green, and Co., 1907.

————. *The Principles of Psychology.* 2 vols. New York: Henry Holt and Co., 1890.

————. *The Varieties of Religious Experience.* New York: Longmans, Green, and Co., 1902.

————. *The Will to Believe and other Essays in Popular Philosophy.* New York: Longmans, Green, and Co., 1897.

————. *The Writings of William James.* Edited by John J. McDermott. New York: Random House, 1968.

Johnson, Howard A., and Thulstrup, Niels, eds. *A Kierkegaard Critique.* New York: Harper and Row, 1962.

Kant, Immanuel. *Critique of Judgment.* Translated by James Meredith. Oxford: Clarendon Press, 1952.

————. *Critique of Practical Reason.* Translated by Lewis White Beck. Liberal Arts Press Edition. Indianapolis: Bobbs-Merrill, 1956.

————. *Critique of Practical Reason and other Writings in Moral Philosophy.* Translated by Lewis White Beck. Chicago: University of Chicago Press, 1949.

_____. *Critique of Pure Reason.* Translated by Norman Kemp Smith. London: Macmillan, 1929. Reprinted, New York: St. Martin's Press, 1965.

_____. *Groundwork of the Metaphysic of Morals.* Translated by H. J. Paton. Harper Torchbooks. New York: Harper and Row, 1964.

_____. *Lectures on Ethics.* Translated by Louis Infield. New York: The Century Co., 1930.

_____. *Religion Within the Limits of Reason Alone.* Translated with an Introduction and Notes by Theodore M. Green and Hoyt H. Hudson with a new essay "The Ethical Significance of Kant's *Religion*" by John R. Silber. Harper Torchbooks. New York: Harper and Row, 1960.

Kierkegaard, Søren. *Attack Upon "Christendom."* Translated by Walter Lowrie. Princeton: Princeton University Press, 1944.

_____. *On Authority and Revelation.* Translated with an Introduction and Notes by Walter Lowrie. Introduction to the Torchbook Edition by Frederick Sontag. Harper Torchbooks. New York: Harper and Row, 1966.

_____. *Christian Discourses.* Translated by Walter Lowrie. Princeton: Princeton University Press, 1940.

_____. *The Concept of Dread.* Translated by Walter Lowrie. 2nd ed. Princeton: Princeton University Press. 1957.

_____. *Concluding Unscientific Postscript to the Philosophical Fragments.* Translated by David F. Swenson and Walter Lowrie. Princeton: Princeton University Press, 1941.

_____. *Edifying Discourses.* Translated by David F. Swenson and Lillian Marvin Swenson. 4 vols. Minneapolis: Augsburg Publishing House, 1943-1946.

_____. *Either/Or.* Vol. I Translated by David F. Swenson and Lillian Marvin Swenson; Vol. II translated by Walter Lowrie with revisions by Howard A. Johnson. Princeton: Princeton University Press, 1959.

_____. *Fear and Trembling and The Sickness Unto Death.* Translated by Walter Lowrie. Revised ed. Princeton: Princeton University Press, 1954.

_____. *For Self-Examination and Judge for Yourselves.* Translated by Walter Lowrie. Princeton: Princeton University Press, 1944.

_____. *The Journals of Kierkegaard.* Translated and selected by Alexander Dru. Harper Torchbooks. New York: Harper and Row, 1959.

_____. *Philosophical Fragments.* Translated by David Swenson.

218   SUBJECTIVITY AND RELIGIOUS BELIEF

2nd ed. Princeton: Princeton University Press, 1962.

————. *The Point of View for My Work as an Author.* Translated by Walter Lowrie, edited by Benjamin Nelson. Harper Torchbook. New York: Harper and Row, 1962.

————. *Purity of Heart Is To Will One Thing.* Translated by Douglas V. Steere. New York: Harper and Row, 1938. Reprinted as Harper Torchbook. New York: Harper and Row, 1956.

————. *Repetition.* Translated by Walter Lowrie. Princeton: Princeton University Press, 1941. Reprinted as Harper Torchbook. New York: Harper and Row, 1964.

————. *Søren Kierkegaard's Journals and Papers.* Translated by Howard V. Hong and Edna H. Hong. Vol. I, A-E. Bloomington: Indiana University Press, 1967.

————. *Søren Kierkegaard's Journals and Papers.* Translated by Howard V. Hong and Edna H. Hong. Vol. II, F-K. Bloomington: Indiana University Press, 1970.

————. *Stages on Life's Way.* Translated by Walter Lowrie. Princeton: Princeton University Press, 1940.

————. *Training in Christianity.* Translated by Walter Lowrie. Princeton: Princeton University Press, 1944.

————. *Works of Love.* Translated by Howard V. Hong and Edna H. Hong. London: Collins, 1962. Reprinted as Harper Torchbook. New York: Harper and Row, 1964.

Kroner, Richard. *Kant's Weltanschauung.* Translated by John E. Smith. Chicago: University of Chicago Press, 1956.

Lovejoy, Arthur O. *The Thirteen Pragmatisms and Other Essays.* Baltimore: Johns Hopkins Press, 1963.

Lowrie, Walter. *Kierkegaard.* 2 vols. New York: Oxford University Press, 1938.

Mackey Louis. *Kierkegaard: A Kind of Poet.* Philadelphia: University of Pennsylvania Press, 1971.

MacMurray, John. *The Self as Agent.* London: Faber and Faber, 1957.

Malantschuk, Gregor. *Kierkegaard's Thought.* Edited and translated by Howard V. Hong and Edna H. Hong. Princeton: Princeton University Press, 1971.

————. *Kierkegaard's Way to the Truth.* Translated by Mary Michelsen. Minneapolis: Augsburg Publishing House, 1963.

Maslow, Abraham. *Toward a Psychology of Being.* 2nd ed. New York: Van Nostrand Reinhold Co., 1968.

Mavrodes, George. *Belief in God.* New York: Random House, 1970.

Miller, E. Morris. *Moral Law and the Highest Good.* Melbourne: Melbourne University Press, 1928.

Moore, Edward C. *William James*. New York: Washington Square Press, 1966.

Novak, Michael. *Belief and Unbelief: A Philosophy of Self-Knowledge*. New York: Macmillan Co., 1965.

Paton, H. J. *In Defense of Reason*. London: Hutchinson, 1951.

————. *The Categorical Imperative*. London: Hutchinson, 1965.

Perry, Ralph Barton. *The Thought and Character of William James*. 2 vols. Boston: Little, Brown and Co., 1935.

Polanyi, Michael. *Personal Knowledge*. New York: Harper and Row, 1964.

————. *Science, Faith, and Society*. Chicago: University of Chicago Press, 1964.

Price, H. H. *Belief*. New York: Humanities Press, 1969.

Ramsey, Ian, ed. *Prospect for Metaphysics*. London: George Allen and Unwin, 1961.

Roth, John K. *Freedom and the Moral Life: The Ethics of William James*. Philadelphia: The Westminster Press, 1969.

Smith, John E. *Experience and God*. New York: Oxford University Press, 1968.

Smith, Norman Kemp. *A Commentary on the Critique of Pure Reason*. 2nd ed., revised and enlarged. New York: Humanities Press, 1962.

Taylor, Richard. *Metaphysics*. Englewood Cliffs, N. J.: Prentice-Hall, 1963.

Thompson, Josiah, ed. *Kierkegaard*. Garden City, N. Y.: Doubleday and Co., 1972.

Thomte, Reidar. *Kierkegaard's Philosophy of Religion*. Princeton: Princeton University Press, 1948.

Tillich, Paul. *Systematic Theology*. Vol. I. Chicago: University of Chicago Press, 1951.

Webb, C. C. J. *Kant's Philosophy of Religion*. Oxford: Clarendon Press, 1926.

Wild, John. *The Radical Empiricism of William James*. Garden City, N. Y.: Doubleday and Co., 1969.

Witter, Charles Edgar. *Pragmatic Elements in Kant's Philosophy*. Chicago: University of Chicago Press, 1913.

Wittgenstein, Ludwig. *Lectures and Conversations on Aesthetics, Psychology and Religious Belief*. Edited by Cyril Barrett. Berkeley: University of California Press, 1967.

Wolff, Robert Paul, ed. *Kant: A Collection of Critical Essays*. Anchor Books. Garden City, N.Y.: Doubleday and Co., 1967.

Wood, Allen W. *Kant's Moral Religion*. Ithaca: Cornell University Press, 1970.

Articles

Blanshard, Brand. "Kierkegaard on Faith," *The Personalist*, 59 (Winter, 1968), 5-22.

Eller, Vernard. "Fact, Faith, and Foolishness: Kierkegaard and The New Quest," *Journal of Religion*, 48, 1 (1965), 54-68.

Evans, C. Stephen. "Kierkegaard on Subjective Truth: Is God an Ethical Fiction?" *International Journal for Philosophy of Religion*, 7, 1 (1976), 288-289.

Gill, Jerry. "Kant, Kierkegaard, and Religious Knowledge," *Philosophy and Phenomenological Research*, 28 (December, 1967), 188-204.

Hare, Peter H., and Madden, Edward H. "William James, Dickinson Miller, and C. J. Ducasse on the Ethics of Belief," *Transactions of the Charles S. Peirce Society*, 4 (Fall, 1968), 115-129.

James, William, "Reason and Faith," *The Journal of Philosophy*, 24 (April 14, 1927), 197-201.

Kennedy, Gail. "Pragmatism, Pragmaticism and the Will to Believe —A Reconsideration," *Journal of Philosophy*, 55 (1958), 115-129.

King-Farlow, John. "Rational Commitment and 'The Will to Believe'," *Sophia*, 8 (1969), 3-14.

King-Farlow, John and Christensen, William N. "Faith — and Faith in Hypotheses," *Religious Studies*, 7 (June, 1971), 113-124.

Lovejoy, A. O. "The Thirteen Pragmatisms," *Journal of Philosophy, Psychology, and Scientific Method*, 5 (1908), 5-12, 29-39.

Mackey, Louis. "Kierkegaard and the Problem of Existential Philosophy," *Review of Metaphysics*, 9 (March and June, 1956), 404-419, 569-588.

Mathur, G. B. "Hume and Kant in Their Relation to the Pragmatic Movement," *Journal of the History of Ideas*, 16 (April, 1955), 198-208.

Mayberry, Thomas C. "God and Moral Authority," *The Monist*, 54 (January, 1970), 106-123.

———. "Laws, Moral Laws, and God's Commands," *The Journal of Value Inquiry*, 4 (Winter, 1970), 287-292.

Meyers, Robert G. "Meaning and Metaphysics in James," *Philosophy and Phenomenological Reasearch*, 31 (March, 1971), 369-380.

Miller, Dickinson S. "James's Doctrine of 'The Right to Believe'," *Philosophical Review*, 51 (November, 1942), 541-558.

———. Review of Bixler's *Religion in the Philosophy of William James, Journal of Philosophy*, 24 (April 14, 1927), 203-210.

———. " 'The Will to Believe' and the Duty to Doubt," *International Journal of Ethics*, 99 (1898-1899), 169-195.

Platt, David. "Is Empirical Theology Adequate?" *International Journal for Philosophy of Religion,* 2 (Spring, 1971), 28-42.

Rotenstreich, Nathan. "Kant's Dialectic," *Review of Metaphysics,* 7 (March, 1954), 389-421.

Schrader, George. "Kant and Kierkegaard on Duty and Inclination," *Journal of Philosophy,* 65 (November 7, 1968), 688-701.

————. "Kant's Presumed Repudiation of the Moral Argument in the Opus Postumum," *Philosophy,* 26 (1951), 228-241.

Sefler, George F. "Kierkegaard's Religious Truth: The Three Dimensions of Subjectivity," *International Journal for Philosophy of Religion,* 2 (Spring, 1971), 43-55.

Silber, John R. "Kant's Conception of the Highest Good as Immanent and Transcendent," *Philosophical Review,* 68 (October, 1959), 469-492.

————. "The Metaphysical Importance of the Highest Good as the Canon of Pure Reason in Kant's Philosophy," *Texas Studies in Literature and Language,* 1 (Summer, 1959), 233-244.

Singer, Marcus G. "The Pragmatic Use of Language and the Will to Believe," *American Philosophical Quarterly,* 8 (January, 1971), 24-34,

Smith, John E. "Religious Insight and the Cognitive Problem," *Religious Studies,* 7 (May, 1971), 97-112.

Vanden Burgt, Robert. "William James on Man's Creativity in the Religious Universe," *Philosophy Today,* 15 (Winter, 1971), 292-301.

Westphal, Merold. "Kierkegaard and the Logic of Insanity," *Religious Studies,* 7 (September, 1971), 193-211.

Whittemore, Robert. "The Metaphysics of the Seven Formulations of the Moral Argument," *Tulane Studies in Philosophy,* 3 (1954), 133-161.

Index

Concepts and proper names which appear pervasively in the text or which are in the table of contents have been generally omitted.